T0176246

TENDING THE HEART OF VIRTUE

VIGEN GUROIAN

TENDING
THE HEART
OF VIRTUE

How Classic Stories Awaken
A Child's Moral Imagination

Second Edition

OXFORD
UNIVERSITY PRESS

OXFORD
UNIVERSITY PRESS

Oxford University Press is a department of the University of Oxford. It furthers
the University's objective of excellence in research, scholarship, and education
by publishing worldwide. Oxford is a registered trade mark of Oxford University
Press in the UK and certain other countries.

Published in the United States of America by Oxford University Press
198 Madison Avenue, New York, NY 10016, United States of America.

Library of Congress Cataloging-in-Publication Data
Names: Guroian, Vigen, author.
Title: Tending the heart of virtue : how classic stories awaken a child's moral imagination /
Vigen Guroian.
Description: 2nd edition. |
New York, NY, United States of America : Oxford University Press, 2023. |
Includes bibliographical references and index.
Identifiers: LCCN 2022046044 (print) | LCCN 2022046045 (ebook) |
ISBN 9780195384307 (hardback) | ISBN 9780195384314 (paperback) |
ISBN 9780197678848 (updf) | ISBN 9780197678831 (epub) | ISBN 9780197678855 (online)
Subjects: LCSH: Children's literature—Moral and ethical aspects. |
Children—Books and reading. | Virtues in literature. | Literature and morals.
Classification: LCC PN1009 .A1 G87 2023 (print) | LCC PN1009 .A1 (ebook) |
DDC 809/.89282—dc23/eng/20220928
LC record available at https://lccn.loc.gov/2022046044
LC ebook record available at https://lccn.loc.gov/2022046045

DOI: 10.1093/oso/9780195384307.001.0001

Paperback printed by Marquis, Canada
Hardback printed by Bridgeport National Bindery, Inc., United States of America

In memory of June Vranian,
wife, mother, and grandmother,
1949–2019

To Virginia, Harris, Louise, George, Vivian, and Elizabeth

I was glad when you arrived in the world
because that was when
the fairies returned to the wood
that hugs Hungry Run.
They came on boats
of broad-fingered tulip poplar leaves
and danced among the trees.

CONTENTS

PREFACE TO SECOND EXPANDED EDITION

More than twenty-five years have passed by since I wrote *Tending the Heart of Virtue*. Over these years, the book has taken me many places to deliver dozens of lectures and to lead many seminars and workshops with teachers, college students, and parents. Along the way, some have asked me if I would consider writing another book of its kind, or, perhaps, do an expanded second edition of *Tending the Heart*. My ideas about what stories and subjects might be included in a new book or a second edition have gone through many iterations. And what I have settled upon hardly begins to reflect all the possibilities that I have contemplated along the way.

For this second edition, I have recast the Introduction because with the passage of time some of my speech in it is anachronistic. For example, my son, Rafi, and daughter, Victoria, are now adults with children of their own. When I was writing *Tending the Heart*, there was much discussion about how to build moral character, teach values, and instill the virtues in children. I wrestled with some of these currents of opinion in Chapter 1. The climate is a little different now and the debate has evolved. Nonetheless, the fundamental issues are the same. So I see no compelling reason to rewrite that chapter. I have limited myself to minor editing and an expansion of my discussion of the moral imagination. As to the remainder of the chapters in the first edition, I have made mainly stylistic revisions. Last, the Conclusion, which serves as a bibliographical essay, has been expanded to include the new topics raised in the added chapters.

Provoked by a trend in the publishing industry to produce bowdlerized versions of the fairy tales and new tellings bent to the latest ideology or social movement, Charles Dickens in 1853 issued an impassioned defense of fairy tales, titled "Frauds on the Fairies." He urged that in "a utilitarian age, of all other times, it is a matter of grave importance that Fairy tales should be respected." Indeed, he could not imagine the survival of English culture itself were these stories to be altered according to the latest fashion, for then the original stories would soon be forgotten and disappear. "Forbearance, courtesy, consideration for the poor and aged, kind treatment of animals, love of nature, abhorrence of tyranny and brute force"—all of these things, and more, are nourished in "a child's heart by this powerful aid" of the fairy tale, he argued.

Were Dickens alive today, I do not doubt that he would protest the persistent bowdlerization, emasculation, and revision of the classic fairy tales. Beware especially when the book you are looking at advertises the contents as a "retelling." It might have pretty pictures but leave out important details in the story or even alter the narrative significantly. Often religious language is expunged. Beware, in particular, of Disney editions. None are faithful to the original. This state of affairs concerns parents and teachers I have met over the years. And I am glad that *Tending the Heart* has encouraged and emboldened them to ask critical questions about the integrity of the texts that are put before them in bookstores, in schools, in libraries, and on the internet.[1]

For practical reasons, I have decided not to write an entirely new book. Instead, I want to give *Tending the Heart* a new lease on life, especially within the worlds of homeschooling and classical schooling, which have expanded exponentially since the first edition. I have also listened to persons who have asked for more reflection on the classic stories. Thus, there are three new chapters in the book.

"The Triumph of Beauty," Chapter 7, is the first addition. In it I return to Hans Christian Andersen. "The Nightingale" and "The Ugly Duckling" are two of Andersen's best stories. "The Nightingale" has been described as a manifesto on art and beauty in fairy-tale form. I agree. More important, however, "The Nightingale" is a stunning parable about how beauty can transform our lives. "The Ugly Duckling" might come as a surprise under the heading of beauty. It has been mercilessly bowdlerized and recast in order to drive home the mistaken notion that, above all else, the story is about bullying or being an underdog. This is wrong. "The Ugly Duckling" is about how a love of beauty can change one's life.

Though I did not include any of the Grimms' fairy tales in *Tending the Heart*, I did not intentionally omit the Grimms. The best of their stories are literary masterpieces. Over the years, I often have spoken on stories such as "Cinderella," "Hansel and Gretel," and "Snow White."

Yet I am limited by topic and by what might reasonably be added to the book without making it cumbersome. I have included in this edition just one story by the Grimm brothers, "Cinderella." Chapter 8, "The Goodness of Goodness," pairs "Cinderella" with John Ruskin's *The King of the Golden River*. Ruskin's tale is a gem of Victorian storytelling, but sadly it has fallen out of the canon. The story's protagonist is the youngest of three brothers whose name is Gluck (German for "luck"). Gluck is a male Cinderella type. This resemblance is not uppermost in my mind, however. The chapter is not a comparative exercise. It is, rather, an exploration of the biblical and religious leitmotifs and rich symbolism that the two stories have in common, especially regarding how goodness is embodied in the two protagonists.

I close the Introduction with a citation from George MacDonald's *The Golden Key*. This is the sort of fairy tale that virtually eludes analysis. The same may be said of several other MacDonald stories. *The Wise Woman* is one. In Chapter 9, "Obedience and the Path to Perfection," I venture, though with trepidation, an interpretation of this remarkable story. *The Wise Woman* was frequently on the syllabus of my college course on children's literature, often paired with Shel Silverstein's *The Giving Tree*. The young men and women in that course continually surprised me with their enthusiastic reception of its message on the virtue of tough love. The wise woman is not cruel but, to the contrary, embodies a divine wisdom and practices a demanding love that beckons us to keep on the difficult path to goodness and perfection. While my undergraduates were divided over whether Silverstein's *The Giving Tree* is a "good" or "bad" story, most agreed *The Wise Woman* is a "good" story.

A final word. In the art of writing literary essays (once called belles-lettres), *how* something is said is almost as important as *what* is said. I am speaking here of the writer's voice and the tonality of it, elements that make his writing distinctive, serve as his signature, and enable the reader to identify with him in a personal way. As I was writing the new chapters for *Tending the Heart*, I often turned back to the original chapters. I had thought to replicate the authorial voice in them, but discovered that, hard as I might try, I could not. I am and I am not the same writer who wrote *Tending the Heart of Virtue* a quarter century ago. My voice has changed, and my vocabulary has too. Nevertheless, I do not think that the difference is so great that it is unrecognizable, jars the mind, or hurts the ears. I certainly hope that this is so. My love and respect for the stories remain the same.

Vigen Guroian
Culpeper, Virginia
Easter, 2022

ACKNOWLEDGMENTS

When I was a child my maternal grandmother, Zabel Keosaian, would come to our home for long stays. That was when my mother, father, brother, and I lived in a small Cape Cod–style home in Stamford, Connecticut. Downstairs there were just four modest rooms, a kitchen, a living room, a small parlor or family room, and one room that served as the playroom for my brother, Michael, and me. In it we kept a fold-up cot for when my grandmother visited.

Upstairs there were two small bedrooms. They seemed even smaller than they were because of the slanted roof that forced even a little person to kneel in order to peer out the dormer windows. When my grandmother stayed with us, I would rise early in the morning and scurry down a steep and very narrow staircase into the kitchen and through it, turning right into a small foyer that led into the living room. On the right-hand wall of this foyer was a mysterious closet with a short child-sized door. The space was under the stairwell, and I was certain a wicked gnome or witch lived in there. To the left was my playroom. On such mornings, I would rush into it and creep under the covers next to my grandmother. I don't recall that I ever woke her. She seemed always to be awake for me.

Once I had snuggled up next to her, my grandmother would tell me *Märchen* (fairy tales) and humorous tales of Armenia and the Middle East. She had fled Turkey with her family after the

First World War. Sometimes she would tell me stories of what she had seen or of things that she had heard from others as a child, things that *really* had happened. I learned later that when she was a young woman in her teens, she would be sent off to smuggle food and provisions to the Armenian freedom fighters who hid in the hills and countryside outside of the Turkish city of Sivas. My grandmother told me stories of great big mountain men, "giants," as she described them, who ambushed people in the passes and catapulted big boulders down cliffsides onto unexpecting travelers. I did not readily distinguish these stories from the fairy tales she told me. I did not know that some of these stories were also her own worst, haunting memories and nightmares of a terrible time of genocide.

My life would have been different—maybe even this book would not have been written—had it not been for my grandmother and her stories. She was indeed a captivating storyteller. Now that I am of an age even greater than was my grandmother when she told me her stories, I realize how much my own imagination and sense of humor were formed by her. It is for these stories that I thank her.

I thank my late parents, Grace and Armen Guroian. They understood that a child whose first language was not English but Armenian needed to be encouraged to read and feel confident about that at a time when there was not much attention paid in schools to the special needs and special gifts of bilingual students. Once a week my father would bring home an armful of books from the library, and it was my mother's job to answer my every plea for a quick definition of this or that word that I did not know.

As I look back, there are two teachers in my past to whom I remain exceedingly grateful for the respect and love of the English language they instilled within me. Helen Rivers taught me English and was my homeroom teacher from seventh through ninth grades. Mrs. Rivers could be a terrifying presence. When she raised her voice she could be heard all the way down into the gym. If you were the object of her outrage or chastisement, you positively shook with fear. Helen Rivers was a taskmistress. I do not know how many poems I had to memorize for her or how many hundreds of sentences I diagrammed for her. But when she gave me a big kiss at the ninth-grade commencement exercises and left her bright red lipstick on my cheek, I knew I loved her. I realized even then how much she had taught me through the discipline she had cultivated within me with love. Later I also realized that she had given me the essential tools to become a writer.

The second teacher I remember with gratitude is John Graham, who was a professor of speech and rhetoric at the University of Virginia, where I earned my bachelor's degree from 1966 to 1970. In his courses, Professor Graham not only taught me the poetics of speech but also impressed upon me and all his students the elements of good style. In simple terms, John Graham taught me how to write.

In the Introduction, I mention the late Russell Kirk and his wife, Annette, and my indebtedness to them both for their encouragement and support in writing this book. But I should also add that Russell helped me procure more than a grant or two that enabled me to take leaves from teaching in order to complete the first edition of this book

Also in the Introduction, I mention St. Paul's School in Brooklandville, Maryland. Both my son, Rafi, and daughter, Victoria, attended St. Paul's School. The headmaster at that time was Robert Hallett, an inspired educator with a vision. Bob welcomed my research and permitted me to engage some of his faculty in the enterprise of bringing together my college students and their elementary and middle school students to read and talk about fairy tales. I remember especially our brown bag lunches together during the years this book took form.

Cynthia Read was editor of religion and philosophy at Oxford University Press in New York when in 1996 or thereabouts I phoned her out of the blue and told her I was writing a book on fairy tales and children's literature and that I had three chapters ready. She requested that I immediately send her those chapters. From there on Cynthia paid close attention to the progress of the book. She put her hand to a first edit of the chapters and helped immensely in improving the text.

Over the ensuing twenty-five years, Cynthia and I kept in touch. I promised her that at some time along the way I would direct my attention to a second, expanded edition of *Tending the Heart of Virtue*. When I had completed drafts of the new chapters for this edition, Cynthia repeated what she had done the first time around. She carefully read the three new chapters and forced me to restructure and rewrite large sections of them. This went on for several months. Because of that, this new edition is a far better book than it might have been had I had an editor who demanded less of me. In my forty-five years of writing I have found none like Cynthia Read. And to her I am profoundly grateful.

Last, I wish to thank the students who enrolled in my course on children's literature for more than a quarter of a century both at Loyola College in Maryland and at the University of Virginia. I remember the many conversations in the classroom from which

I learned so much. Some of the discussions remain vivid in my memory. And among the literally thousands of papers that my students wrote for me, there were some gems. Some of them I have saved to this day and have taken instruction from in writing this book. In that regard I gladly give credit where credit is due.

INTRODUCTION

Children are vitally concerned with distinguishing good from evil and truth from falsehood. This need to make moral distinctions is a gift, a grace that human beings are given at the start of their lives. Of course, we mustn't mistake this grace for complete innocence. Children are not pure innocents, as every new parent quickly discovers. The guile of even the smallest child can make one wonder: "Where did she learn that?" Becoming a responsible human being is a path filled with potholes and visited constantly by temptations. Children need guidance and moral road maps, and they benefit immensely from the example of adults who speak truthfully and with moral strength.

Our society is finding it difficult to meet these needs of children. Some well-meaning educators and parents want to drive the passion for moral clarity out of children rather than use it to shape their character. We want children to be tolerant, and we sometimes seem to think that a too sure sense of right and wrong only produces fanatics. Perhaps we have become so resigned to flailing about in the culture's murky waters of moral compromise and ethical obscurantism that it is hard for us to imagine other possibilities for our children. I was no exception as a young parent, and I sometimes fall into similar habits as a grandparent. I find myself doing

Tending the Heart of Virtue. Second Edition. Vigen Guroian, Oxford University Press.
© Vigen Guroian 1998, 2023. DOI: 10.1093/oso/9780195384307.003.0001

what I often criticize in others, nervously rationalizing my laziness or unwillingness to cultivate conscience and moral sense in my grandchildren. Mostly, we all fall back on the excuse that we are respecting our children's freedom by permitting them to determine right from wrong and to choose for themselves clear goals of moral living. But this is the paean of a false freedom that pays misdirected tribute to a deeply flawed notion of individual autonomy. We end up forfeiting our parental authority and failing to be mentors to our children in the moral life. This, I fear, is the actual state of things.

Every parent who has read a fairy tale to a young son or daughter is familiar with what I venture to say is a universal refrain of childhood: "But is he a good person or a bad one?" or "Is she a good fairy or an evil fairy?" What stronger proof or assurance could we want that God and nature have endowed even the youngest human beings with a moral constitution that needs to be nurtured and cultivated? Yet our society embraces an anti-human trinity of utilitarianism, subjectivism, and relativism that denies the existence of a moral sense or moral law.

Almost eighty years ago, C. S. Lewis, author of the popular Narnia Chronicles, diagnosed this state of affairs in his brilliant little book *The Abolition of Man*. In it Lewis discussed the forces that starve the moral imagination and replace it with moral relativism and utilitarian reason. He warned of a rising philosophy of education and childrearing that undermines confidence in moral certitudes and substitutes the dogma that morality is relative to individual desire and cultural context. We are reaping the dreadful harvest of that trend in our day. Such is the *Weltgeist* that captures the minds of many modern people. And yet even as we submit ourselves to this "new morality," we continue to want and expect children to grow up to be *good* people. This "is the tragicomedy of our situation," Lewis comments, that while "we clamour for those very qualities [of character and virtue]" in our children, "we are rendering [them] impossible.... In a sort of ghastly simplicity we remove the organ and demand the function. We make men without chests and expect of them virtue."[1]

Perhaps it is not surprising that someone who detected such things in the culture went on to write a series of remarkable children's fantasy stories—the first and best-known of these being *The Lion, the Witch and the Wardrobe*—that invite modern children into a world where the "old morality" reigns and retains its compelling vigor. Lewis, of course, was heir to the Victorian retrieval of the fairy tale. And he followed in the footsteps of the great nineteenth-century inventors of fairy tales and fantasy stories, among whom we can certainly count the Grimms, Hans Christian Andersen, and George MacDonald.

The Victorians brought fairy tales into the nursery because they saw in them a wisdom and a capacity to stimulate and instruct the moral imagination. In our day we have witnessed a resurgence of this interest in the fairy tale. The renowned psychiatrist Bruno Bettelheim lent an important impetus to this movement almost fifty years ago with his publication of *The Uses of Enchantment: The Meaning and Importance of Fairy Tales* (1975). "[It] hardly requires emphasis at this moment in our history," Bettelheim wrote, that children need "a moral education ... [that teaches] not through abstract ethical concepts but through that which seems tangibly right and therefore meaningful ... The child finds this kind of meaning through fairy tales"[2]

As parents raising small children in the 1980s, my wife, June, and I looked for guidance in choosing stories to read to our son, Rafi, and our daughter, Victoria, as they do today raising their own children. When Rafi and Victoria were between the ages of five and twelve, we read most of the stories I discuss in this book. Then I took these stories into the college classroom, where I taught for a quarter century a course titled Religion in Children's Literature.

This all began with a conversation one evening in the fall of 1983 in the lounge of a hotel in Washington, D.C. I had arranged to meet the late writer and man of letters Russell Kirk and his wife, Annette. They were in town for a lecture Russell was to give. Russell had written on occasion about children's literature and practiced on his four daughters his own exceptional talent for telling what he liked to call ghostly tales. That evening I asked him what children's stories were his favorites. And he was obliging. He mentioned to me George MacDonald's *The Princess and the Goblin,* Carlo Collodi's *Pinocchio,* a personal favorite of his, and Lewis's Narnia Chronicles. He added such favorites as John Ruskin's *The King of the Golden River,* Oscar Wilde's "The Selfish Giant," and of course the classic tales of the Grimm brothers and Hans Christian Andersen. Most of the books and fairy tales Russell mentioned to me that evening are in this book. In writing this book, I have tried to give my readers similar help to make the right choices.

In time, as I explored further, I was surprised to discover that there were very few books written in an accessible way on children's literature for parents and teachers. I mean books that take care to discuss the content and meaning of these stories in relation to the child's understanding and parents' and teachers' concerns about raising children to be ethical persons.

Literary criticism on children's literature is still a relatively new field and has not contributed much to the readers I have in mind. And while this is another matter that I have addressed elsewhere, much of what the critics have to say I disagree with.[3] Much of it is social constructionist, based on a theory that all meaning is subjective, not objectively real, and changes as society changes; or it wears the blinders of one school of thinking or ideology, whether that be Marxist, Freudian, Jungian, or feminist.

One might have thought ethicists could do better. Yet ethicists, whether religious or philosophical, have not done better. There is a paucity of reflection on children as moral learners or actors. Ethicists have written very little on the virtues as taught and communicated in fairy tales and children's stories. Perhaps this is because, like so many others, ethicists too subscribe to the mistaken notion that childhood is more about socialization than moral formation. In any case, it is far safer to presume that the moral agent is an adult when discussing morality. After all, in a very real way, we adults have difficulty entering into the inner moral experience of the child.

Thus, my task in this book is a rather simple one. My principal objective is to be a helpful guide through some of the most beloved fairy tales and classic and contemporary stories written for children. I have tried to be of assistance to parents and teachers who want to explore the moral and religious significance of these stories with their own children or students. By and large I have left definitions of childhood and what actually constitutes children's literature to others.[4] All of the stories that I discuss in this book fall one way or another into the category of fairy tale and the related modern genre of fantasy story. My experience in the classroom with persons ranging from eighteen to eighty has proven to me the wisdom in C. S. Lewis's observation about the best test of a children's story. In an essay on writing children's stories, Lewis quips: "I am almost inclined to set it up as a canon that a children's story which is enjoyed only by children is a bad children's story. The good ones last. A waltz which you can like only when you are waltzing is a bad waltz."[5]

I am a theologian by trade and so, as might be expected, I have been alert not just to moral themes but also to the great religious questions that have been raised by some of the most popular and honored authors of children's stories. More often than not contemporary writers and critics have avoided these religious themes or discussed them with embarrassment, if not outright antagonism. Thus, I have taken up the challenge to explore seriously some of these religious topics. Most of the chapter headings signal this interest. Themes such as love, beauty, immortality, evil, and redemption are at the heart of many of the best fairy tales and children's stories, and these themes ought not to be overlooked or minimized. I hope this book is that much better for its serious attention to the religious and moral aspects of these stories.

As I already have mentioned, this book began with my own children. That is to say that it came to be in large measure because, like other parents, I thought it was important to read stories to my children and to select the right ones. I searched for stories that would enrich their imagination and provide them with some memories that might positively influence their character and conduct throughout the whole of their lives. I have continued this practice with my grandchildren, to whom I have dedicated this edition.

I believe that my children became better readers and writers, even better speakers, because we spent special time together reading the fairy tales of the Grimm brothers and George MacDonald, or the *Märchen* and humorous tales from the Middle East and Armenia that my maternal grandmother told me when I was a child. I think that my son's willingness to go to a remote village in Armenia in the summer of 1996 to complete reconstruction of an ancient church toppled by the catastrophic earthquake of December 1988 was helped by the fact that I had told him my grandmother's stories. In his application to colleges, I discovered a short essay that Rafi wrote in answer to the question about which books of his childhood meant the most to him. He responded that C. S. Lewis's Narnia Chronicles were the most memorable because they left him standards to live by. And in his high school senior English course, Rafi decided to read all the Narnia books again and to write a final paper on Lewis's use of the elements of classical epic in the stories. As for Victoria, there happened a wonderful confluence of our early reading with her passion for ballet. She learned through dance how much the fairy tale genre has influenced music and art. Over the years she danced to the music of such musical compositions as *The Nutcracker, Swan Lake,* and the ballet version of *Alice in Wonderland.*

I think that the great fairy stories lend themselves naturally to dance and dramatic enactment. When Victoria was in fourth grade I approached her English teacher with the idea of bringing my undergraduate seminar on children's literature into her classroom. We decided that our common reading would be *Pinocchio,* and that late in the spring session my students and I would meet with her fourth graders at St. Paul's School in Brooklandville, Maryland, for conversation and to share poster drawings depicting scenes from the story. We would conclude by breaking off into smaller groups to rehearse dramatic enactments of these scenes or episodes and then gather together to perform these skits for each other.

Even more than a quarter century later, I can recollect vividly the reaction of my Loyola College students to this experience. They were struck by how much detail the fourth graders remembered and by the "sophisticated" lessons they drew from what they read. In an essay titled "Children and Literature," the renowned child psychiatrist Robert Coles has commented: "The truth is that many of us (certainly many in my field of child psychology) don't give enough credit to the natural, normal everyday development of narrative interest, narrative sense, narrative response, narrative competence in boys and girls."[6] My college students made this very discovery for themselves. They also confessed with open embarrassment that the fourth graders had grasped better than they much of the meaning in the story. For example, the fourth graders seemed to recognize from personal knowledge the nature and source of Pinocchio's temptations and backslidings, and were much less prepared than they to excuse him for the behavior and decisions that got him into so much trouble and caused Geppetto such grief. The fourth graders did not yet believe, as contemporary college students are apt to do, that growing up is a straight line— twelve years of primary and secondary education, four years of college, and then with a degree in hand one is well on the way to becoming a complete and successful human being.

Whereas my college students admitted they sometimes got bored with the repetition in the story, the elementary school children became absorbed in that repetition. It reminded the children of their own experience of trying and failing and trying again. G. K. Chesterton observes in *Lunacy and Letters*, "For it is a mark of the essential morality of fairyland (a thing too commonly overlooked) that happiness, like happiness anywhere else, involves an object and even a challenge; we can only admire scenery if we want to get past it."[7] The repeated attempts and failures of Pinocchio and the challenges he faces over and over again to reunite with the object of his affection and love—Geppetto, his father and maker—made immediate sense to the fourth graders and held their attention. My college students began to suspect that maybe they had lost something in growing up—a sense of wonder and a yearning for a taste of the other—that might have been better tended and retained if they had been brought up on more of what we were reading in class. Perhaps the fourth graders they had met were actually nearer than they to the wellsprings of human morality and were better served by reading *Pinocchio* than they had been by a required course in ethics.

Repetition signified one other thing to the fourth graders, the importance of which also dawned on my college students. Chesterton comments that when we grow up we tend to think that repetition is a sign of deadness, like "a piece of clockwork. People feel that if the universe was personal it would vary, if the sun were alive it would dance." To the contrary, "variation in human affairs is generally brought into them, not by life, but by death; by the dying down or breaking off of their strength or desire. A man varies his movements because of some slight element of failure or fatigue." Whereas repetition, far from signifying monotony and deadness, may signify delight, desire, and vitality. And this is what it seemed to mean for the children of St. Paul's School who read *Pinocchio*. "A child kicks his legs rhythmically through excess, not absence, of life. Because children have unbounding vitality, because they are spirit fierce and free, therefore they want things repeated and unchanged. They always say, 'Do it again'" because there is such delight in that thing or activity. "It may be," Chesterton concludes, "that God makes every daisy separately, but has never got tired of making them. It may be that He has the eternal appetite of infancy, for we have sinned and grown old, and our Father is younger than we. The repetition in Nature may not be a mere recurrence;

it may be a theatrical *encore*."[8] Perhaps we need more intergenerational learning of the sort my college class and I experienced back then at St. Paul's School. Perhaps fairy tales ought not only to take a bigger place in American childhoods but ought to be read by college students as well.

In Chapter 1, I discuss what I believe are some of the serious shortcomings of contemporary education when it comes to the moral instruction of our children and the important role that fairy tales and fantasy stories could play in this instruction. My views have been formed and confirmed by my experience with my own children, with my grandchildren, and in the classroom. The candor, honesty, and intelligence of the college students I taught for decades have added to my conviction that things must be done differently.

I have also taught graduate students, parents, and teachers over the years. During the 1990s I taught graduate-level courses at the Ecumenical Institute of Theology of St. Mary's Seminary and University in Baltimore, Maryland. I offered workshops and seminars on fairy tales and children's stories. Those experiences remain very special in my memory. The seminars were attended by public and parochial school teachers, seminarians, religious sisters, and priests and pastors. Much of my inspiration for this book grew from these workshops and seminars.

While attending one of these seminars, a Black pastor of an inner-city Baltimore church was moved to commence a series of sermons for adults and children that explored some of the fairy tales we read in class. He related the fairy tales to stories in the Bible and the social ethical concerns of his ministry. I recall how he in the seminar compared "Beauty and the Beast" with the Old Testament story of Ruth and Naomi. He compared Ruth's love for her mother-in-law, Naomi, and refusal to abandon her to Beauty's love and loyalty toward her father. And he went on to explain that in her marriage to Boaz, Ruth yet manages to keep her promise never to abandon Naomi. Likewise, even as Beauty keeps her promise to the Beast and finally marries him, she reconciles this with her love for and duty toward her father. Another Black minister found the resources in "Hansel and Gretel" useful for his work with abandoned and abused children. As he put it, "On any given day of the week we find more than one Hansel or Gretel on a street corner downtown."

An Invitation

Thus stimulated by both my readings to my children and my classroom experiences, I wrote this book (in its first edition and now in an expanded form in this second edition). Over the years, I have listened very closely to the "non-experts": my children, my grandchildren, and my students at Loyola and later at the University of Virginia. And I have tried my very best to draw on what I have learned from my children and my students in writing this book, from their fresh encounters with the stories I discuss. Frankly, they have taught me much more than the so-called experts.

Also, I have striven to assist parents and teachers in finding norms and standards in these stories that they might not have seen on their own. I hope this book gives them confidence they might otherwise not have had in presenting these stories to children. But I also have wanted not to spoil the pleasure of reading these stories for either the first or the tenth time. The deep truths of a good story, especially fairy tales, cannot be revealed through discursive analysis alone—otherwise why tell the story? Rather, these truths must be experienced through the story itself and savored in the immediacy of the moment that unfolds with the impending danger of the quest or the joy of reunion with the beloved. In George MacDonald's haunting tale *The Golden Key*, the young heroine of the story encounters the Old Man of the Earth:

> Then the Old Man of the Earth stooped over the floor of the cave, raised a huge stone from it, and left it leaning. It disclosed a great hole that went plumb-down.
> "That is the way," he said.
> "But there are no stairs."
> "You must throw yourself in. There is no other way."[9]

This is also the way with fairy tales.

May your own reading of this book be a beginning and not an end, not a closure but an invitation to unceasing explorations of the imagination. And may our children be the final beneficiaries.

1

AWAKENING THE MORAL IMAGINATION

> When Mendal was already the far-famed and much-hated rabbi of Kotzak, he once returned to the little town in which he was born. There he visited the teacher who taught him his alphabet when he was a child and read the five books of Moses with him. But he did not go to see the teacher who had given him further instruction, and at a chance meeting the man asked his former pupil whether he had any cause to be ashamed of his teacher. Mendal replied: "You taught me things that can be refuted for according to one interpretation they can mean this, according to another, that. But my first teacher taught me true teachings which cannot be refuted, and they have remained with me as such. That is why I owe him special reverence."
>
> —*Martin Buber, Tales of the Hasidim*

Flannery O'Connor, that marvelously gifted American writer of the past century, spoke a simple though profound truth when she said that "a story is a way to say something that can't be said any other way. You tell a story because a statement would be inadequate."[1] The great fairy tales and fantasy stories communicate the

Tending the Heart of Virtue. Second Edition. Vigen Guroian, Oxford University Press.
© Vigen Guroian 1998, 2023. DOI: 10.1093/oso/9780195384307.003.0002

meaning of morality through vivid depictions of the struggle between good and evil, where characters must make difficult choices between right and wrong, or heroes and villains contest the very fate of imaginary worlds. Not didacticism but rather the narrative, the dramatic action, makes the fairy tales meaningful. Narrative supplies the imagination with important symbolic information about the shape of our world and appropriate responses to its inhabitants. The contemporary moral philosopher Alasdair MacIntyre sums this up eloquently:

> It is through hearing about wicked stepmothers, lost children, good but misguided kings, wolves that suckle twin boys, youngest sons who receive no inheritance but must make their own way in the world and eldest sons who waste their inheritance ... that children learn or mislearn both what a child and what a parent is, what the cast of characters may be in the drama into which they have been born and what the ways of the world are. Deprive children of stories and you leave them unscripted, anxious stutterers in their actions as in their words.[2]

G. K. Chesterton muses about the wisdom and ethics of the fairy tale. He writes: "I am concerned with a certain way of looking at life, which was created in me by the fairy tales, but has since been meekly ratified by mere facts."[3] This way of looking at life that Chesterton identifies I in this book call the *moral imagination*. This is illustrated when he continues: "We can say why we take liberty from a man who takes liberties. But we cannot say why an egg can turn into a chicken any more than we can say why a bear could turn into a fairy prince. As *ideas*, the egg and the chicken are further from each other than the bear and the prince; for no egg itself suggests a chicken, whereas some princes do suggest bears."[4] Likewise, we may say that values are set by the free market or by the state and measure what we are up against and how we should trade our wares or parlay our talents. Yet we cannot know, except within the context of the entire story, that what initially seemed to be the enlightened discernment of a character was actually a stupid cleverness, courage a stupid bravado, or disloyalty creative fidelity to a greater good.

The Virtues and Moral Character

Moral living is about being responsive and responsible toward other people. And virtues are those traits of character that enable persons to use their freedom in morally responsible ways. The mere ability, however, to use moral principles to justify one's actions does not make a virtuous person. The brilliant twentieth-century Jewish philosopher Martin Buber tells the story of how he fell into "the fatal mistake of *giving instruction* in ethics" by presenting ethics as formal rules and principles. Buber discovered that very little of this kind of education gets "transformed into character-building substance." In his little gem of moral and educational philosophy, an essay appropriately entitled "The Education of Character," Buber recalls:

> I try to explain to my pupils that envy is despicable, and at once I feel the secret resistance of those who are poorer than their comrades. I try to explain that it is wicked to bully the weak, and at once I see a suppressed smile on the lips of the strong. I try to explain that lying destroys life, and something frightful happens: the worst habitual liar of the class produces a brilliant essay on the destructive power of lying.[5]

Mere instruction in morality is not sufficient to nurture the virtues. It might even backfire, especially when the presentation is heavily exhortative and the pupil feels coerced. Instead, a compelling vision of the goodness of goodness itself needs to be presented in such a way that it is attractive and stirs the imagination. A good moral education addresses both the cognitive and affective dimensions of human nature. And stories are an irreplaceable medium for this kind of moral education, by which I mean the education of character.

The Greek word for character means literally an impression. Moral character is an impression stamped upon the self. Character is defined by its orientation, consistency, and constancy. Today we often equate freedom with morality and goodness. But this is naive because freedom is transcendent and the precondition of choice itself. Depending upon his or her character, an individual will be drawn toward either goodness or wickedness. Moral and immoral behavior is freedom enacted for good or ill.

In the Case of "Beauty and the Beast"

The great fairy tales and children's fantasy stories attractively depict character and virtue. In these stories the virtues glimmer as if in a looking glass, and wickedness and deception are unmasked of their pretensions to goodness and truth. The stories make us face the unvarnished truth about ourselves and compel us to consider what kind of people we want to be.

"Beauty and the Beast" is one of the most beloved of all the fairy tales because it contrasts goodness with badness in a way that is appealing to the imagination. It is also a story that depicts with peculiar force the mystery of virtue itself. Virtue is the "magic" of moral life, for it often appears in the most unexpected persons and places and with surprising results. At the beginning of the story, we learn that a very rich merchant had three "daughters [all of whom] were extremely handsome, especially the youngest; [so she was] called 'The little Beauty.'" But nothing more is said about Beauty's physical attributes. Instead, our attention is drawn to her virtuous character. Beauty's moral goodness—her inner beauty—is contrasted with her sisters' pride, vanity, and selfishness—their inner ugliness. Although Beauty's sisters are physically attractive, they "had a great deal of pride, because they were rich. They gave themselves ridiculous airs . . . and laughed at their youngest sister [Beauty], because she spent the greatest part of her time in reading good books." By contrast, Beauty is "charming, sweet tempered . . . spoke so kindly to poor people," and truly loves her father.[6]

Because she is virtuous, Beauty is able to "see" in the Beast a goodness that his monstrous appearance belies. At her first supper in the monster's castle, Beauty says to the Beast: "That is true [that I find you ugly], for I cannot lie, but I believe you are very good-natured." And when the Beast tries her even more with his repeated self-deprecating remarks, Beauty responds emphatically: "Among mankind . . . there are many that deserve [the] name [Beast] more than you, and I prefer you, just as you are, to those, who, under a human form, hide a treacherous, corrupt, and ungrateful heart" (p. 190). The sharp contrast between Beauty's goodness and her sisters' badness, which is masked by their physical attractiveness, parallels the irony that the Beast, who is repulsive physically, is good and virtuous. "Beauty and the Beast" teaches the simple but important lesson that appearances can deceive, that what is seen is not always what it appears to be.

Similarly, this great fairy tale also bids us to imagine what the outcome might have been had Beauty's sisters been placed in her position. No doubt they would not have recognized or appreciated the goodness beneath the Beast's monstrous appearance. Nor does it seem at all likely that they would have made Beauty's courageous and fortuitous choice. The paradoxical truth that the story portrays is that unless virtue is present in a person she will not be able to find, appreciate, or embrace virtue in another.

"Beauty and the Beast" embraces one last important moral truth: a person's decisions in life will define what kind of person she becomes. In this sense also our destinies are not fated, for we decide our own destinies. At the end of the story, the "beautiful lady" who has visited Beauty in her dreams appears at the Beast's castle and brings with her Beauty's entire family. The fairy then says to Beauty: "Beauty . . . come and receive the reward of your judicious choice; you have preferred virtue before either wit or beauty, and deserve to have a person in whom these qualifications are united; you are going to be a great queen" (p. 195). Beauty's sisters, however, are unhappy in their marriages because they chose their spouses solely on the basis of good looks and wit. Through greed, jealousy, and pride their hearts have become like stone. So they are turned into statues, but retain their consciousness that they might behold their sister's happiness and be moved to admit their own faults.

Awakening the Moral Imagination and Teaching the Virtues

Like all the great fairy tales, "Beauty and the Beast" invites us to draw analogies between its imaginary world and the world in which we live. It provides the imagination with information that the self may use to distinguish what is true from what is not. But how, we might ask, is the imagination itself awakened, and how is it made moral? These are important questions for the moral educator, and they are not so easily answered.

Buber's frank discussion of the mistakes he made when he first taught ethics helps us to see how difficult awakening and nurturing the moral imagination can be. Buber's mistakes are not uncommon. They are often committed, especially when the role of reason in human conduct is overestimated and the roles of the will and the imagination are underestimated. This hazard is increased by a utilitarian and instrumentalist ethos that has seeped to the taproots of our culture. Despite evidence that we are failing to transmit morality effectively to our children, we persist in teaching ethics as if it comes from a how-to manual for successful living. Moral educators routinely introduce moral principles and even the virtues themselves to students as if they are practical instruments for achieving success. When we tell our children that standards of social utility and material success are the measurements of the value of moral principles and virtues, then it is not likely that our pedagogy is going to transform the minds or convert the hearts of young people. As Buber observed in his own classroom, all that we will accomplish is to confirm the despair of the weak, darken the envy of the poor, justify the greed of the rich, embolden the deceitfulness of the liar, and encourage the aggression of the strong.

Much of what passes for moral education fails to nurture the moral imagination. Yet, only a pedagogy that awakens and enlivens the moral imagination will persuade the child or the student that courage is the ultimate test of good character, that honesty is essential for trust and harmony among persons, and that humility and a magnanimous spirit are goods greater than the prizes gained by selfishness, pride, or the unscrupulous exercise of position and power.

The moral imagination is not a *thing*, not even so much a faculty of the mind, but rather the very process by which the self makes metaphors out of images that memory supplies. It then employs these metaphors to suppose correspondences in experience and to make moral judgments. The twentieth-century philosopher George Santayana explains this process with his own use of metaphor: "Perceptions fall into the brain rather as seeds into a furrowed field or even as sparks into a keg of powder. Each image," in turn, gives birth to more images, "sometimes slowly and subterraneously, sometimes (when a passionate train is started) with a sudden burst of fancy."[7]

The important question is not so much whether imagination is waxing or waning in youth today. For wherever there are human beings imagination exists and is exercised, much as wherever there are spiders webs are spun. The important question is what kinds of imagination our contemporary culture is engendering. There are other undesirable forms of imagination, such as the idyllic, the idolatrous, and the diabolic.[8] And these unhealthy forms of imagination are on the rise in a culture dominated by a pervasive media and ubiquitous advertising.

We needn't be concerned that spiders will cease spinning their webs properly. Spiders act by instinct. Human beings, however, exercise their imaginations freely. Indeed, it is every bit as correct to say that human beings are imaginative creatures as to say they are reasoning ones. The moral imagination is active for well or ill, strongly or weakly every moment we are living, whether we are awake or asleep. Yet it needs proper nurture and proper exercise. Otherwise, the moral imagination will atrophy like a muscle that is not used. Furthermore, the richness or poverty of the moral imagination is dependent upon the richness or poverty of experience. When human beings are young and dependent upon parents and others who assume custodial care for them, they are especially open to formation through experiences that these adults may provide. When we argue or discuss what kind of education or recreation our children should have, we are acknowledging these realities.

Sadly, too often our society fails to provide children with the kinds of experiences that cultivate and build up the moral imagination. A measure of the impoverishment of the moral imagination in the rising generation is their difficulty in recognizing, making, or using metaphors that will enable them to act responsibly and morally. College students today do not lack an awareness of morality, although they often are confused or puzzled about its basis or their personal ownership of it. Nonetheless, I have found that many are perplexed when reading a novel or short story because they have not learned how to find and follow the inner connections of character and action, the narrative itself, and the moral meaning that is communicated. This is a failure of imagination, not of knowledge that can be tested.

Some years ago, I administered a surprise quiz in a course on theology and literature, in which I asked the students to list and explain five metaphors that they had found in John Updike's *Rabbit, Run*. The majority of the class could not identify five metaphors. Some did not even identify the metaphor in the book's title, which I had purposely discussed as such in a previous class meeting. It was not that these young people lacked a practical definition of a metaphor. They had been provided with a definition in their English courses. They lacked, however, a personal knowledge of metaphor that an active imagination provides. I suspect that in the past these students had gotten the idea that all they needed to do was look for the so-called facts in a book. Facts are things whose meaning belongs to their use and whose use requires relatively little interpretation. We are living in a culture in which metaphor is discarded for these so-called facts. We train minds to detect these facts much as one breaks in a baseball glove. Meanwhile, the moral imagination suffers.

Nature, Imagination, and *Poesis*

George MacDonald, that great storyteller of the Victoria era, was of the persuasion that an acquaintance with nature may be even more important than story for the formation of the moral imagination. This point was brought home to me more than two decades ago, when I was teaching at Loyola College of Maryland. I had assigned in my ethics course the twentieth-century American writer Walker Percy's novel *The Thanatos Syndrome*. The protagonist of the novel is a psychiatrist whose name is Thomas More. More has a theory about human types that he, as the first-person narrator, reveals to the reader at the start of the novel. More places all of his patients into one of two categories: they are either bluebirds or blue jays. During a classroom discussion of the novel, it dawned upon me that More's classificatory metaphors had escaped my students' comprehension. So I raised these questions: "Have you observed these birds in nature? And are you at all familiar with the distinctive habits and temperaments of bluebirds and blue jays? Perhaps, for starters, you could identify for me the physical attributes of each bird."

My students had a difficult time with this, for they lacked habits of observation and *poesis*. *Poesis* is an activity of making that is imaginative. It is the earmark of play itself, which seems to come naturally to young children, not so easily to college-age youth. I can only guess that the young men and women in my classroom had spent far too much time looking at a screen and not out the window—or, better still, spending time out of doors. MacDonald urged that even the youngest children be encouraged to observe nature closely in order to put the world together and to speculate from what they see to what they do not see. This sort of attentiveness to nature differs from the empirical method of the natural sciences. It is not so much an activity of reason as of the imagination. It enables not the prediction of phenomena, as science strives to achieve, but rather the invention of literature and poetry, and an appreciation of the same.

MacDonald maintains that we assimilate the natural world through our imagination and also uncover in it an inexhaustible treasure house of forms and images. He cites Thomas Carlyle in *Past and Present*: "'The coldest word was once a glowing new metaphor and bold questionable originality. Thy very attention, does it not mean an *attentio*, a stretching-to?'" MacDonald adds: "All that moves in the mind is symbolized in Nature. Or, to use another more philosophical, and certainly not less poetic figure, the world is a sensuous analysis of humanity. . . . Take any word expressive of emotion—take the word *emotion* itself –and you will find that its primary meaning is of the outer world," as the rustling and agitation of the trees is analogized to the self in its inner disturbances.[9] In other words, that which is "outside" of us is the necessary precondition for understanding ourselves inwardly.

And when we put into words this experience of the external world with its forms and images and relate that to our inner experience, our humanity in all its depth and complexity of meaning flowers and is unveiled. The imagination lights the way. The very essence of things and the world in its wholeness are revealed to us, along with our relationship to that world. What would we do without the lion to remind us of the nobility that belongs to our nature or the owl for the wisdom into which we must mature as human beings?

What Fairy Tales Do for the Moral Imagination

Fairy tales and fantasy stories transport the reader into other worlds that are fresh with wonder, surprise, and danger. They challenge the reader to make sense out of those other worlds, to navigate his or her way through them, and to imagine oneself in the place of the heroes and heroines who populate those worlds. The safety and assurance of these imaginative adventures is that risks may be taken without having to endure all of the consequences of failure; the joy is in discovering how these risky adventures might eventuate in satisfactory and happy outcomes. Yet the concept of self is also transformed. The images and metaphors in these stories stay with the reader, even after he has returned to the "real" world.

After a child has read Hans Christian Andersen's "The Snow Queen" or C. S. Lewis's *The Lion, the Witch and the Wardrobe,* her moral imagination is bound to have been stimulated and sharpened. These stories offer powerful images of good and evil and show her how to love through the examples of the characters she has come to love and admire. This will spur her imagination to translate these experiences and images into the constitutive elements of self-identity and into metaphors she will use to interpret her own world. She will grow increasingly capable of moving about in that world with moral intent.

When the moral imagination is wakeful, the virtues come to life, filled with personal and existential as well as social significance. The virtues needn't be the dry and lifeless stuff of moral theories or the ethical version of hygienic rules in health science classes; they can take on a life that attracts and awakens the desire to own them for oneself. We desperately need to adopt forms of moral pedagogy that are faithful to the ancient and true vocation of the teacher—to make persons into mature and whole human beings, able to stand face-to-face with the truth about themselves and others, while also desiring to correct their own faults and to emulate goodness and truth wherever it is found. We need to take greater advantage of the power in stories to humanize the young, whether these be Buber's beloved tales of the Hasidim or the stories we commonly refer to as fairy tales.

The Deception of Values in the Contemporary Debate over Education and Morality

"Values" is an often-invoked buzzword in contemporary education. It carries with it the full burden of our concerns about morality. But can it carry those concerns to a successful conclusion? Teaching values, whether family values, democratic values, or religious values, is touted as the remedy for our moral confusion. Of course, this consensus about the need for stronger moral values immediately cracks and advocates retreat when the inevitable question is raised as to which values should be taught. I do not think that the debate over values lends much promise of clarifying what we believe in or what morality we should be teaching our children. Values are not the answer to moral relativism. Quite the contrary, values talk is entirely amenable to moral relativism.

In *The Demoralization of Society: From Victorian Virtues to Modern Values*, Gertrude Himmelfarb exposes what some students of Western morals have known for some time, which is that "values" is a rather new word in our moral vocabulary. Its use reaches back not much farther than the late nineteenth century. The German philosopher Friedrich Nietzsche seems to have been the inventor of our modern use of the term as a category of morality. Nietzsche was opposed to what he called "effeminate" Christianity and advocated the "Übermensch" or superior human being with the courage to defy conventional religious morality and invent his own values. In his famous book *Beyond Good and Evil*, Nietzsche used "values" in this new way—not as a verb meaning to value or esteem something, or as a singular noun meaning the measure of a thing (the economic value of money, labor, or property), but in

26

the plural form, connoting the moral beliefs and attitudes of a society or an individual.[10] In his phrase "transvaluation of values," Nietzsche summed up his thesis about the "death of God" and the birth of his new "noble type of man." Nietzsche described this new kind of human being as "a determiner of [his own] values" who judges right from wrong on the basis of what is good or injurious to himself. Thus, the values of conventional morality were false values bound to be replaced by the self-made values of the truly autonomous and free individual.

Nietzsche's innovative use of the term "values" did not gain immediate approval or acceptance. Even as late as the 1928 edition, the *Oxford English Dictionary* did not list "values" in the plural form referring to moral qualities. More recently, the 1992 edition of the *Oxford Modern English Dictionary* not only defines "values" in the modern sense of moral qualities, but also assigns them a subjectivistic character. The dictionary's editors give this definition: "values" refers to "*one's* standards, *one's judgement* of what is valuable or important in life" (the emphases are mine). Another way of putting it is that "values" belong to those things we call individual lifestyles, and in common discourse a lifestyle is something we choose and even exchange for another according to our personal preferences and tastes, much in the same way that we might replace one wardrobe with another. Himmelfarb justifiably says: "'Values' [has] brought with it the assumptions that all moral ideas are subjective and relative, that they are mere customs and conventions, that they have a purely instrumental, utilitarian purpose, and that they are peculiar to specific individuals and societies."[11]

In our consumerist society moral values may even take on the characteristics of material commodities. We easily assume that personal freedom is about *choosing* values for oneself in an unregulated and ever-expanding marketplace of moralities and lifestyles. Choosing values turns out to be not much different from shopping for groceries at the supermarket or selecting building supplies at the home improvement store. As a society, we are learning to regard morality and values as matters of taste and personal satisfaction. For some people, married heterosexual monogamy is a value, whereas for others it is romantic relationships with one or several lovers, male or female or both. Some people say abortion is wrong and they do not approve of it, but these same people also say that for others abortion may be all right. This is possible only if values are the creation of the self and are not universally binding moral norms. If one scratches just beneath the surface of the moral outlook of many Americans, one bumps into the rather naively but also often vehemently held assumption that the individual is the architect of his or her own morality, built out of value "blocks" that the individual independently picks and stacks. We suddenly run into the ghost of Friedrich Nietzsche.

There are real and very important differences between what we now call values and the virtues as they were traditionally understood. Let me put it this way. A value is like a smoke ring. Its shape is initially determined by the smoker, but once it is released there is no telling what shapes it will take. One thing is certain, however. Once a smoke ring has left the smoker's lips it has already begun to evaporate into thin air. Volition and volatility are characteristics of both smoke rings and values. By contrast, a virtue might be compared to a stone, whose nature is permanence. We might throw a stone into a pond, where it will lie at the bottom with other stones. But if at some later date we should want to retrieve that stone from the bottom of the pond, we can be sure that the shape of the stone has not changed and that we will be able to distinguish it from the rest of the stones.

The virtues define the character of a person, his enduring relationship to the world, and what will be his end. Whereas values, according to their common usage, are the instruments or components of moral living that the self chooses for itself and that the self may disregard without necessarily jeopardizing its identity. Accordingly, values are subordinate and relative to the self's own autonomy, which is understood as the self's highest value and essential quality. But when we say in the traditional speech of character that Jack is virtuous and that he is a courageous person, we are saying that the virtue of courage belongs to the very essence of who and what Jack is. Being courageous is not subject to a willing for it to be so or a willing for it not to be so. Virtues and vices define the will itself and also properly describe the willing person. The color orange is both a quality of an orange and an inescapable description of it. If we find an object, however, that looks like an orange but is brown, either it must be an orange that has gone bad or it is not an orange at all. Similarly, it makes no moral sense to say that a courageous man has decided to be a coward. We cannot say on the basis of some subsequent behavior we have observed in Jack that he must have decided to become a coward. If Jack's recent actions were indeed cowardly and not courageous, then we are obliged to revise our original description of Jack.

Thus, I am contending that what seems so self-evident to many of our contemporaries about the centrality of values to moral living might not be true, might not be consistent with human nature, or might not adequately take into account the larger share of human reality over which we each personally have little or no choice or control. Rather, the best sources in the Western tradition have argued that morality is much more than, indeed qualitatively different from, the sum of the values that an essentially autonomous self chooses for itself. Classical, Jewish, and Christian sources, such as Plato, Aristotle, Cicero, St. Augustine, St. Basil of Caesarea, St. John Chrysostom, Maimonides, St. Thomas Aquinas, and John Calvin, insist that morality is neither plural nor subjective. Instead, they maintain that human morality is substantial, universal, and relational in character, founded and rooted in a permanent good, in a higher moral law, or in the being of God. From this standpoint, values and decisions whose claims of legitimacy extend no further than individual volition are as effervescent as the foam that floats on top of the waves. They cannot be reliable guides to moral living.

The great teachers of our historical culture insist that morality is deeper and more substantial than effervescent foam. It stands to reason, they insist, that where there are waves and foam there is a deeper body of water. These sources describe a sea of substantial morality that lies beneath the ephemeral and ever-changing surface expressions of emotion, taste, and satisfaction in ordinary human intercourse. They describe character as the gravity that keeps us afloat and virtues as the sails that propel us and the instruments that help us to maintain our course, even when the ship is being rocked by stormy waters and high seas.

Sailors need to know when to use ballast or throw down the anchor, lest the ship sink and they drown. In like manner, the virtues enable us to respond correctly to those moments of life that are the moral equivalents to such conditions at sea. However, an ability to discern these moments and respond appropriately entails more than formal techniques of decision-making, just as successful sailing requires that one know more than just the techniques of good navigation. As the latter requires a knowledge of and familiarity with the sea that cannot be taught in books but can only be learned from seafaring itself, so the moral life requires that we *be* virtuous. The virtues are not just the moral equivalent of techniques of good sailing; rather, they are the way as well as the end of goodness and happiness. If we assume, however, as so many of the textbooks would have us believe, that problems and quandaries are the whole subject matter of ethics and that the decisions we make are the purpose of morality, then we are likely to interpret even the virtues in the same superficial, utilitarian way in which we already think of values. But if we pay heed to the ancient sources, we will recognize that the virtues are related to a much thicker and deeper moral reality. We will see the virtues as the qualities of character that we need in order to steer our way through the complicated and mysterious sea of morality into which we all have been placed. For such journeying, a pocketful of values is neither sufficient ballast nor a substitute for sails, compass, or sextant.

Conclusion on Moral Pedagogy: A Response to the Contemporary Debate over Moral Education

Years ago in a series of essays entitled, simply enough, "Education, or the Mistake About the Child," G. K. Chesterton entered into a debate that then was no less important than it is today.[12] That debate is about what counts for moral education. In conclusion, I want to review what Chesterton had to say, thus bringing this conversation around full circle to the claim I made at the start: that stories, especially fairy tales, are invaluable resources for the moral education of children.

Modern educators have not been well disposed toward traditional fairy tales and their like. They write them off as too violent
or not contemporary enough, and so forth. They favor "practical" and "realistic" stories—stories about the lives children live
today that easily lend themselves to distillation into useful themes,
principles, and values. What some educators can't find they create.
From the pens of those writing textbooks on values spill stories
whose sole purpose is to clarify so-called moral problems or
draw out reasons for making intelligent moral decisions. These
stories are of the disposable kind, made to be discarded like empty
cartons once the important "stuff" that was packed in them has
been removed. Teaching reasoning skills, rather than the virtues,
is considered the means to a moral education; values clarification,
not character, is regarded as the goal.

These educators think that moral education is like teaching children reading or arithmetic. But even that is not quite accurate, because in the case of moral education children are supposed to be
permitted to discover and clarify for themselves their own values
and personal moral stance in the world. Yet we do not permit children to invent their own math; rather, we teach them the multiplication tables. Nor do we encourage children to make up their
own personal alphabets; rather, we teach them how to read. What
might be the outcome of an education that did permit children to
invent their own math and alphabets? No doubt the result would
be confusion or chaos. Should we be surprised at the outcome of
our recent efforts to help children clarify their own values—in
fact, invent their own personal moralities?

In his own inimitable way, G. K. Chesterton exposed the flaw
and deception in this modern approach to moral education. And
he identified the dogmatizing in its anti-dogmatic rhetoric. In our

day this modern approach is justified by prior commitments to certain psychological theories that elevate personal autonomy and self-realization above what we dismissively call "external authority." The teacher must not introduce values into the classroom but instead should work to "draw out" from children their own moral beliefs and through a process of clarification help them to better formulate their own values. But here is how Chesterton characterizes this historical debate:

> The important point here is only that you cannot anyhow get rid of authority in education. . . . The educator drawing out is just as arbitrary and coercive as the instructor pouring in; for he draws out what he chooses. He decides what in the child shall be developed and what shall not be developed. He does not (I suppose) draw out the neglected faculty of forgery. He does not (so far at least) lead out, with timid steps, a shy talent for torture. The only result of this pompous and precise distinction between the educator and the instructor is that the instructor pokes where he likes and the educator pulls where he likes.[13]

In answer to the skeptics, Chesterton states what he thought to be obvious. Whether we admit it or not, education is bound to indoctrinate and bound to coerce. Rabbi Mendal especially thanked and praised his first teacher because he faithfully inculcated in his young student the necessary rudiments of culture and passed on the essentials of a religious and moral way of life. The *Oxford English Dictionary* defines "indoctrination" as to imbue with learning or bring into a knowledge of something, such as a dogma. Chesterton argues that an authentic moral education is not possible unless something like this occurs. He speaks of the responsibility to affirm "the truth of our human tradition and handing it on with a voice of authority, an unshaken voice. That is the one eternal education; to be sure enough that something is true that you dare to tell it to a child."[14]

The real corruptions of moral education are an imperious moralizing, on the one hand, and the indulgence of spurious argument and undisciplined opinion, on the other. Nevertheless, a valid and effective moral education is bound to be coercive at times and even do a kind of violence, whether or not opinion is "drawn out" from the student or dogma is "put into" him.

> Exactly the same intellectual violence is done to the creature who is poked and pulled. Now we must all accept the responsibility of this intellectual violence. Education is violent because it is creative. It is creative because it is human. It is reckless as playing on the fiddle; as dogmatic as drawing a picture; as brutal as building a house. In short, it is what all human action is; it is an interference with life and growth.[15]

But Chesterton was not an advocate of the blunt and heavy instrument. Nor am I. This is one reason fairy tales appealed to him so much. Fairy tales might not qualify as scientific hypotheses or theories, but they do resonate with the deepest qualities of humanness, freedom, and the moral imagination. At the same time, they deny the psychological and material determinism that lurks behind much of the modern talk of human liberation, and they discredit the hubris of reason and rationality that displaces faith and confidence in truth. Again, they show us a way of envisioning the world—a world in which everything that is need not have been, and in which the *real* moral law connotes freedom and not necessity. The fairy-tale philosopher, writes Chesterton, "is glad that the leaf is green precisely because it could have been scarlet. . . . He is pleased that snow is white on the strictly reasonable ground that it might have been black. Every colour has in it a bold quality as of choice; the red of garden roses is not only decisive but dramatic, like suddenly spilt blood. He feels that something has been *done*," that there is something *willful* in all of it, as if someone decided that things ought to be this way instead of another way and that these things are repeated either in order to improve them or simply because they are a source of delight in their repetition.[16] The fairy-tale philosopher respects the deeper mystery of freedom in its transcendent source.

Second, fairy tales show us that there is a difference between what is logically possible and what is morally felicitous, between what is rationally doable and what is morally permissible. In fairy tales the character of real law belongs to neither natural necessity nor rational determinism. Rather, real law is a comprehensible sign of a primal, unfathomable freedom and of a numinous reality and will. Real law, the realest law, can be obeyed or broken, and in either case for the very same reason, because the creature is both subject of and participant in this primal freedom. Fairy-tale heroes are called to be both free and responsible, thus virtuous and respectful of the moral law.

Fairy tales and modern fantasy stories project fantastic other worlds, but they also pay close attention to real moral "laws" of character and virtue. These laws ought not to be high-handedly shoved down the throats of children (or of anyone else). More accurately, they are norms of behavior that obtain in patterns of relation between agent, act, other, and world. Rational cognition is capable of grasping these norms. They become habit, however, only when they are lived, or, as in the case of fairy tales, experienced vicariously and imaginatively through the artful delineation of character and plot in story. Thus, while fairy tales are not a substitute for life experience, they have the great capacity to shape our moral constitution without the shortcomings of either rigidly dogmatic schooling or values-clarification education. By portraying wonderful and frightening worlds in which ugly beasts are transformed into princes and evil persons are turned to stones and good persons back to flesh, fairy tales remind us of moral truths whose ultimate claims to normativity and permanence we would not think of questioning. Love freely given is better than obedience that is coerced. Courage that rescues the innocent is noble, whereas cowardice that betrays others for self-gain or self-preservation is worthy only of disdain. Fairy tales say plainly that virtue and vice are opposites and not just a matter of degree. They show us that the virtues fit into character and complete our world in the same way that goodness naturally fills all things.

I realize that the views I have expressed defy what the advocates of late modernity or postmodernity insist on—that there is no such thing as a common human condition or a perennial literature that lends expression to the experience of that condition. I do not expect to persuade those who are entrenched in these positions to change their minds. I can only appeal to that certain "stuff" of human existence that the human imagination takes hold of and makes moral sense of in fairy tales. I mean such things as the joy in the birth of a first child and the crippling sorrow of illness and deformity; childhood fears of getting lost and childhood desires to escape parental authority; the love that binds siblings together and the rivalry that tears them apart; the naming we do that gives identity and the naming we also do that confuses identity; the curses of dread malefactors and the blessings of welcome benefactors; the agony of unrequited love and the joy of love that is reciprocated.

I could go on. But the skeptics and critics will not be satisfied. The skeptics say there is nothing of commonality in such things, just individual lives and the particular conditions in which these lives flourish or fail. I am not convinced. Nothing of what these people say is proven, and as I have grown old and become more traveled and my memory fills with so many different lives and human faces, the wisdom of fairy tales, the wisdom of a common human condition underlying and running through all of the diversity and difference, seems far more reasonable than moral and cultural relativism.

One last thing in which I agree with Chesterton. Fairy tales lead us toward a belief in something that, if it were not also so veiled in a mystery, common sense alone would affirm: if there is a story, there must surely also be a storyteller.

2

ON BECOMING A REAL HUMAN CHILD

Pinocchio

In the Disney animated film version of Carlo Collodi's classic, Geppetto wishes upon a star that the wooden marionette he has made might become a real boy. In the end, Geppetto's wish is granted by the Blue Fairy because Geppetto has "given such happiness to others" and because Pinocchio has proven himself to be "brave, truthful, and unselfish." The contemporary children's story writer Maurice Sendak judges that Disney's Pinocchio "is good; [and that] his 'badness' is only a matter of inexperience."[1] Sendak likes it this way, as he also dislikes Collodi's *Pinocchio* because the puppet "is *born* bad" into a world that is itself "a ruthless, joyless place, filled with hypocrites, liars, and cheats." According to Sendak, Collodi created a character who is "innately evil, [a] doomed-calamity child of sin" who "doesn't stand a chance . . . a happy-go-lucky ragazzo, but damned nevertheless."[2]

I strongly disagree with Sendak's reading of Collodi. Yet his remarks raise important questions about the meaning of

Tending the Heart of Virtue. Second Edition. Vigen Guroian, Oxford University Press.
© Vigen Guroian 1998, 2023. DOI: 10.1093/oso/9780195384307.003.0003

childhood and about the nature of moral perfection. These matters pertain to Collodi's story and, as I will show, contrary to Sendak's opinion, make it one of the great works of literature for children.

What Is Meant by "Growing Up"

Sendak explains that he likes Disney's version of *Pinocchio* because Disney establishes the puppet's desire to grow up as the central concern of the story, rather than emphasizing the imperative to be good. "Pinocchio's wish to be a real boy remains the film's underlying theme, but 'becoming a real boy' now signifies the wish to grow up, not [as in Collodi] the wish to be good."[3] I agree with Sendak that "growing up" is a primary concern in the film, as it is in the book. But his contrast between this desire to grow up and the imperative to be good is troublesome. Surely, Sendak would agree that normally when we say to a child, "It's time you grow up," we mean that in order to become a mature human being, a person must also be morally responsible.

What kind of a story would *Pinocchio* be, after all, if all that was entailed in the fulfillment of Pinocchio's (or Geppetto's) wish is that his wooden frame be magically transformed into human flesh without the accompaniment of an increase in his moral stature? Actually, neither the Disney film nor the Collodi story portrays Pinocchio's wish and transformation into a flesh-and-blood child this way. In both stories Pinocchio wants to be more. He wants to be a *real* boy, a good boy, a genuine *human* son.

All children, excepting Peter Pan, want to grow up. And, in fact, all healthy children will grow to be adult individuals whether they want to or not. Pinocchio certainly has a special problem that Collodi casts as an allegory about moral growth. Pinocchio is a wooden puppet, and as the blue-haired fairy says to him, puppets never grow: "They are born puppets, they live puppets and die puppets."[4] The deeper meaning belongs to the metaphor of "woodenness." The woodenness of his mind and will, not that he is made of wood, is Pinocchio's most difficult obstacle to "growing up." Sendak has this part right at least: Collodi's Pinocchio is no mere innocent, and the wrongs he commits are, more often than not, not just the mistakes of ignorance but the consequences of a hard head, undisciplined passions, and a misdirected will that resists good advice.

In the Disney animation, real boyhood is bestowed on Pinocchio as a reward for being good by the Blue Fairy with a touch of her magic wand—or, as the Blue Fairy herself says, because Pinocchio has proven himself "brave, truthful, and unselfish." In Disney's imagination this is magic. In theological terms this is works righteousness. By moral description, the Disney story presents the virtues as the completion and very essence of Pinocchio's humanity: once he has proven himself "brave, truthful, and unselfish," he is transformed into a real boy. Collodi views things differently. In his story, Pinocchio becomes a real flesh-and-blood human child after he awakens from a dream in which the blue-haired fairy forgives him for his former waywardness and present shortcomings, while she also praises him for the good path he has taken by demonstrating a son's love for his father. For Collodi, real boyhood is not so much a reward as it is the visible sign of a moral task that has been conscientiously pursued, a task that even at that moment when Pinocchio is transformed from wood into flesh and blood is not yet wholly completed. Pinocchio's filial love, obedience, truthfulness, and self-expenditure for the sake of others ultimately triumph over his primal propensity to be selfish and self-centered. His good heart with its innate capacity to love finally dominates over his wooden head. The flesh he acquires represents a significant stage in the perfection of his humanity— that is, childhood—when filial love and obedience toward parents are appropriate. These and the other virtues are the preconditions for becoming a real human being, but they do not constitute our humanity as such. Collodi is clear that Pinocchio's good heart is the source and substance of his humanity and that responsible relationships with others are that humanity's path to perfection. Grace assists but does not compel the moral maturation of the puppet, since the puppet, despite Sendak's opinion, is essentially good, and since grace is not the same as Disney's magic.

Tin Soldiers and Marionettes

In *Mere Christianity*, C. S. Lewis asks this hypothetical question:

> Did you ever think, when you were a child, what fun it would be if your toys could come to life? Well suppose you could really have brought them to life. Imagine turning a tin soldier into a real little man. It would involve turning the tin into flesh. And suppose the tin soldier did not like it. He is not interested in flesh: all he sees is that the tin is being spoilt. He thinks you are killing him. He will do everything he can to prevent you. He will not be made into a man if he can help it.[5]

In the Disney film, Geppetto wishes that the wooden puppet would become a real boy. In the Collodi fairy tale, it is Pinocchio who makes the wish, not Geppetto, and what Pinocchio actually wishes for is that he become a fully grown man. The blue-haired fairy then explains to Pinocchio that he has to "begin by being a good boy" (p. 132) and that this involves obedience, truthfulness, an education, and consoling one's parents.

Collodi wants his child readers to understand that being a good boy or girl means being in a proper relationship to one's parents. This is the real genius of his story. Pinocchio refers to Geppetto as his father throughout the story. Some of the first trouble he gets into is prompted by his at least half-innocent desire to bring back to his father a fortune that will make Geppetto's life easier. When Pinocchio is separated from his father, his intention is to return. When Pinocchio "loses" his father, his intention is to find him. Over and over, however, Pinocchio is sidetracked by the allurements of quick gain and easy pleasure. He is tested and tried and repeatedly fails to resist temptation. His wooden head—his laziness, selfishness, and rebelliousness, in no small way compounded by his inexperience—overrules his good heart, his innate capacity to love and act responsibly.

C. S. Lewis continues, "What would you have done about that tin soldier I do not know. But what God did about us was this. The Second Person in God, the Son, became human Himself."[6] In this way God not only has called us into the full maturity of being human but has shown us the way and given us his own strength to see us through. Collodi sends the blue-haired fairy to Pinocchio, and at critical moments in the puppet's journey back to his father she comes to his assistance. Early in the story, she appears as a young maiden who saves Pinocchio from death by hanging on a tree (an allusion to Christ's crucifixion) and then adopts him as a brother. Nevertheless, the fox and the cat lure him away from the fairy child. Later, when Pinocchio returns, he finds that the little house in which the child had lived is no longer there. "Instead there was a little piece of white marble on which these sad words were engraved: HERE LIES THE BLUE-HAIRED CHILD WHO DIED OF SORROW ON BEING DESERTED BY HER LITTLE BROTHER PINOCCHIO." Poor Pinocchio is devastated. He drops to the ground, "kissing the cold stone a thousand times" (pp. 117–18). He counts the fairy child's death as the loss of a sister, now added to the loss of a father. And he blames himself for both deaths.

This is a turning point in the story. The fairy child's mysterious death and the inscription on her gravestone are signs of a grace that does not coerce but, nevertheless, insists that the wooden puppet become a responsible person. Although Pinocchio lapses again and endures some of the worst consequences of his misbehavior, including being turned into a donkey, something is stirred in his heart, and a memory is lodged there that ultimately contributes to his conversion and transformation into a real human child.

The blue-haired fairy is an immortal who does not abandon Pinocchio. She appears again in the story, for, as Pinocchio discovers, she is yet alive and grown into a young woman. This re-union occurs immediately after an episode in which Pinocchio has failed to rescue Geppetto from the sea and is carried to Busy Bee Island by a friendly dolphin. Pinocchio is ravenously hungry yet refuses to work for a meal—that is, until he comes upon a young woman who offers him bread if he will carry a pail home for her. At first Pinocchio does not recognize the young woman. Later, when he has finished eating, he looks up at her with "eyes wide open as if he had been bewitched" (p. 130).

"What is the matter with you?" asked the good woman, laughing.

"Because, it's . . . ," stammered Pinocchio, "it's . . . it's . . . you are like . . . you remind me of . . . Yes, yes, yes. The same voice . . . the same eyes . . . the same hair . . . You have blue hair too, just as she had! O dear fairy, O dear fairy, tell me, is it you? Is it really you?" (p. 130)

Collodi has recast St. Luke's post-resurrection story of two of the disciples encountering the resurrected Christ on the road to Emmaus (Luke 24:13–31). At first the disciples do not recognize him. But when Christ invites them to break bread with him, their eyes are opened. So it goes in Collodi's story also. This episode of hidden and revealed identity clarifies the providential and nurturant role of the blue-haired fairy. The fairy subsequently asks Pinocchio how he was able to recognize her, and he responds, "It was love for you that told me" (p. 131). Having lost a sister and, he believes, a father also, Pinocchio declares that he will call her mother. "Now I am a woman, nearly old enough to be your mother," she says. "I like that very much," he says, "because instead of calling you little sister, I shall call you mother." He adds, "A mother, as other *boys* [have]" (pp. 131–32, my emphasis).

The theme of filial love and responsible relationship with parents and siblings is, as I have stated already, at the very core of Collodi's story. Being a real human child means being a responsible and beloved son or daughter. Being good is not a means to gaining boyhood or girlhood as a reward. Rather, being good is a quality of respect and responsibility toward others you love, firstly and especially one's parents and siblings. This, insists Collodi, is essential to becoming a complete human being. A status as son or daughter, brother or sister, and mother or father deeply defines our humanity.

The Meaning of the "Heart"

In this connection it is also easy to commit another mistake that Sendak makes. Sendak is uncomfortable with what he describes as Collodi's excessive emphasis on moral rules. And Collodi certainly does pepper his tale with proverbs and moral precepts that are delivered by such colorful characters as the blue-haired fairy, a cricket who meets an early demise at Pinocchio's hands but returns as a ghostly source of wisdom and conscience, a parrot, and a white blackbird. Yet these proverbs and moral precepts are in service to the much greater ends of love and moral responsibility. Their externality is taken into Pinocchio's good heart and they are translated into the "flesh" of his humanity as the puppet learns to live in the spirit of mature sonship with an inward desire to be good.

Collodi gives us a Christian and catholic interpretation of the "heart." He makes it the seat and source of integral personhood, the innermost self or "I." The heart represents all that is potential in us that is wholly human, as we are created in the very image and likeness of God. But the heart, while it is essentially good, is also susceptible to corruption; there good and evil struggle for dominance. In Collodi's story, we follow this struggle through a puppet pilgrim's progress until at last goodness triumphs in the heart, as it should, as is natural, and Pinocchio is moved toward obedience and compassionate care of his father and mother.

In the book's final chapters, Pinocchio not only bravely saves Geppetto from the belly of the great shark but also turns over a completely new leaf by devoting all of his energies to provide for his sick father. When he hears that the blue-haired fairy is also very ill in the hospital and without a penny to buy a piece of bread, he gives over the extra money he has saved to purchase himself a new suit so that his "kind mother" will be cared for (p. 228). The evening of the same day, Pinocchio retires exhausted and dreams that the fairy visits him. She kisses him and says, "Brave Pinocchio! In return for your good heart, I forgive you all your past misdeeds. Children who love their parents, and help them when they are sick and poor, are worthy of praise and love, even if they are not models of obedience and good behaviour. Be good in the future, and you will be happy" (pp. 228–29).

Sendak describes this as "dreary" sermonizing. He calls the fairy's love a "castrating love" and describes Pinocchio's obedience to Geppetto as an unhealthy "yield[ing] up of himself entirely, unquestioningly, to his father."[7] Which moves me to ask: Have we come so far that we readily regard selfless filial love, conscientious respect of parents, and diligent obedience to them as suspect, as the unsavory products of extreme parental severity and abusive dominance over the child?

Pinocchio's Journey: How He Became a Real Human Child

In the end, as the reborn flesh-and-blood Pinocchio looks at the marionette, his former self, leaning lifeless against a chair, he exclaims: "How ridiculous I was when I was a puppet! And how happy I am to become a real boy!" (p. 232). This is a startling image—a metaphor for life lived to its completion, wherein life's complete measure is God's own judgment mirrored in our conscience. In Collodi's story, Pinocchio's humanity is present from the start within that mysteriously animate piece of wood out of which Geppetto fashions the puppet—a prehistory not told by Disney. The wood is Pinocchio's own recalcitrant nature, a nature affected by a will turned against that nature's own good. The puppet must overcome this destructive willfulness in order to become a faithful son and real human child.

Truthfulness and Self-Narrative

Collodi combines the parable of the prodigal son with the story of Jonah and the whale and Bunyan's *Pilgrim's Progress*. To that mix he adds his own genius. His story verges on merely the episodic—a rogue's tale—but so do our lives if we think about it. It is up to Pinocchio to make more of his life than just a rogue's tale. To do so he must become able to interpret his world and his own purposes truthfully. Collodi employs self-narrative to carry this out. Thus, at critical moments in his adventures, Pinocchio endeavors to tell his story. These are benchmarks in his moral and spiritual journey of self-discovery, conversion, and transformation. He is able to tell his story more truthfully as time goes on, until, finally, he narrates the true story of a prodigal son who has found his way back to his father and is forgiven. This is the same story the reader has read.

Just as important, Collodi demonstrates that there is a connection between this truthful self-narration and the ability Pinocchio gradually acquires to interpret reality accurately and to respond to it successfully. Very early in the story, Pinocchio makes his first try at a self-narrative. He attempts to explain to Geppetto what has happened to him after running away from home. The misadventure reaches its miserable end when Pinocchio returns home tired and cold and burns his feet on the coal heater. Pinocchio's account of the sequence of events is confused and deceiving. His inexperience combined with a propensity to shift blame onto others makes for a rather bizarre narrative. Pinocchio mixes up physical or natural causality with moral causality. He exclaims: "I got more and more hungry; and for that reason the little old man with the nightcap opened the window ... [and] I got a kettle of water on my head" (p. 35).

The innocence or naiveté of a small child might be all that is involved here. Yet more seems to be suggested than that. "It thundered and lightninged," Pinocchio continues, "and I was very hungry, and the talking cricket said, 'It serves you right; you have been wicked and deserve it.' And I said, 'Be careful, cricket!' And he said, 'You are a puppet, and you have a wooden head!' And I threw a hammer at him, and he died; but it was his fault, for I didn't want to kill him" (p. 35). In the second instance, Pinocchio lies, or at least twists the truth, about what the cricket has said to him and in so doing shifts blame for the cricket's demise onto the cricket. Even at this early stage of his life, Pinocchio exhibits the rudiments of conscience. Children learn these strategies of excuse-making and transposition of blame onto others early and they can readily identify with Pinocchio. They, like the puppet, also experience themselves as often at the mercy of external forces. The notion that who I am is mostly what is done to me and what happens to me rings true to a young child's subjective experience. Pinocchio is a puppet. But being a young child is very much like being a marionette.

When my now fully grown son and daughter were in grade school, I read *Pinocchio* to them. And as I mention in the Introduction, I discussed the story with my daughter's fourth-grade class at St. Paul's School in Brooklandville, Maryland. I remember especially well the incidents in *Pinocchio* that my children and the fourth graders brought up. First, they recalled the cricket's admonitions and good advice and how he rebukes Pinocchio for his mendacity and unwillingness to listen. Second, they took a great interest in what comes to pass as Pinocchio turns into a donkey, which the cricket prophesies happens to children who are lazy and disobedient. And last, they were anxious to discuss the nature of Pinocchio's misbehavior and the reasons for his repentance.

In his little gem, *A Brief Reader on the Virtues of the Human Heart,* the philosopher Josef Pieper recalls a popular saying of the Middle Ages: "A man is wise when all things taste to him as they really are."[8] This sums up why people need to look at reality without deceiving themselves. So long as self-deception is at the source of a person's perception of things, he or she cannot mature into the fullness of being human or lead a successful course through life. In *Pinocchio,* the physiological metaphor of hunger represents the many other passions and desires that lead children astray. Like all small children, Pinocchio is often driven by uncontrollable hunger. This gets him into much of his early trouble, while undisciplined passions and wanderlust eventually land him in the false paradise of Playland. But Pinocchio's longing to be a real boy with a mother and father lies deeper still and is the source of his eventual salvation.

Imagination and the Moral Self

The complete truth about being a human being is often falsified or at least partially obscured by a young child's subjective experience. A person has to grow as a moral self in order to transcend this childlike subjectivity and primitive narcissism. He must begin to take a view of the world that is conditioned by an internal discipline of the passions and a "receptivity to teaching [and] . . . willingness to accept advice."[9] This is certainly what Pinocchio's pilgrimage toward maturity is about. This mature way of experiencing and knowing the world is not the objective knowing normally associated with physical science, nor is it the subjectivity of solipsism. It is an intersubjective and relational way of experiencing and knowing. It is a way of interpreting the world that requires memory and a moral imagination; otherwise a moral self cannot come into being.

Just as the appetites require discipline that they may be directed toward their proper ends, so the imagination needs to be guided by reason, sound memory, and the common stock of human wisdom about the world and its possibilities. Pinocchio's journey to real boyhood and sonship is dependent upon the presence and appropriation of these things, which serve his deep desire to be a real boy and human son. As we have seen from his first try at accounting for his behavior and the world around him, Pinocchio initially lacks a robust moral imagination. The rudimentary imagination he has is corrupted by phantasmagoria. Initially, the vain imaginings of Pinocchio's own egocentricity dominate. Freud calls this the "imaginary," thus suggesting a disconnection with reality; earlier philosophical and literary sources merely call it "fancy." But the phantasmagoria of unrestrained appetite and wild passion arise as if willing themselves into existence. The moral imagination is different. The analogies and sentiments of the moral imagination need to be nurtured and cultivated.

In order to abscond with the few gold pieces that the showman Fire-eater gave to Pinocchio, the fox and the cat persuade the inexperienced puppet that if he buries his gold pieces in the Field of Miracles a money tree will grow that will make him and his father wealthy. Pinocchio's imaginings become wild and fantastic:

> Suppose, instead of a thousand gold pieces, I find two thousand on the branches of the tree? Oh, what a fine gentleman I shall be then! I shall have a magnificent palace, and a thousand wooden ponies and a thousand stables to play with, a cellar full of lollies, and cordials, and a library brimful of candies, and tarts, and cakes, and almond biscuits, and cream puffs! (p. 98)

These and other phantasmagoria of the untrained imagination lead Pinocchio into many of his misadventures and leave him deaf to voices of good counsel. But Pinocchio eventually outgrows these vain imaginings. As his experiences accumulate—relationships with responsible moral agents, the discomforts of following foolish whims and being driven by blind fear, and the spontaneous acts of his good heart when he rescues his fellow puppet Harlequin from Fire-eater's stove or the mastiff Alidoro from drowning—Pinocchio gains a moral imagination. He begins to associate his experiences in a mutually interpretive manner and to see correspondences between these experiences denoting regularities in the ways persons relate to one another and things interact in the world. He especially embraces the moral obligations and responsibilities that connect him vitally to father, mother, sister, neighbors, and even strangers.

Truthful Story and the Real Self

As I have said, Pinocchio's ability to piece together an accurate account of himself and his adventures increases from beginning to end. The last two accounts are his most successful. Nor do I think it is accidental that they are elicited by events that recapitulate the biblical motifs of drowning and rebirth, as well as penance and baptism into new life.

The first of these occasions follows Pinocchio's misadventure in Playland, where he is changed into a donkey. Pinocchio arrives at a circus, where again misfortune follows him when he becomes lame in a performance. Of no use now to his owner, the donkey is sold to a man who intends to use his thick skin to make a drum for the village band. The man ties a stone to Pinocchio's neck and throws him into the sea to drown, "so that he might skin him" afterward (p. 199). When the man pulls Pinocchio out, he discovers to his amazement and utter dismay that there is a wooden puppet at the end of the line.

> When [the man] recovered he could only stammer, "Where...where is the little donkey I threw in the water?"...
>
>   "I am the little donkey!" answered the puppet, laughing....
>
>   "But how can it be that you, who were a little donkey a short while ago, have now become a wooden puppet?"
>
>   "It must be due to the sea water. It does, sometimes, work real miracles!" (p. 201)

The spirited puppet then asks the man if he would like to hear "my *true* story" (p. 201, my emphasis). This is the first time that Pinocchio prefaces his remarks with "my true story." The fall into beastliness is reversed. The puppet who was created in the image of a real boy is returned to his original form. But more seems to have occurred inwardly than even the miraculous transformation of appearance. Pinocchio has become a new person who tells the story of his adventures truthfully. This truth is more, however, than merely a quality of literal accuracy. Truth comes from the heart. And Pinocchio now speaks from the heart:

> "A couple more words, and I'll have finished. After buying me, you brought me here to kill me; and as you pitied me, you preferred to tie a stone to my neck, and throw me into the sea. . . . [But] you reckoned without the fairy."
>
> "And who is the fairy?"
>
> "She is my mother and, like every mother, she loves her child dearly, and never loses sight of him, and helps him in all his troubles, even when, because of his foolishness and his naughty ways, he deserves no help. So, as I wanted to say, as soon as the good fairy saw I was in danger of drowning she sent an immense shoal of fish who thought that I was a dead donkey, and began to eat me. . . . [And] you must know that when the donkey's hide that covered me from head to foot, was eaten away, naturally the bones remained—or, to be exact, the wood; for as you see, I am made of very hard wood." (p. 203)

Pinocchio acknowledges the great mystery of his transformation in the ocean waters and that nothing less than the providential and motherly love of the blue-haired fairy accounts for it and for his salvation. This confession reflects an inward conversion of heart manifested outwardly by the metamorphosis from a donkey back into a puppet and finally into a real human child.

Love and Courage: Becoming a Real Human Child at Last

Pinocchio manages to escape from the man by diving into the sea and is guided by the blue-haired fairy, who has taken the shape of a she-goat standing atop a rock that juts from the water. As he swims toward the rock, Pinocchio encounters the great shark and is swallowed. Like Jonah in the belly of the whale, he is stricken with fear and desolation. And like Jonah, he laments his condition and pleads for salvation. "At first Pinocchio tried to be brave; but when he knew for certain that he was inside the shark's body, as in a prison, he began to weep and sob" (p. 207). But this desperate situation turns out to be the occasion when his father forgives him. For Pinocchio is reunited with Geppetto in the belly of the great shark and when he sees him exclaims: "Yes, yes, it's really me! And you've already forgiven me, haven't you? Oh dear Father how good you are! And to think that instead I ... oh!"[10] Pinocchio repents and insists on telling his whole story to Geppetto, and it is a truthful telling. In complete command of his memory, he is able to look upon himself without self-deception. The puppet lets go of his old self completely in order to save the life of his father, as he gains the courage, in the face of certain death, to plan a successful escape.

This entire episode inside the shark's body is reminiscent of St. Augustine's thoughts in his *Confessions*, when Augustine speaks penitently of his abandonment of God and self: "But where was I when I looked for you? You were there before me, but I had deserted even my own self. I could not find myself, much less find you."[11] One can hardly doubt, in this instance, the influence of Collodi's early religious training.

After Geppetto expresses his complete despair of ever escaping to safety, Pinocchio consoles his father and gives him hope that they can escape from their imprisonment in the shark's belly. Pinocchio already has experienced the horror of death and the redeeming hand of a loving and forgiving providence. Thus he says to his father, "Give it a try, and you'll see. In any case, if it's written in Heaven that we must die, at least we'll have the great consolation of dying clasped together."[12] Josef Pieper writes, "Every brave deed draws sustenance from preparedness for death, as from the deepest root."[13] And Pieper continues:

> To be brave is not the same thing as to have no fear. To be sure, fortitude excludes a certain kind of fearlessness, namely, when it is based on a mistaken appraisal and evaluation of reality. This sort of fearlessness either is blind and deaf toward actual danger or else stems from a reversal in love. For fear and love limit one another: one who does not love does not fear either, and one who loves falsely also fears falsely.[14]

The modern abridgments and retellings of *Pinocchio,* of which Disney's is only the most well known, soften the violence of death in Collodi's original tale and as a result sweeten and sentimentalize the love that grows within Pinocchio. Thus, they also fail to capture the gritty nature of the puppet's courage and endurance. Pinocchio's close calls with death, whether when dangling over the showman's fire, hanging from a tree, or being plunged into the dark depths of the sea, are also the hard lessons he learns about the true value of life, the reality of reciprocal love, and the necessity of self-expending love in the face of evil and danger.

TENDING THE HEART OF VIRTUE

All of this is beautifully and forcefully captured in the scene that immediately follows the expulsion of father and son from inside the belly of the sea monster.

While Pinocchio was swimming towards the land as quickly as he could, he noticed that his father, sitting on his back with his legs in the water, was trembling violently, as though feverish.

Was he shivering because of cold, or of fright? Who knows?...But Pinocchio thought he was frightened, and tried to comfort him, "Courage, daddy! In a few minutes, we shall reach land, and be safe."

"But where is the land?" asked the old man.... Poor Pinocchio pretended to be cheerful, but was rather discouraged.

He swam until he could breathe no longer: then he turned to his father, and said, "Daddy, help me...I am dying."

Father and son were about to drown together, when a voice, like a badly tuned guitar, said, "Who is dying?"

"I, and my father!"

"I recognize your voice! You are Pinocchio!"

"Right. And who are you?"

"I am the tunny fish, your pal in the shark's body."

"How did you escape?"

"I did the same as you, but you showed me the way. I followed you, and I, too, escaped."

"Dear tunny, you've come just in time! I beg you, for the love you have for your own children, the little tunnies, to help us, or we are lost."

"Of course! With all my heart."

Reaching land, Pinocchio jumped down first, and then he helped his father. Then he turned to the tunny, and said in a trembling voice,

"My dearest friend, you have saved my father's life! I cannot find words to thank you. May I give you a kiss as a token of my eternal gratitude?"

The tunny put his nose out of the water, and Pinocchio, kneeling on the ground, pressed a loving kiss on its mouth. At this sign of real, unaffected love, the tunny, who was not used to such things, was so moved that, ashamed to be seen crying like a babe, he dived under the water, and disappeared.

Meanwhile, the sun had risen. (pp. 217–18, 219)

Perhaps the profoundest lesson that Carlo Collodi teaches in his magnificent tale is that death too must be faced honestly if love is to become completely real in our lives and in the lives of those who are the recipients of that love. Death *is* the great despoiler of life, but there is the even greater truth that death is powerless over life if love is received and love is returned. I agree with Collodi's deep sentiment here that it is our great human task to learn and believe this truth about life, love, and death; otherwise, how can we possibly grow into better and more perfect human beings? Indeed, if we fail to take this truth to heart, we risk devolving into jackasses or, worse still, wild apes dressed up in men's and women's clothes. As Lucy fears in C. S. Lewis's *Prince Caspian,* "Wouldn't it be dreadful if some day in our own world, at home, men started going wild inside, like the animals here [in Narnia], so that you'd never know which was which?"[15] Comically, tragically, and, sometimes, ruthlessly, Collodi explores this mystery. In spite of that, his book is not so dark as Sendak would have us believe. We all must experience some darkness, otherwise how can we appreciate the light? We all must experience the nearness of despair, otherwise how can we know when to celebrate the triumph of hope? We all must at some time or another face forthrightly the tragedy of love and death, so that one day the pain of separation might be replaced by the joy of reunion with the beloved one.

Pinocchio puts his true courage in the service of a self-emptying love that saves his father's life. He thanks the tunny humbly on his knees for rescuing not *himself* but his *father.* His gratitude is the natural reaction of a loving heart that wholly embraces goodness, represented so movingly in the kiss that Pinocchio presses on the tunny's mouth. And from this moment on, Pinocchio's loving heart is linked with the sequence of all his actions in such a manner that the natural and supernatural virtues of courage, obedience, truthfulness, industry, charity, and compassion surpass his "wooden" propensities for laziness, lying, and selfishness. Already before his wooden frame turns into flesh and blood, Pinocchio is a good son. Thus Pinocchio's transformation into a real boy is accomplished not through some final magical action, as Disney has it, but by the inner working of a grace that converts the heart and moves the self toward acts of genuine love.[16]

LOVE AND IMMORTALITY IN *THE VELVETEEN RABBIT* AND "THE LITTLE MERMAID"

I had at first considered including a discussion of Margery Williams's modern classic *The Velveteen Rabbit* in the preceding chapter. After all, the interest in this wonderful fairy tale is sustained by the Velveteen Rabbit's desire to become real. He gains his first knowledge of what that means from the wise old Skin Horse in the nursery. But we must not overlook the fact that it is the Velveteen Rabbit himself who brings up the question and that *his* desire to become real lies at the heart of Margery Williams's story.

In *Pinocchio,* Collodi emphasizes the need for the puppet to love others and in so doing overcome a deadly self-centeredness. Williams emphasizes the other pole of love's reciprocity—being loved by another. Loving and being loved make us *real,* say these authors, and the stories they have written state that fact powerfully. Yet, in my view, Williams's story explores an even deeper meaning of becoming *real*: immortality. This can be said also of Hans Christian Andersen's universally loved story "The Little Mermaid," to which I will turn in the second half of this chapter.

Tending the Heart of Virtue. Second Edition. Vigen Guroian, Oxford University Press.
© Vigen Guroian 1998, 2023. DOI: 10.1093/oso/9780195384307.003.0004

I do not think that modern people have outgrown the yearning for immortality, even if it might be the case that the traditional religious answers to the question of immortality are proving less persuasive to many people today than in preceding times. And there is no doubt in my mind that *The Velveteen Rabbit* and "The Little Mermaid" continue to address the need that children have for satisfying answers to such questions as "What happens to us after we die? And where do we go?" The renowned psychiatrist Robert Coles, who has devoted a long career to the care and study of children, writes concerning the deep curiosity that his child patients have about immortality. In his book *The Spiritual Life of Children,* Coles comments:

> The questions Tolstoy asked, and Gauguin in, say, his great Tahiti triptych, completed just before he died ("Where Do We Come From? What Are We? Where Are We Going?"), are the eternal questions children ask more intensely, unremittingly, and subtly than we sometimes imagine.[1]

Meanwhile, it is remarkable how little serious attention educators and literary critics give to these themes, as if religion does not exist in children's lives or, if it does, is off-limits. It is my contention that Williams and Andersen have written stories that are profound allegories of love and immortality. And I think it is more than worthwhile to explore the messages in these two stories.

On the Meaning of Becoming "Really Real" in *The Velveteen Rabbit*

> One day the Velveteen Rabbit asks the Skin Horse, "What is REAL? Does it mean having things that buzz inside you and a stick-out handle?"

> "Real isn't how you are made," said the Skin Horse. "It's a thing that happens to you. When a child loves you for a long, long time, not just to play with, but REALLY loves you, then you become Real."[2]

The Skin Horse, who has lived in the nursery longer than any other toy, certainly speaks from a wisdom about what becoming real really means. Since his arrival in the nursery as a Christmas gift, the Velveteen Rabbit has wondered whether the mechanical wind-up toys are more "real" than he. He assumes this is so since they replicate the movements of real living things and boast of the same to him.

The Skin Horse quickly corrects this misperception. " 'Real isn't how you are made,' said the Skin Horse." Indeed, the fate of most of these new mechanical toys is to break and be thrown out. "He [the Skin Horse] knew that they were only toys, and would never turn into anything else." The sources of their very pretensions to being real are ironically also why they will never "turn into anything else." Their complicated workings leave them easy to break, and they are not soft or lovable like the Velveteen Rabbit. They simply do not possess the traits that will engage the imagination and win the love of a child over a long time. The Skin Horse again puts these matters plainly:

> You become [Real]. It takes a long time. That's why it doesn't often happen to people who break easily, or have sharp edges, or who have to be carefully kept. Generally, by the time you are Real, most of your hair has been loved off, and your eyes drop out and you get loose in the joints and very shabby. But these things don't matter at all, because once you are Real you can't be ugly, except to people who don't understand.

The Skin Horse tells the Velveteen Rabbit that he was made real by the uncle of the boy who now lives in the nursery. He has lost much of his brown coat and the hairs from his tail, but he explains that looking worn-out, having failing eyes and weakened limbs, and losing one's hair are the emblems of having been loved and having given oneself in love to another over a lifetime. In time the Velveteen Rabbit, too, becomes old and shabby. The Boy "loved him so hard that he loved all his whiskers off, and the pink lining to his ears turned grey, and his brown spots faded ... [But] he didn't mind how he looked to other people, because the nursery magic had made him Real, and when you are Real shabbiness doesn't matter."[3]

This is how in this story the question of what it means to become real is raised. Yet the answer is not simple. In fact, Williams introduces several levels of meaning. First, the Velveteen Rabbit is quite literally a "real" stuffed animal. This literal meaning of "real" is taken for granted, however, and is not what the drama and mystery in the story are about. The Velveteen Rabbit wants to become real in quite another sense. He wants to be loved. The Skin Horse testifies that to be loved brings about "realness." In Martin Buber's terms, an "I" embraces another as "Thou" and "realness" comes into being.

This once happened to the Skin Horse, and it also happens to the Velveteen Rabbit. For the Boy eventually tires of the mechanical toys, and embraces the neglected stuffed animal in imaginative play, as if the rabbit were a living being, a person, a "Thou" and not an "it." As Buber says, "Real living is meeting."[4] The Boy's love for the Velveteen Rabbit is analogous to the love shared between two "real" persons in a relationship of mutual affirmation and responsibility. This, in turn, is analogous to the love of God that gives each one of us being and, according to biblical faith, draws us through our own response to his love into immortal life.

Of course, Buber's concept applies to this "real world," in which toys like the Skin Horse and the Velveteen Rabbit are merely inanimate objects and do not possess the powers of thought and speech. And while fairyland and this world hold some things in common, not all things that are possible in fairyland are possible in the "real world." It is not likely that in the "real world" a prince and a pauper could look so alike that through a series of accidents they trade places, but it is possible, whereas only in fairyland can a wooden hobbyhorse grow wise or a stuffed rabbit become a creature of real flesh and blood. When a child is drawn imaginatively into fairyland, toys become playmates that are to him every bit as "real" and "alive" and "responsible" for their behavior as himself. Every true nursery or playroom is a piece of fairyland, a place where metaphors may shade into full-blown allegories of the world outside.

The Meaning of Immortality

Margery Williams surely intended for her story to find its way into the nursery and the playroom, where it could stir the child's imagination to make allegory out of metaphor. After the Velveteen Rabbit becomes real like the Skin Horse, one would suppose the story might end. What greater joy in fairyland is there than for a stuffed animal to be made real by the love of a child? Instead, the story takes a turn that strongly suggests, indeed invites, allegorical interpretation. Love lends encouragement to the heart's desire for immortality. Williams believes in that yearning and beckons children—and willing adults—to freely exercise their imaginations in such a way that the metaphor of becoming real expands into an allegory of immortality.

One day long after the Velveteen Rabbit had become real, the Boy becomes ill with scarlet fever and the doctor orders that everything that has come in contact with him be put into a sack and burned. The Velveteen Rabbit spends the night out in the garden in the sack along with lots of old picture books and all sorts of odd rubbish. As he lies covered in darkness, the Velveteen Rabbit longingly remembers his life with the Boy, the love and the play that they had shared together in this garden, and the happiness that he had known in becoming real.

On one occasion, the Boy had left the Velveteen Rabbit in a cozy spot by the bracken. He was approached by some rabbits who moved like the mechanical toys, yet they were not mechanical at all. Evidently they were "a new kind of rabbit altogether." And they, in turn, quickly discovered that the Velveteen Rabbit had "no hind legs," and that he didn't "smell right" either. They dared him to dance. But, of course, he could not. So he said, "'I don't like dancing' . . . But all the while he was longing to dance . . . and he would give anything in the world to be able to jump about like these rabbits." Worst of all, one of the rabbits had called out, "He isn't a rabbit at all! He isn't real!" The Velveteen Rabbit protested, "I *am* Real!" But he suspected that there was a difference between his realness when with the Boy and being real like these rabbits who ran free and danced in the garden. And he wanted to be like those rabbits.

Williams locates this scene midway in the story, but it foreshadows the ending also. As the Velveteen Rabbit lies in a heap in the garden that last night, he thinks sadly, "Of what use was it to be loved and lose one's beauty and become Real if it all ended like this?" His soulful lament soon is answered in an unexpected way. He does not realize that becoming real in the nursery is itself just a shadow or image of being wholly real like the rabbits he met that day, and that his return to the garden, his true home, ensures he will become one of them.

During the night, the Velveteen Rabbit crawls out of his death sack to have a view of the garden he loved. "A tear, a real tear," writes Williams, "trickled down his little shabby velvet nose and fell to the ground." Where this *real* tear falls a flower grows up unlike any other flower in the garden, and out of the blossom of that flower steps a fairy who with one kiss bestows on the Velveteen Rabbit the gift of life. " 'I am the nursery magic Fairy,' she said. 'I take care of all the playthings that the children have loved. When they are old and worn out and the children don't need them any more, then I come and take them away with me and turn them into Real.' " The Velveteen Rabbit asks if he wasn't real already. And she answers, "You were Real to the Boy because he loved you. Now you shall be Real to everyone." And so she flies him into the wood where the "real" rabbits dance and play.

Readers young and old are able to grasp easily the figurative meaning that Williams gives "real" in the first instance. When you love someone long and hard enough, something new is brought into existence by that relationship that deepens and adds meaning to one's life, and an "I-Thou" relationship is established. This kind of relationship can even exist between a person and an inanimate object. But what of this final realness, the life that the fairy bestows on the Velveteen Rabbit in the end? One way to explain it is to subsume it under the magic that happens in fairyland. This magic transforms the Velveteen Rabbit from an image or replica of a rabbit into a living and breathing rabbit. These things happen in fairyland.

Yet many of the students I have taught over the years thought that Williams may have written an allegory not just of love but of immortality. In other words, the transformation of the Velveteen Rabbit from a worn-out stuffed animal into a real rabbit is an allegory of our translation into the eternal life. After all, the fairy says to the rabbits in the wood: "You must be very kind to him [the Velveteen Rabbit] and teach him all he needs to know in Rabbitland, for he is to live with you *for ever and ever!*" (my emphasis).

The Skin Horse achieves the first stage of being real, but for all his wisdom, he cannot imagine the next stage that would make him real "for ever and ever." The Velveteen Rabbit, however, is set on a path to this second kind of realness. This is by no merit of his own but rather through his intense desire to be a real rabbit, and by a Greater Love that cares for the toys in the nursery too much to allow them to be just thrown away after they are "used up."

"The Little Mermaid": Hans Christian Andersen's Allegory of Immortality

> Do fish complain of the sea for being wet? Or if they did, would that fact itself not strongly suggest that they had not always been, or would not always be, purely aquatic creatures?
> —Letter from C. S. Lewis

Some years ago, Disney Studios gave "The Little Mermaid" their highest compliment: they made it into a full-length animated movie. Nevertheless, as is typical of Disney, the film version betrays the original story while it also adroitly exploits our society's obsessions with physical beauty and romantic love. But the literary critics have faulted Andersen's original tale for somewhat different reasons than the distortions I have alluded to in the Disney retelling.

Roger Sale is one such critic, and his opinions about "The Little Mermaid" are typical. Sale does not just argue that Andersen's story demeans womanhood. He also objects to its religious content.[5] In the Little Mermaid, says Sale, Andersen created a female character who not only is naturally inferior to human beings but must suffer senselessly for the likes of "a dense and careless" male character, the prince, whose life the Little Mermaid saves and whose love she unsuccessfully pursues. Andersen tells his reader that merpeople do not possess an immortal soul, Sale continues, yet "he cannot say what this means . . . since the mermaids seem to lack nothing possessed by human beings except legs. . . . To make socially inferior into sexually inferior, and to make sexually inferior into naturally inferior, is bad enough, but to make naturally inferior into religiously inferior is sheer desperation." Worse yet, her grandmother tells the Little Mermaid that to gain an immortal soul she must win the love of a man. This, Sale maintains, "reduces 'soul' to a romantic and sexual prize."[6]

Sale also objects to "explicit religion" in fairy tales. He argues that this gets authors into the kind of mess that in this story Andersen is in. I disagree. I do not think that the religious theme weakens Andersen's story. I more than suspect, however, that religion confounds this interpreter. Perhaps if Sale and other critics like him—for he is not alone in his judgments—were better able to recognize and appreciate the care and artistry with which Andersen employs religious language and symbolism in his storytelling, they might reconsider their objections to his work. Instead, these critics have poured their energies into psychological and sociological interpretations of Andersen's person and work, so his religion is almost always interpreted as the rationalization of his own feelings of rejection in personal life, especially in his relations with women, and his failure to gain social acceptability among the upper class.

Jack Zipes's discussion of Andersen in his study *Fairy Tales and the Art of Subversion* is another example of this social-psychological approach to Andersen and his work. Zipes argues that "Andersen never tired of preaching self-abandonment and self-deprivation in the name of bourgeois laws. The reward was never power over one's life but security in adherence to power." As for the Little Mermaid, Zipes dismisses her religious yearning as denial and rationalization. Stripped of its camouflage, her pursuit of the prince's love reveals an ego that has become "dissociated because she is attracted to a class of people [human beings] who will never accept her on her own terms. . . . Thus she must somehow justify her existence to herself through abstinence and self-abnegation."[7]

But what if we were to take Andersen's religion at face value and not as a psychological cover for his personal insecurities about social status and acceptance? Then, I submit, we might interpret "The Little Mermaid" differently, with an appreciation for its allegorical qualities and valuable moral lessons. In this reading the Little Mermaid's virtues of courage, forbearance, and unselfish love may be seen as the admirable attributes of a healthy and strong character.

The Little Mermaid's Longing for Immortality

Right from the start of the story, Andersen distinguishes the Little Mermaid from her five older sisters. The sisters are the daughters of the Merking, who is a widower. They live with him and his mother at the bottom of the sea in a beautiful palace with walls of white coral. The royal grandmother promises the princesses that on their fifteenth birthdays they may "go up out of the sea" and look at the world above.[8] Andersen adds: "None of them [the princesses] was so full of longing as the youngest, and she was the very one that had the longest to wait and was so quiet and thoughtful" (p. 80). The Little Mermaid longs to see the world above with its land and sea and human cities. However, Andersen artfully gives her longings symbolic importance. He expands metaphor into full-blown allegory.

"Outside the palace there was a great garden," Andersen writes. "Over everything down there lay a wonderful blue glow; you would think that, instead of being on the bottom of the sea, you were standing high up in the air with nothing but sky above and below you. In clear calm weather you could see the sun looking like a purple flower with all that light streaming out from its center" (p. 77). Like Williams in *The Velveteen Rabbit*, Andersen uses the paradisical symbolism of the garden as a principal leitmotif for his allegory. He describes a garden suffused with the color blue, which symbolizes mystery and eternity. The sun shines below "like a purple flower with all that light streaming out from its center," evocative of a numinous reality and the Little Mermaid's attraction to it.

Andersen explains that each of the princesses "had her own little plot of the garden, where she could dig and plant whatever she liked." Each gave her bed the shape of something, a whale or a mermaid. The Little Mermaid, however, made "hers quite round and would only have flowers that shone red like the sun." The circle replicates the sun and connotes eternity. Similarly, the

Little Mermaid's love of the scentless flowers that she plants in her garden mirrors her deep desire to see the flowers up above and smell their fragrances. "She found her greatest delight in hearing about the world of men up above.... What she thought especially wonderful and beautiful was that up on earth the flowers had a sweet scent" (p. 79).

Eventually, we need to make sense of what Andersen might have intended by making merpeople without souls. But I am reminded here of something C. S. Lewis says in *Letters to Malcolm*. Lewis writes: "What the soul cries out for is the resurrection of the senses."[9] Now, great harm can be done to the enjoyment of a story when it is treated like a container filled with symbol treats. And I want to avoid that mistake. Yet I also believe that a full appreciation of Andersen's artfulness and intention in making the Little Mermaid what she is, with the desires she has, cannot be understood without paying serious attention to the symbolism he puts into this story.

The following passage, which again describesthe Little Mermaid's garden and her relationship to it, is especially significant:

> She was a strange child, quiet and thoughtful, and when the other sisters decorated their gardens with the most wonderful things they had got from wrecked ships, she would only have, apart from the rose-red flowers which looked like the sun high up above her, a beautiful marble statue, a handsome boy carved out of clear white stone and come down to the bottom of the sea with the wreck of a ship. She planted by it a rose-red weeping willow which grew magnificently and hung its fresh branches right over the statue down to the blue sand of the ground, where its shadow showed violet and was in constant motion like its branches—its top and its roots seemed always to be playing at kissing one another. (pp. 78–79)

The Little Mermaid deeply yearns for something more in her life than her familiar world provides. Her curiosity and sense of mystery help her to discover clues of the "otherness" that she seeks long before saving the prince's life or learning from her grandmother that what the prince has that she does not is an immortal soul. When she does lay her eyes on the prince, the Little Mermaid immediately associates him with the statue. He is its living archetype. And the beauty she sees in the prince reflects the glory of the world above to which she is so strongly attracted. The rose-red willow tree alludes to blood and tears and the passion of the cross. This prefigures the Little Mermaid's own suffering, especially her final act of self-sacrificial love, when she chooses death rather than take the prince's life in order to save her own.

In *Orthodoxy*, his masterly work of Christian apologetics, G. K. Chesterton argues the following propositions that I believe bear directly on our consideration of the story of "The Little Mermaid" as an allegory of love and immortality:

> First, . . . some faith in our life is required even to improve it; second, . . . some dissatisfaction with things as they are is necessary even in order to be satisfied; third, . . . to have this necessary content and discontent it is not sufficient to have the obvious equilibrium of the Stoic. For mere resignation has neither the gigantic levity of pleasure nor the superb intolerance of pain.[10]

The Little Mermaid invites great pain and suffering upon herself. That is because she imagines more for her life and is dissatisfied with the limitations of life under the sea. She will not be resigned to the clear implications of her grandmother's explanation of the conditions of her existence and the difficulty, indeed near impossibility, of transcending those conditions.

Her grandmother tells her that in order to gain an immortal soul a man must "fall in love with you so deeply that you would be more to him than father and mother." She and the man must be wed by a priest "with a vow of faith here and for all eternity; then his soul would overflow into your body, and you, too, would have your share in human fortune. He would give you a soul and yet keep his own" (pp. 90–91).

In pursuit of this end, the Little Mermaid makes a deal with the sea-witch. At the witch's behest, she trades her beautiful voice for legs. She willingly takes upon herself the awful burden of having to endure the excruciating pain when she walks, as if she were stepping on "a sharp knife that cuts [her] and makes [her] blood flow" (p. 94).[11] The reader will be warned not to make such deals with the "devil." And just in case we need to be persuaded of the potentially tragic consequences that may come from such acts, Andersen paints vividly the suffering and grief that the Little Mermaid undergoes for that mistake. In addition, there are the ominous terms of her quest for the heart of the prince. If she fails, she not only will forfeit her three hundred mortal years as a mermaid but will not gain an immortal soul and must die on the first morning after the prince weds another. Nonetheless, Andersen does not permit his reader simply to conclude that taking her sisters' path and being content with remaining a mermaid is the more admirable or desirable choice. His ability to awaken our moral and religious imagination certainly cannot be overlooked. He uses all of his narrative skills to evoke within his readers the same feelings and struggle with those feelings that the Little Mermaid goes through. And despite her suffering, he makes it difficult for the reader to disapprove of the Little Mermaid's decisions, to dismiss her courage as foolishness, or to deny her deepest yearnings and where those might lead her.

Romantic Love and the Desire for Immortality

Sale argues that Andersen reduces gaining "a 'soul' to a romantic and sexual prize."[12] But I don't think that is it at all. Yes, romantic love is part of what moves the Little Mermaid to her decisions and undertakings. But a desire for the beloved and a yearning for an even greater love and communion are mingled in this haunting tale. Andersen leaves us to ponder which the Little Mermaid wants more, a man or a soul, or whether it is even possible to disentangle her attraction to his beauty from her desire to have a soul and enjoy immortality.

   This is not a flaw in the story. Rather, Andersen brilliantly puts the theme of romantic love into the service of his allegory. Peter Kreeft astutely observes that "an image can easily become an idol, and romantic love [can become] an unusually powerful idol because it is such a powerful image." He adds, however, that "romantic love is [also] a powerful image of the love of God because, unlike lust, it does not desire a possessable and consumable thing (like a body)."[13] We are reminded of Dante's attraction to Beatrice in *The Divine Comedy* and, of course, the ancient tale of the love between Psyche and Cupid that has been interpreted through the ages as an allegory of the soul's journey through life and final union after suffering and death with the divine. Kreeft also reminds us that romantic lovers often mistakenly expect that the joy they seek can be found solely in the beloved, whereas wisdom teaches that the beauty that belongs to the beloved is bound to fade and his embrace, which is, after all, merely mortal, must inevitably release. "Because romantic love is only a prophet," Kreeft instructs, "it breaks when it turns into a god."[14]

Andersen's story does not make romantic love into an idol. To the contrary, the story communicates a serious admonition about the harm that such an idol can bring upon its worshiper. After she saves the young prince from drowning, the Little Mermaid sets him on a beach where a young girl finds him. Knowing that he is now safe and that there is nothing more that she can do for him, the Little Mermaid retreats to the sea. After her arrival home, she grows "even more sorrowful than before. Her one comfort was to sit in her little garden and throw one arm round the beautiful marble statue that looked so like the prince." Andersen adds that she "no longer looked after her flowers" (p. 88) and that the garden grows wild and twisted with vines that climb among the branches of the willow tree and cast darkness over the place. An inordinate erotic attraction to the beloved is bound to lead to unhappiness and ruin. A marble statue is the first object of the Little Mermaid's desire and yearning for something "beyond"; the young prince is the second. But when she embraces the prince as the final object of her love and desire for happiness, the path of her life becomes twisted and dangerous. She makes the desperate deal with the sea-witch.

The Rising of the Sun and What Is Meant by Gaining an Immortal Soul

The Little Mermaid makes choices, and these choices decide her destiny. Others might have made different choices. But she contributes vitally to her final destiny and the person she eventually becomes. Through her attraction to the beauty of the statue and the young prince, the Little Mermaid is drawn toward a wholly other reality. In the end, the life she thinks she has given up and the promise of immortality she thinks she has lost are returned, in spite of her mistakes, because goodness and mercy and unselfish love conquer within her. That is how I would put it, and this way of putting it reveals an allegory.

After the Little Mermaid makes the pact with the sea-witch, a tale unfolds of unrequited love, heartbreaking disappointment, and silent suffering. While the prince holds great affection for the Little Mermaid and lovingly takes her into the protection and comfort of his household, eros is missing in his fondness for her, and she begins to realize that he will never marry her. Her heart slowly breaks as she continues to endure the frustration of not being able to speak and the terrible agony of walking as if on sharpened knives. There comes a time when the prince must go to a nearby kingdom to meet the young princess of that land. The prince is certain that he will not be able to love her, for his obsession is with the face of the young girl he saw when he first awoke on the beach the morning after his ship sank. He does not know that he confuses that memory with his memory of the Little Mermaid, who he says reminds him of that girl. When his eyes fall on the princess, he recognizes her instead as the young maiden who he thinks saved his life, and a marriage is swiftly arranged.

The prince, who joyfully tells the Little Mermaid of his discovery, does not know that his decision to marry seals a terrible fate for her. Her life must end at the sunrise after the wedding and her body will be dissolved into oblivion in the sea foam. Bravely and without complaint, the Little Mermaid accepts her fate. Following the wish of the prince, she participates in the wedding, which is held on board a ship, and she dances more brilliantly than ever before. "Sharp knives seemed to cut into her delicate feet," writes Andersen, "but she did not feel it, for the pain in her heart cut yet more sharply. . . . She laughed and danced with the thought of death in her heart." Later she stood alone on board ship and "looked towards the east for the first red of morning—the first ray of the sun, she knew, would kill her" (pp. 103–4). Andersen joins together the governing symbols in his story in such a manner that the pathos swiftly yields to a profound situational irony, which secures the allegorical meaning.

The symbolism is unmistakably religious. Andersen repeats the images of the rising sun and the red sky. In this manner he alludes strongly to the beginning of his story, when he acquainted the reader with the Little Mermaid's attraction to the sun, the hope it stirred in her heart, and her love of the "rose-red flowers" that shone in her garden like that sun (pp. 78–79). Now at the close of the story the sun appears once more and, instead of a new life, it seems to promise only death. This is what the mermaid and the reader would believe. But just before the arrival of dawn, her sisters emerge from the deep. They inform her that they have struck a deal with the sea-witch. In return for their long tresses, she has arranged for a way that the Little Mermaid can save her own life. They tell their sister:

> She [the sea-witch] has given us a knife—here it is! Can you see how sharp it is? Before the sun rises, you must thrust it into the prince's heart, and as his warm blood splashes on to your feet, they will grow together into a fishtail and you will be a mermaid again, and then you can come down to us in the water and live your three hundred years before you turn into the dead salt foam

of the sea. Hurry! Either he or you must die before the sun rises!
(p. 104)

The wisdom of evil is this: that it uses our personal suffering as well as our greatest hopes and fears to tempt us to sin. The sea-witch offers the Little Mermaid the opportunity to wreak a splendid revenge on the prince in a perverse mockery of ritual sacrifice and eucharistic offering. She can take his life and save her own with a knife that is figuratively connected to the piercing pain in her feet that has afflicted her since she journeyed up above. The Little Mermaid's refusal brings to mind the biblical stories of David and Saul and the several opportunities to kill Saul that David relinquishes. In the David and Saul stories, Saul's irrational jealousy and anger move him repeatedly to throw his spear at David. In the last instance, David, who has become a hunted man, is given the chance to see to it that Saul is killed with Saul's own spear as he lies sleeping in an encampment. But David will not permit his lieutenant to carry out the ugly deed. The spear, of course, symbolizes all of the pain, suffering, and injustice that David has endured at the hands of Saul, whom he loved as a father.[15] The knife that the Little Mermaid is given serves a similar purpose in Andersen's story.

David's decision to spare Saul saves his soul from darkness. Likewise, we may say that the mermaid's decision to spare the prince at the cost of her own life ironically gains her the immortality she believes she has given up. Midway through the story, the Little Mermaid makes her greatest wish, which is also a prophecy of her future conduct and the direction that her life takes henceforth. She says to her grandmother, "I would give all the hundreds of years I have to live to be a human girl for just one day and then to receive my part in the Kingdom of Heaven" (p. 90). This also is, no doubt, just the sort of "religious" writing that Sale finds objectionable.

I cannot answer for the critic's prejudices. I can point out, however, the skill with which Andersen draws out the meaning of the mermaid's final decision to spare the life of the prince. He makes it at once both the culmination of her life and the fulfillment of her religious quest. When the Little Mermaid's sisters beseech her to kill the prince and come back with them, they finish with the plea, "Do you not see the red streak in the sky? In a few minutes the sun will rise, and then you must die!" (p. 104). Andersen does not need to explain the Little Mermaid's feelings. We can easily imagine what they are. It was not easy for her to leave her family the first time. Now she must repeat that decision. But she remains true to her deepest yearnings for the Kingdom of Heaven, even, ironically, by making a decision that she can only believe seals her own death and extinction.

> The little mermaid drew aside the purple hangings of the tent, and she saw the lovely bride sleeping with her head upon the prince's breast, and she bent down and kissed his fair forehead. She looked at the sky where the red of morning was shining more and more brightly; she looked at the sharp knife and gazed once again upon the prince who murmured his bride's name in his dreams. She alone was in his thoughts, and the knife quivered in the mermaid's hand—but she flung it far out into the waves which shone red where it fell and looked as if drops of blood had spurted up out of the water. Once more she looked with half-glazed eyes upon the prince, threw herself from the ship down into the sea, and felt her body dissolving into foam. (pp. 104–5)

Sale calls the prince a "dull and careless man." I disagree. The prince certainly does not "see" what we want him to see, but he does not lack affection or sympathy. As mentioned before, he takes the Little Mermaid in and acts always with kindness toward her. Nor does he lack the important characteristic of gratitude. He is truly grateful for the act of kindness that saved his life, and to the extent that the Little Mermaid reminds him of the face of the girl he thinks saved him, he is moved to compassion. Needless to say, the prince's "blindness" is disappointing, and the romantic in each of us wants to fault him for not loving her as a lover and taking her as a wife. Unwittingly, he causes the Little Mermaid great suffering and sorrow. But this is precisely what makes her final decision to spare his life at what she believes will be the cost of her own life such a powerful lesson of love and forgiveness. The Bible's understanding of love echoes throughout—"If you love those who love you what credit is that to you? For even sinners love those who love them" (Luke 6:32). "No one has greater love than this, to lay down one's life for one's friend" (John 15:13).

Perhaps Andersen ought to have ended his story with the passage cited above and its symbolism of sacrifice and rebirth, and left sufficient ambiguity and inconclusiveness to keep the reader wrestling with its meaning. But much like Dostoevsky in his novels, Andersen felt compelled to spell out the way toward the happy resolution of his irony. And certainly that was not such a bad decision if Andersen had child readers in mind, because they would want more to be said about the fate of the Little Mermaid.

The mermaid and the reader soon learn that the sun to which the mermaid has been so drawn throughout will not become, as she fears, the cause of her dissolution into nothingness. For just as the mermaid throws herself into the sea and feels herself dissolving in it, the sun rises out of the sea. "[Its] rays fell gently and warmly on the death-cold sea-foam; and the little mermaid had no feeling of death upon her." She looks up to that sun and is greeted with a vision of "hundreds of lovely transparent forms" (p. 105), and her body is transformed into one like theirs as she ascends into the air to join them.

"'To whom am I coming?' she asked. . . . 'To the daughters of the air!' answered the others." The daughters of the air then tell the Little Mermaid that they, like a mermaid, "have no eternal soul" and, like her, they depend "upon the power of another" to finally possess one. But by good deeds, they continue, they can gain a soul after three hundred years. "You, poor little mermaid, have striven with your whole heart for the same thing as we strive for. You have suffered and endured, and raised yourself into the world of the spirits of the air. And now you, too, through your good deeds can create an immortal soul for yourself in three hundred years" (pp. 105–6).

These passages might cause more than a little consternation in theological quarters. Is Andersen committed to the heresy of works righteousness? Then again, he seems to contradict himself, because he also says that mermaids and their kind depend upon another to gain an immortal soul. Which is it? Is immortality a gift or the product of one's own good works? But the legitimate theological objections that might be raised here are probably as misleading and beside the point as the claims made by literary critics that the story and its main character are the products of Andersen's personal feelings of social and sexual inferiority. Andersen's stories have gained their own immortality because generations of ordinary readers have not thought these quirks in Andersen's character or his apparent deviations from theological orthodoxy to be nearly so important as the truths about human nature and human destiny that they explore. Sale and Zipes would dissolve this wisdom in the solvent of their own disbelief. They would have us ignore these central truths about life and love and death and immortality. But the readers whom they almost begrudge for standing by this story and its endearing character are not likely to be persuaded.

At the ending, Andersen reveals the meaning of the central metaphor that is behind the allegory. He reports that after listening to the daughters of the air, "the little mermaid lifted her bright arms up towards God's sun" (p. 106). In this great and profound fairy tale, Hans Christian Andersen challenges every reader to contemplate his or her fate if love does not endure and personal immortality is just an illusion. From the start, the Little Mermaid is not content with the answer that she is given. "We can live until we are three hundred years old," says the Merking's mother to the Little Mermaid, "but then when our life is finished here, we are only foam upon the water" (p. 90). That is why the Little Mermaid sets her eyes always on the rising sun, even when she fears that it will be her death. And so we should also ask ourselves: why would we want our children or ourselves to be content with that answer when immortality has been proffered?

4

FRIENDS AND MENTORS IN *THE WIND IN THE WILLOWS, CHARLOTTE'S WEB,* AND *BAMBI*

Aristotle said it a long time ago: "Without friends no one would choose to live."[1] Friendships bring a goodness and grace into our lives whose value transcends material measure. Of what value are wealth or possessions, Aristotle challenges us to consider, without companions with whom to share them? And friendships can make us better persons also by prompting us to think of others besides ourselves. "It is more characteristic of a friend to do well by another than to be well done by," Aristotle continues.[2]

Virtue and the moral imagination are practically inconceivable apart from the rich soil of friendship to grow upon. Certainly, childhood would not be childhood without friends: that seems an incontrovertible truth. And so one is bound when writing on children's literature to consider stories the principal subject of which is friendship. In this chapter, I consider three of the most beloved stories in the entire corpus of children's literature: *The*

Tending the Heart of Virtue. Second Edition. Vigen Guroian, Oxford University Press.
© Vigen Guroian 1998, 2023. DOI: 10.1093/oso/9780195384307.003.0005

Wind in the Willows, Charlotte's Web, and *Bambi.* Each of these stories explores different qualities of friendship; however, *Charlotte's Web and Bambi* move our reflection on the meaning of friendship toward a consideration of that special kind of friend who is a mentor.

The Wind in the Willows: On the Nature of Friendship

Of all the classics of children's literature none, in my opinion, captures the meaning of friendship as profoundly and with such utter simplicity and whimsicality as Kenneth Grahame's *The Wind in the Willows. The Wind in the Willows* is about friendship in perhaps its purest form, where no one friend is superior to the other, while each friend stands to benefit from the unique gifts of the other. Such reciprocity is the principal theme of the relations of the four main characters in Grahame's story. Mole, Water Rat, Badger, and Toad are very different in makeup and disposition. Yet this is what lends such richness to their common undertakings and texture to their life together. Complementarity and not uniformity is the spice that adds flavor to good friendships, with special needs and unique gifts mixed and matched to create strong bonds of companionship. Aristotle argues that a friendship may be called perfect not because the friends are perfect but because the existence of the friendship itself makes possible their moral perfection. The call of friendships to a perfection of one's character is a theme that ought to be introduced to children, and *The Wind in the Willows* is a good place to start.

The Call to Friendship

Mole is the primal "child" of Grahame's story. We watch him mature to claim an equal footing in friendship with Rat, Badger, and Toad. It is Mole that I turn to mainly. Mole is the first character to whom we are introduced in *The Wind in the Willows*. At the beginning he is mysteriously drawn out of his familiar way of life underground. "The Mole had been working very hard all the morning, spring-cleaning his little home.... Something up above was *calling* [my emphasis] him imperiously, and he made for the steep little tunnel which answered in this case to the gravelled carriage-drive owned by animals whose residences are nearer to the sun and air."[3] This is how Mole's rite of passage begins as he enters upon a world greater than any he has ever known, one that is filled with new and exciting smells and sounds and sights. More important, Mole joins a community of animal persons that forever will change his life and make him a better and stronger animal.

Grahame thinks of friendship as a calling. By grace and not just chance are we sent forth into the world for fellowship and communion with others. Friendships even sound the call to a higher and transcendent communion with God. Mole and Rat hear this call in the wind in the willows. It is no accident that Mole's growth into full equality with his new friends is marked by an experience of this higher calling. One night he and Ratty set out onto the river to search for their friend Otter's son, Portly, who has been missing for several days. Just before the breaking of dawn, Rat and Mole hear music among the willows, the pipe of Pan, the "Friend and Helper." They follow that music to its source and find little Portly safe under the protection of Pan. While Grahame employs motifs and characters of pagan myth, the theme of spiritual love, which is the highest form of friendship, taps a deep and ancient tradition of spirituality. That tradition successfully relates friendship to agape and that love to the desire for God.

On their mission of charity, the two friends enter together into this spiritual reality of friendship. On the one hand, this higher friendship is an ascetical achievement. Grahame makes a metaphor out of their boating activity. Rat rows while Mole steers accordingly midstream, carefully following "a narrow track [of moonlight] that faintly reflected the sky" (p. 118) in search of the lost and helpless child. On the other hand, the friends' journey is a mystical sojourn. Nature provides the essential metaphors, as the two searchers are carried downstream by wind and water. Mole and Rat "glided onwards . . . Never had they noticed the roses so vivid, the willow-herb so riotous, the meadow-sweet so odorous and pervading . . . and they felt a consciousness that they were nearing the end, whatever it might be, that surely awaited their expedition." Just before dawn, they arrive at a hallowed ground where the nature god resides. "In midmost of the stream, embraced in the weir's shimmering arm-spread, a small island lay anchored, fringed close with willow and silver birch and alder. Reserved, shy, but full of significance, it hid whatever it might hold behind a veil, keeping it till the hour should come, and, with the hour, those who were called and chosen" (p. 122).

Most contemporary interpreters of Grahame's story dislike this chapter. They argue that it neither captures religious experience accurately nor depicts the artistic imagination faithfully. These critics regard the entire episode as an unnecessary and disruptive interpolation into the narrative. But I think Grahame deliberately planted this episode right in the middle of his story. It matters little that his own religious beliefs were heterodox or that he disagreed with some of the essential teachings of the Christian faith. Nevertheless, "Pipers at the Gate of Dawn" parallels the Judeo-Christian understanding of the spiritual perfection of friendship. His hero-friends are rewarded with the numinous presence of the nature god.

> Perhaps he [Mole] would never have dared to raise his eyes, but that, though the piping was now hushed, the call and the summons seemed still dominant and imperious. . . . Trembling he obeyed, and raised his humble head; and then, in the utter clearness of the imminent dawn, while Nature, flushed with fullness of incredible colour, seemed to hold her breath for the event, he looked in the very eyes of the Friend and Helper . . . saw, last of all, nestling between his very hooves, sleeping soundly in utter peace and contentment, the little, round, podgy, childish form of the baby otter. (p. 124)

We see this vision through Mole's eyes, and it is a crucial moment in his maturation. From here on, Mole assumes a much more active and equal role with his friends.

Pan mercifully erases the memory of Mole and Ratty's encounter with him, "lest the awful remembrance should remain and grow, and overshadow mirth and pleasure" (p. 125). But the little otter's continuing presence no doubt often reminds the two friends of the good service to which they once put their friendship. Grahame also emphasizes the manner in which Mole and Rat responded that day to the vision of the demigod: "Then the two animals, crouching to the earth, bowed their heads and did worship" (p. 124). Communion and worship are friendship's proper end when it is raised to its highest spiritual level. Whatever else his critics have had to say about this chapter, Grahame got this just right.

Leisure and the Imagination

> This day was only the first of many similar ones for
> the emancipated Mole, each of them longer and full
> of interest as the ripening summer moved onward. He
> learnt to swim and to row, and entered into the joy of
> running water; and with his ear to the reed-stems he
> caught, at intervals, something of what the wind went
> whispering so constantly among them.
> —*The Wind in the Willows*

In an age in which people obsessively shift back and forth from
work to working at making recreation, we are in jeopardy of
forgetting the value of unplanned leisure and spontaneous play.
When the child leaves home, we believe, he leaves play and goes
to work. We say that play is for children. But is this really true?
There is an ancient wisdom that says, quite to the contrary, that
play is the necessary condition for the establishment and health of
a truly social world and the role that friendship plays in it. Kenneth
Grahame reminds us of that wisdom in *The Wind in the Willows*.
When we take time off from work we sometimes say that we are
"killing a little time," as if leisure and play are "breaks" from work
or "escapes" from responsibility. Grahame, on the other hand,
thinks of play and leisure as preconditions of real selfhood and social belonging and as the very best use that we can make of time
because this is when friendships are forged.

We rarely see Grahame's coterie of friends working except, one
might say, at being good companions. For friendships to prosper,
leisure and play are necessary. Friendships need the space and time
represented by the open country and the river in *The Wind in the
Willows*. Friendships thrive in the open air and wind and sun. Their
value is missed or misunderstood in a world in which money is

mistaken as the measure of nearly everything and utility becomes the sole test of value. Friendships exist for their own sakes. Yet a healthy social world and culture itself are the felicitous outcome of robust friendships.

The world of leisure and play that Rat, Mole, Toad, and Badger inhabit used to be familiar to children. However, we have grown suspicious of this kind of leisure and play, even for children. The opinion spreads that even children's play ought to be organized and properly supervised. It does not occur to us that this might not be true play. We blur the differences between recreation and pure play. But perhaps we are not yet so far from the experience of the Victorians that we cannot still learn from their wisdom about the meaning and nature of childhood and the role of free and imaginative play. Mole is called out of his womblike home to become a friend to others, and he grows into a mole of character precisely because he plays and makes friendships in the doing. Indeed, he seems to be a character destined for friendship. That is what I think makes him so attractive. He gives us the hope that our lives might prosper and be filled in the same way.

In the first chapter of *The Wind in the Willows*, Grahame describes how Mole discovers the river and happens upon Rat.

> He [Mole] thought his happiness was complete when, as he meandered aimlessly along, suddenly he stood by the edge of a full-fed river. Never in his life had he seen a river before. . . . As he gazed, something bright and small seemed to be twinkling down in the heart of it. . . . Then, as he looked, it winked at him, and so declared itself to be an eye; and a small face began gradually to grow up around it, like a frame round a picture. (p. 29)

The river is where leisure is taken and enjoyed. In the Victorian era, the waterways and estuaries of the English landscape were transformed into places of play and recreation. At one point, Grahame describes Mole with a metaphor of the river. Mole "meander[s] aimlessly" until he arrives at the river's banks. Rat takes Mole boating and teaches him the ways of the river, the life of this leisure, the opportunities and fruits of which are friendship and real happiness. Friendships—unlike, for example, coworker relationships—are not supervised by another party or assigned to a specific task or pursued for profit. Mole and Rat meet accidentally or by destiny, but not according to a plan. He who goes looking for a friend is the least likely of persons to find a friend.

The river symbolizes a world of leisure and play in which friendships are made and enjoyed. Likewise, it also supplies the significant "stuff" of the moral imagination: it is the inspiration of mental images of self and world that the self then can use to relate successfully with others in friendships, common undertakings, and a shared vision of life. Grahame describes Mole's first encounter with the river this way:

> The Mole was bewitched, entranced, fascinated. By the side of the river he trotted as one trots, when very small, by the side of a man who holds one spell-bound by exciting stories; and when tired at last, he sat on the bank, while the river still chattered on to him, a babbling procession of the best stories in the world, sent from the heart of the earth to be told at last to the insatiable sea. (p. 29)

Soon Mole meets Rat, who becomes his principal interpreter of the "stories" the river tells. Rat is Mole's guide to the world of imaginative play hosted by the river. Mole, for his part, assimilates these experiences to steer his way successfully in the wider world. He takes the initiative that sets in motion the triumphant assault upon Toad Hall that drives out the renegade band of unsavory stoats and weasels who have taken possession of it. Toad Hall is not just the elegant home of Mr. Toad; it is the symbol of the friends' social world that Toad foolishly and selfishly puts at risk.

Play is not "killing time" or an "escape" from work; it is an activity that gives life to the moral imagination. If we are deprived of play, the moral imagination is stunted. But play also can be misused or wasted, or it can become an obsession that subverts the social world. And this is, of course, what is the matter with Toad's behavior as he pursues fancies that feed uncontrolled appetites. Toad's kind of play is entirely set loose from responsibility, and this is why the friends ultimately act severely in order, as the tough-minded but lovingly wise Badger puts it, to "convert" and "reform" Toad. What else are friends for? Aristotle says of friendship: "It helps the young to keep from error; it aids activities that are failing from weakness; those in the prime of life it stimulates to noble actions—'two going together'—for with friends men are more able to think and to act."[4]

Needfulness and Friendship

As Aristotle also observed, friendships help to satisfy the neediness we have in common as finite creatures and social animals. If we were gods and entirely self-sufficient, we might be able to do without friends. But we are not gods and so we need friends in order to flourish and be happy. Ironically, this neediness, which is sometimes mistakenly thought of as weakness, is the soil in which the mutuality and reciprocity of friendship grow. As I have already suggested, Mole is especially attractive to children precisely because he is so childlike himself and so helpless at the start. As if from a womb, Mole emerges from under the ground into the sun and the fresh air, open to new experiences but still having needs. Instinctively, he seems to know that only friends can answer those needs. And so he sets off into the world.

Indeed, Grahame shows us through Mole's experience how friendships form us into stronger and more integrated persons. We begin on a lesser plane and through friendships grow into something greater. When Mole first tunnels his way into the light, he is an inexperienced and timid animal. He journeys through woods and meadows and is frightened by unfriendly creatures, yet his natural curiosity and the "call" to friendship spur him on. Life underground has been comfortable. But aboveground, Mole experiences an exhilarating freedom that he has not known before. He is "emancipated," as Grahame puts it. When Mole strikes a friendship with Water Rat and the others, his life takes a new turn.

Children are born needful. We do not condemn the infant's need for her mother's milk or describe the child's efforts to gain parental affection and care as selfishness. We know that these things must necessarily be provided if children are going to grow from young, dependent human beings into healthy and responsible adults. Modern psychology confirms the common stock of human wisdom that says children ought to have friends, and not just any friends, but the best of friends—not perfect friends, for there are no such persons, but friends with real virtues that in combination contribute to the moral growth of all the friends. In *The Wind in the Willows*, Kenneth Grahame gives us a quartet of endearing characters, friends who together show us the value and importance of this truth.

Charlotte's Web: A Friend as Mentor

In the closing pages of E. B. White's memorable children's story, Charlotte endeavors to explain to Wilbur why she responded to his need for a friend and dedicated herself to saving his life through the ingenious ploy of spinning words in her web.

> "You have been my friend.... That in itself is a tremendous thing. I wove my webs for you because I liked you. After all, what's a life, anyway? We're born, we live a little while, we die. A spider's life can't help being something of a mess, with all the trapping and catching flies. By helping you, perhaps I was trying to lift up my life a trifle. Heaven knows anyone's life can stand a little of that."[5]

Even she, whom Wilbur regarded as so wise and so ingenious, was not without real needs. She in her own fashion needed a friend. Nevertheless, Charlotte and Wilbur's friendship is different from the friendship of Mole, Rat, Badger, and Toad. From the beginning, Charlotte and Wilbur are not equals. Charlotte is wiser and knows more about the ways of the world than Wilbur, and she cares for him with something that resembles maternal love. Fern, the young daughter of the farmer John Arable, opposes her father's intention to mercifully put the runt pig to death, and so she is the first to save Wilbur's life and to care for him like a mother. But Wilbur is moved to her uncle Homer Zuckerman's farm and there, separated from Fern for most of each day, Wilbur needs closer and more constant care and company. Charlotte supplies this, and she becomes the object of Wilbur's greatest love.

As a surrogate mother, Charlotte tells Wilbur bedtime stories and sings him lullabies, teaches him manners, tells him to chew his "food thoroughly and eat every bit of it" (p. 64), encourages him when he is down, and builds up his confidence for the day when he must stand on his own four feet without the benefit of her care. But Charlotte, unlike a natural mother, is able to keep a decided distance from Wilbur. This is symbolized by the fact that her web is beyond Wilbur's reach. Thus, something more is suggested about their relationship that needs naming.

Whereas parents do not choose who their children are or children their parents, Charlotte chooses Wilbur as a friend and Wilbur willingly accepts that friendship. That is, Charlotte is a *mentor* to Wilbur and theirs is a *mentoral friendship*. This takes into account the fundamental inequality in their friendship, while it also keeps in view the important characteristic of mutual affection that belongs to all true friendships. Again, Aristotle is our best guide. In his *Nicomachean Ethics*, he discusses relationships of inequality like Charlotte and Wilbur's and defines these as friendships of a special sort. "But there is another kind of friendship," Aristotle notes, "that which involves an inequality between the parties, e.g. that of father to son and in general of elder to younger" and the like. In such friendships the love that the lesser gives to the greater makes up the difference. In other words, "when the love is in proportion to the merit of the parties, then in a sense arises equality, which is certainly held to be characteristic of friendship."[6] Without wanting to understate Charlotte's true affection for Wilbur, we still are bound to say that Wilbur's love is of greater intensity and is the more all-consuming, just in the same way that his need for a friend is greater. Yet, according to Aristotle, this is as it should be: a proportionality in love appropriate to kind establishes ground for a true friendship.

But what is a mentoral friendship, and how does such a description help us to understand this story and the special ways in which it is able to speak to children? "Mentor" has a long history and an-cient etymology. It comes from the Greek *menos,* which means mind or spirit, and suggests a strong sense of purposefulness and agency. Mentor is the guise and name the goddess Athena assumes as a counselor to Odysseus's son, Telemachus, in Homer's epic poem *The Odyssey.* Athena is prompted to take this strategy because Odysseus's delay in reaching home has left Telemachus despairing and unsure. She seeks to encourage him, to counsel him, to make him wiser and better aware of his own inner resources, resources he will later draw upon to defeat his mother's unscrupulous and ambitious suitors and guarantee for his father a happy return.

The mentor, therefore, is someone who brings the student to self-knowledge and instills confidence in her charge to pursue a successful course in life. The relationship is not unlike a teacher toward a pupil, and, at least as much as in that kind of relation-ship, the mentoral relationship is characterized by a fundamental inequality. This describes Charlotte's relationship to Wilbur. She is wiser than Wilbur and is able to give him far more than he can offer to her in return, except his love. By her constant counsel and by spinning such words as "some pig," "terrific," and "radiant" into her web, she builds up his self-esteem.

> Ever since the spider had befriended him, he had done his best to live up to his reputation. When Charlotte's web said SOME PIG, Wilbur had tried to look like some pig. When Charlotte's web said TERRIFIC, Wilbur had tried to look terrific. And now that the web said RADIANT, he did everything possible to make himself glow. (p. 114)

Charlotte chooses her role quite intentionally and with a sin-gleness of purpose that would ordinarily contradict the free spirit of friendship. She must find a way to save Wilbur's life while also guiding him through the performance of tasks that will contribute to that end. Nor does her stake in Wilbur's survival include the futurity of parenthood. Measured by the life expectancy of a pig, her summer's role in his life is but a short span. In this case the special needs of the "lesser" party call out from the mentor just what he or she possesses that the "lesser" party needs at the present moment. Charlotte says to Wilbur, "By helping you, perhaps I was trying to lift up my life a trifle." And this is no doubt true in some sense. But it does not explain why Charlotte responded in the first place to Wilbur's anguished plea for a friend and someone to save him from death. Charlotte wanted to help Wilbur live and be happy, and she felt within herself that she had the ability to do so. Nothing he might have added would have made a difference in her determination.

So Charlotte gives constant thought to how she will fulfill her promise to save Wilbur's life. "Day after day the spider waited, head-down, for an idea to come to her. . . . Charlotte was naturally patient" (p. 66). And like a wise teacher, Charlotte gives her pupil as much as he can absorb and not more. She guides him to the point when he must take possession of himself and make independent decisions.

That process of mentoring comes to a close at the state fair, when Charlotte's life is wholly spent and she is near death. Until this time there has been little that Wilbur could do to reciprocate in kind for what Charlotte has done for him. When he realizes, however, that Charlotte will not return to the farm and that there is nothing he can do about that, Wilbur takes an initiative that bridges the significant gap between mentor and pupil, sufficient to the requirements of true friendship. Wilbur sees to it that Charlotte's egg sac is brought back to the Zuckerman farm, where it will be safe. Yet even this act of loving reciprocity is conditioned and limited by the enduring qualities of the mentoral relationship itself. It cannot change Wilbur's role in the relationship with Charlotte from "lesser" to "greater." Wilbur cannot teach the teacher; nor is he able to share in Charlotte's experience of being his guide. The mentor stands at both ends of the mentor-mentee relationship, the mentee only at one end. Wilbur waits through the long winter until the spring to enter into a role toward Charlotte's children that is similar to what she was toward him. Yet Charlotte's special role of mentor and friend to Wilbur is irreplaceable and unrepeatable. At the end of the story we are told:

> Wilbur never forgot Charlotte. Although he loved her children and grandchildren dearly, none of the new spiders quite took her place in his heart. (p. 184)

If we are able to look back on our lives and say that there was a Charlotte in it, we are most fortunate, but an even greater good fortune is if we become a mentor and friend to someone else, as Charlotte A. Cavatica was for Wilbur the runt pig.

Bambi: What Mentors Are For

Walt Disney so radically altered Felix Salten's *Bambi: A Life in the Woods* that it is difficult not to worry that the reader will keep wanting to return to the Disney animation rather than follow the lines of the original story. Yet Salten's book is one of the most beautifully written of children's stories. And Disney did not capture the depth of its wisdom. It is a tale spun with great force and majesty. As I have done with *Charlotte's Web*, in *Bambi* I look closely at one particular character, Bambi the deer and his relationship with the mysterious old stag. For it is within this relationship that Bambi matures and assumes a special role among the deer. This relationship is at the center of Salten's story, and not Bambi's love for Faline, the young doe, as Disney has it.

Thus far, I have led the reader from a discussion of pure friendship in *The Wind in the Willows* through the mentoral friendship in *Charlotte's Web*. In *Bambi*, Salten shows us the meaning of pure mentorship. Whereas friendships necessarily entail equality of one sort or another, mentorship presupposes a fundamental inequality between mentor and pupil. The mentor's selection of the pupil is the defining act in such a relationship, since the mentor has a vital stake in choosing the right pupil.[7] He wants to ensure that the special knowledge and skills he possesses are transmitted to another.

As I have suggested in my discussion of *Charlotte's Web*, the office of teacher is inherently suited to the role of mentor. Yet we have so democratized and bureaucratized education that genuine mentoral possibilities are nearly precluded in teaching. Contemporary institutionalized forms of education bend to an egalitarian impulse that inhibits the teacher from discriminating among students. The renewed contemporary interest in mentorship as an aspect of professional training is strongly affected by this same egalitarian prejudice. In society at large it is virtually assumed that the pupil initiates the relationship with a mentor of her choice. While this might be a legitimate and worthwhile practice in various spheres of public life, it is not genuine mentorship. In a true mentoral relationship, the mentor chooses the mentee, and for very good reasons.

Not surprisingly, mentoral relationships still happen in the performing arts, such as in dance or music. The market and a hyperegalitarian ethos have chipped away at the master- protégé relationship but have not completely eliminated it. Most anyone with the financial resources can purchase ballet or violin lessons, but in the end the master still chooses the protégé for special attention and instruction. It is hard to imagine how the arts would survive if this were precluded.

Thus the mentor's selection of the pupil is the crucial and defining act of the mentoral relationship. The relationship is from the start asymmetrical and discriminative. By means of physical gesture, tone of voice, and behavior, the mentor communicates his special knowledge and skill and also a piece of his own character. There is no such thing in this relationship as being informative without also being formative. The mentor has a vital stake in choosing the right mentee. And so he dedicates himself to engendering in the mentee essential qualities of character or skills that are not merely private or personal but ultimately crucial to the continuance of a practice, special art form, or way of life.

May we still call this kind of relationship a friendship? If we take Aristotle's lead, I believe that the mentoral relationships in White's and Salten's stories may be called "friendships," but of a very special sort. In both stories a relationship of unequals increases affection, trust, and mutuality—all essential earmarks of friendship. Yet unlike *Charlotte's Web*, in *Bambi* the private lives of the central characters are not the primary concern, and so in that story the qualities of friendship that develop within the mentoral relationship are subordinated to and strictly serve the purposes of mentorship. The old stag gives himself over to producing in Bambi essential qualities of character that are not merely personal but ultimately crucial to the continuance of a way of life. In this way, Salten illumines a form of relationship the conspicuous lack of which in modern society may also help to account for the crisis of morality and culture that we face.

The Solitary Life and Life in the Woods

Early in *Bambi* the reader learns that the old stag is the spiritual head and protector of the deer herd, even though he is absent and removed most of the time from their daily lives. Salten echoes the biblical theme of a calling to "separateness." He also incorporates characteristics of both the Stoic sage and the Christian office of the holy elder of monastic origins. The other deer of the woods refer to the stag as the "old Prince." He is a solitary guardian who appears suddenly—usually, as we learn, when the deer and other smaller creatures need to be warned of danger, especially of the hunter. He is the ideal embodiment of the virtues and practical skills necessary for deer to prosper. The stag is vigilant and has studied and put to memory the physical topography of the woods so as to be able to avoid or escape immediate danger. "He uses trails none of the others ever use. He knows the very depths of the forest. And he does not know such a thing as danger."[8] He also knows the spiritual geography of life and death in the woods. He practices the virtues of attentiveness and watchfulness, which extend and deepen life and living for all of the deer.

The stag commands profound respect and even awe from the other deer. "There isn't anybody that compares to him. Nobody knows how old he is. Nobody can find out where he lives. Very few have seen him, even once. At times he was thought to be dead because he hadn't been seen for so long. Then someone would see him again for a second and so they knew he was still alive. Nobody had ever dared ask him where he had been" (p. 57). The other deer do not mistake him for a god, as they do Man, but he is admired as the model of what is highest and noblest in the deer.

The secret of the stag's wisdom and longevity resides in his ability to be alone, to spend time with himself whereby he achieves self-mastery and perfects his special powers of discernment and insight into the rhythm of life in the woods. He has perfected a special sixth sense of knowing or anticipating when human beings, the hunters, will interrupt that rhythm and rain death upon the animal inhabitants of the forest. We are not given an explanation for why the stag chooses Bambi as his protégé and successor. This choice is wrapped up in the mysterious character of the stag himself. He initiates a mentor-protégé relationship between himself and Bambi that serves all the deer by guaranteeing the succession of a new guardian and protector.

The Importance of Knowing How to Be Alone

Salten introduces the theme of knowing how to be alone early in the story, and throughout he explores its importance for survival in the woods. In one sense being alone is what any young buck or doe must learn in order to mature. It is a part and parcel of personal autonomy, and it necessitates the courage and confidence to successfully live apart from the mother. This is a precondition for mating and perpetuation of the species. Salten is a careful observer of the life and behavior of deer. Yet he is not a naturalist who records the animals' life cycle. He is a moralist who uses his knowledge of nature to tell a moral tale. In his book knowing how to be alone has ethical and spiritual significance.

Early in the story the stag suddenly confronts Bambi, who has gotten lost and is wandering through the woods and thickets. Bambi is frightened and calling for his mother. "What are you crying about?" the stag says to Bambi. "Your mother has no time for you now.... Can't you stay by yourself? Shame on you!" (p. 55). This timely reproach sows a seed of desire in the youngster. He wants to be like the old stag and wants to prove himself better in his eyes. For a long time afterward the stag is absent. Bambi struggles on his own to mature and act independently absent fear. He learns some hard lessons about life in the woods, especially about the reality of death. He witnesses the bloody deaths of some of his animal companions. He also discovers another presence in the woods—human beings, who kill with an unpredictability and wantonness that terrify all of the forest creatures.

On one occasion a young adult buck is shot. Salten describes Bambi's reaction:

> He [Bambi] felt himself threatened by something dark. He did not understand how the others could be so carefree and happy while life was so difficult and dangerous. The desire seized him to go deeper into the woods. They lured him into their depths. He wanted to find some hiding place where, shielded on all sides by impenetrable thickets, he could never be seen. (pp. 68–69)

Man, the hunter, represents the irrationality of evil that always threatens to rob life of meaning. Bambi needs to understand the nature of this destructive force. In the face of danger and even death he has to learn a discipline of vigilance and self-possession in order to survive and be heir to the stag. His desire to go deep into the woods is not merely an impulse to escape. He is driven to be truly free and not a captive to the blinding and incapacitating fear that he has observed in the other deer and inhabitants of the woods.

By the end of the story, Bambi has learned how to be alone, The old stag's role and his responsibility for the lives of the deer and other animals in the woods will now devolve upon him as the stag goes off to die alone. Salten again emphasizes the importance of knowing how to be alone: "When he [Bambi] was still a child the old stag had taught him that you must live alone. Then and afterwards the old stag had revealed much wisdom and many secrets to him. But of all his teachings this had been the most important: you must live alone. If you wanted to preserve yourself, if you understood existence, if you wanted to attain wisdom, you had to live alone" (pp. 175–76).

This aloneness is not the homelessness or the desolation that the other creatures experience in the face of danger or evil. Of all the animals and deer, the old stag is the most at home in the woods and the least afflicted by desolation. This is because he understands the order of existence and trusts in its Source. The aloneness to which Bambi is called is a way of learning important skills of survival. In this manner Bambi is prepared to become the guardian of the herd—not that he rules by might, but rather that he leads like the biblical prophet, through discernment and familiarity with the way of Being itself. The old stag brings up Bambi in this singleness of life for the good of all. And the last and most important lesson he teaches Bambi is about the true order of Being. At the close of the story, the old stag leads Bambi to the still and bloodied body of a poacher:

"Do you see, Bambi," the old stag went on, "do you see how He's lying there dead, like one of us? Listen, Bambi. He isn't all-powerful as they say. Everything that lives and grows doesn't come from Him. He isn't above us. He's just the same as we are. He has the same fears, the same needs, and suffers in the same way. He can be killed like us, and then He lies helpless on the ground like all the rest of us, as you see Him now."

There was silence.

"Do you understand me, Bambi?" asked the old stag.

"I think so," Bambi said in a whisper.

"Then speak," the old stag commanded.

Bambi was inspired, and said, trembling, "There is Another who is over us all, over us and over Him."

"Now I can go," said the old stag. (pp. 187–88)

This is the final and most important truth that the old stag teaches to Bambi. With this truth Bambi takes the stag's place as the new guardian of the herd. His new status has been built upon the sure foundation of his obedient relationship to the old stag.

The Special Qualities of the Mentor

In *Bambi* Salten depicts a special form of love and relationship that the English word "friendship" does not quite cover, and yet mentorship and friendship are related. Before the stag leaves Bambi to go off and die, he says to him: "Good-bye, my son, I loved you dearly" (p. 188). Never before did the old stag state his love in such words, yet in all of his actions toward Bambi he manifested this love. The mentor is a special friend. What makes the friendship special is that the stag reserves it in his heart until his role as mentor is completed.

There is a poignant moment in the novel that never ceased to draw attention from my students. Roughly midway through the story, Bambi happens upon the old stag grazing in a clearing. He decides to approach the stag and introduce himself. As he approaches, he feels the stag's strength. The stag returns a haughty look that misrepresents the stag's own feelings. Bambi is discouraged by what he takes to be the stag's indifference toward him. This, however, is a miscommunication. In actuality the stag is thinking: "What should I say to him? I'm not used to talking. I'd say something stupid and make myself ridiculous" (p. 120). Thus he decides to walk off, leaving Bambi "filled with bitterness" (p. 121). On the one hand, we might interpret this interlude as a missed opportunity for the initiation of an intimate friendship. No doubt Bambi is greatly disappointed; the stag might have handled things differently. On the other hand, we could conclude that, however awkwardly he has handled this encounter, the stag has acted appropriately in his refusal to strike up a conversation. He has chosen the higher good of remaining at a distance from the youngster to whom he intends to pass on his skills of survival and guardianship.

In this scene, we are reminded that the stag is only a deer, a mortal, not a god. His self-isolation is in some real way "unnatural." Yet for the sake of the other deer it is necessary. Had the stag indulged his own need for companionship, his role as mentor might have been compromised. Even the old stag is still learning and maturing in the role of mentor, and he is giving something up in order to succeed in that role. Being a mentor requires *ascesis*, a special struggle of discipline and self-denial.

The mentor has to be tough and withhold a full expression of friendship in order that his skill and wisdom are passed on to his protégé. Effective parenthood also requires elements of the mentoral relationship. Children need parents who are good mentors, but they also need mentors who are not parents, who like Charlotte and the old stag are able to keep a studied distance from their young charges. As I have repeatedly suggested, the office of mentorship runs against our democratic and egalitarian ethos. The paucity of genuine mentoral relationships in contemporary society, however, should give us reason for concern. That is because this special form of "friendship" is necessary for the maturation of the individual as well as the health and growth of community and culture.

EVIL AND REDEMPTION IN "THE SNOW QUEEN" AND *THE LION, THE WITCH AND THE WARDROBE*

A person's goodness or badness is a valence and measure of one's humanity or inhumanity. Because this is true we do not hesitate to call individuals like Adolf Hitler and Ted Bundy monsters, and persons like Mohandas Gandhi and Mother Teresa saints. For sure, in the moral realm most things are not entirely black or white. In most of us goodness and badness are complicatedly mixed. That is why most of us deserve neither the condemnation of "monster" nor the appellation "saint." But there is no mistaking the whiteness of white for the blackness of black. And if that sounds childlike, so be it.

Even in this jaded age a grown-up comes along every now and then who, like a child, affirms this truth without apologies. The late Lebanese statesman Charles Malik was one such childlike grown-up. Malik said:

> There is truth, and there is falsehood. There is good, and there is evil. There is happiness, and there is misery. There is that which

Tending the Heart of Virtue. Second Edition. Vigen Guroian, Oxford University Press.
© Vigen Guroian 1998, 2023. DOI: 10.1093/oso/9780195384307.003.0006

ennobles, and there is that which demeans. There is that which puts you in harmony with yourself, with others, with the universe, and with God, and there is that which alienates you from yourself, and from the world, and from God. These things are different and separate and totally distinguishable from one another.

I take these Malik's sentiments to be the product not of naiveté and untested idealism but of moral character tried in the human struggle for justice and peace. Malik lends expression to a deep knowing that evil is real and loose in the world and that redemption from the hurt and violence of evil is part our doing and part the grace of God. This struggle is what life is finally all about. Or in the words of the eldest brother, Dmitri, of Fyodor Dostoevsky's great novel *The Brothers Karamazov*: "The devil is struggling with God and the battlefield is the human heart."[1]

The Redemptive Truth of the Heart

"Man is broad, even too broad, I would narrow him," adds Dmitri (p. 108). Dmitri is moved to say such a thing by the intensity of his own personal suffering. Ironically, however, this is the expression of a man whose heart is so complex and whose nature is so broad that he could not possibly be other than who he is. The irony is indicated by the very title of the chapter in which this speech is located: "The Confession of an Ardent Heart: In Verse." The heart represents the center of personal existence, the unifying power of the self, the center of willing and purposive action.

Hans Christian Andersen and C. S. Lewis respected the "broadness" of human nature and believed that if the heart is pure, then goodness will prevail. But if our heart is impure, then more than likely you or I will rationalize and justify our own selfishness and misdeeds. It is not surprising, therefore, that both Andersen and Lewis wrote profoundly about the struggle between good and evil that is waged within the human heart. Through their stories, these two writers explore how the heart becomes dark and hardened when it follows evil, as well as how redemption from this "fall" is possible through the power of active goodness and love.

"The Snow Queen": Whence Evil and How Love?

> Now the heart speaks readily and warmly where it is
> at home. The coldness of the outer spaces chills it into
> silence.
> —Austin Farrer, *Love Almighty and Ills Unlimited*

On one level, Hans Christian Andersen's "The Snow Queen" is a romantic's response to the eighteenth-century Enlightenment's emphasis on abstract and utilitarian reason. It is also a satire aimed at a philosophy of education that sharpens the intellect while it starves the emotions. "The Snow Queen" transcends romanticism, however, and reclaims a vision of the integral self in communion with others and with the whole of creation. In "The Snow Queen," Andersen shows us wherein evil lies and how it robs life of joy, but he also celebrates how goodness and love restore wholeness and happiness to life.

The story is in seven parts and is about two young children, a boy and a girl, who live in apartments right next to each other. They are the best of friends, until one day the boy is stolen away by the mysterious Snow Queen.

The Origin and Nature of Evil

Andersen begins his novella-length fairy tale with a prologue. A good frame can illumine and enhance even the best of paintings, and Andersen's prologue accomplishes this for his story.

It does so by telling this tale: Once upon a time the devil invented a magic mirror that had a strange power. It made anything that was good or beautiful that was reflected in it look horrid, while everything that was wicked and ugly appeared desirable and attractive. The devil was the headmaster of a school for demons, and his pupils soon broadcast the news that "for the very first time . . . you could see what the world and mankind really looked like."[2] In the end, they decided to fly with the mirror to heaven in order to ridicule the angels and God himself. But as they flew higher and higher, the mirror laughed so hard that the demons lost their grip on the object. And so it fell all the way to earth, where it shattered into billions of pieces, some so small that the wind blew them to every corner of the world.

This was the worst thing that could have possibly happened because every piece and sliver of the mirror possessed precisely the same power to distort beauty and goodness as the whole mirror. Whenever pieces "got into people's eyes, there they stayed, and then the people saw everything distortedly, or else they had eyes only for what was bad in things . . . Some people even got a little bit of the mirror in their hearts, and then it was really dreadful, for their hearts became just like lumps of ice" (p. 229).

Andersen's prologue is reminiscent of the story of the tower of Babel. In that biblical myth human beings, who speak a single language, try to build a tower that reaches to the heavens in order "to make a name" for themselves and rival God (Gen. 11:1–9). God sees that they are grasping beyond their creaturely limits and so he resorts to confusing their speech, thus forcing them to abandon their Promethean project. But, of course, as the book of Genesis testifies, human beings remain proud and rebellious and pursue other means to gain godlike superiority and control over their fellows.

Andersen's myth of the demons and the broken mirror illuminates the brokenness and discordancy of human existence. Thus while resembling the story of the tower of Babel, it draws also from the biblical story of the Fall and the legend of the proud angel Lucifer's rebellion against God (e.g., Isa. 14:12–15, Zech. 3:1–2). These biblical tales teach that pride, inordinate desire, and egoism interrupt and shatter the harmony and communion of innocent life.

The biblical themes in the prologue thus frame and interpenetrate the story Andersen tells of the love shared between the young girl, named Gerda, and the little boy, Kay, and the strange events that test that love. He begins with a description of a garden paradise in which the two children play.

> In the big city, where there are so many houses and people that there is not room enough for everyone to have a little garden, and where, therefore, most people must content themselves with flowers in pots, there were two poor children, who had a garden that was a little bigger than a flower-pot. They were not brother and sister, but were just as fond of one another as if they had been. Their parents lived right next to each other; they lived in two attics; where the roofs of the two neighbouring houses met and the gutter ran along under the eaves, the two little windows faced one another, one from each house. All you need do was step over the gutter and you could get from one window to the other.

> Their parents had a large wooden box outside each window, and in it grew vegetables for their use and a little rose-tree.... Then their parents found that if they placed the boxes across the gutter they reached almost from one window to the other, and looked for all the world like two banks of flowers. As the boxes were very high and the children knew they must not clamber upon them, they often got leave to climb out to one another and sit on their little stools under the rose-trees where they played wonderful games together. (p. 231)

So in the beginning, the boy and girl are an indivisible couple. They hold each other's hands and kiss the roses and look "up towards God's bright sunshine" and speak "to it as though the Christ Child were there Himself" (p. 233). They are like Adam and Eve in the Garden of Eden before the Fall, where they walked with God and were in unbroken communion with each other and with the whole of creation.

One afternoon, however, as Kay and Gerda are gazing with wonder and appreciation at a picture book of animals and flowers, Kay is suddenly stricken. A splinter of the devil's mirror pierces his heart and another enters his eye. Immediately, he sees and responds to things differently. He tells Gerda she looks ugly when tears well in her eyes as she fears for him in his cry of pain. He looks up at a beautiful rose and sees a grotesque worm-eaten flower. All of the roses begin to look ugly. And as the summer shades into fall and winter, Kay's heart turns into a lump of ice.

Andersen portrays what traditional religion calls diabolical possession. It is the inverse of love and communion. The self is imprisoned within its own egoism. It is inordinately attracted in an all-consuming manner to some *thing* or *object*. As a result, it is drawn away from the presence of others. Instead, there is only "the burdensome presence of one obsessed by himself, a self-idol."[3]

This is what happens to Kay as he gradually grows mean-spirited and separates himself from Gerda and the world they have shared. Some who think that Andersen is best understood from the vantage of Jungian or Freudian psychology or one or another theory of child development have argued that Kay's behavior after the splinters enter his eye and heart are "normal" signs of male aggressive behavior and of a healthy ego seeking autonomy after the dependency of early childhood. Andersen writes that Kay became bored with his old picture books and said they are for babies. He takes to standing behind the grandmother's chair when she reads, cruelly imitating her characteristic gestures. And "his games had become quite different . . . from what they had been before, they were so intelligent" (pp. 234–35). One recent psychological interpreter contends that all of this is simply evidence that Kay is nearing adolescence.[4]

It is worth noting, however, that illustrators of the story have portrayed the children as preadolescent. The tone of the story from beginning to end would justify this artistic judgment. In any case, Andersen the allegorist was not content with literal meanings. Even if he accurately reflects patterns of child development in this story, he transforms these into symbols that probe the deeper meaning of good and evil. His personal faith may have fallen short of the contemporary standards of Christian orthodoxy, but Andersen believed fervently in a liberal version of Christianity that emphasized Jesus's life as a moral model and his teachings of the kingdom of God as an ethic to live by.[5]

Near the end of "The Snow Queen," Andersen cites a biblical verse from the gospel of Mark (Mk. 10:15) that becomes the spiritual centerpiece of the story: "Whosoever shall not receive the Kingdom of God as a little child shall not enter therein" (p. 262). If we pay heed to this saying, we cannot miss Andersen's deeper moral message. He would not have us tolerate Kay's meanness toward Gerda or the grandmother. Kay is being transformed into a little beast. God is the source of goodness and unity. That is why it is so devastating when Kay turns against Gerda and the grandmother who represent goodness and nearness to God.

The Appearance of the Snow Queen

The grandmother mentions the Snow Queen to the two children on one stormy day in winter when Gerda and Kay ask her if the snowflakes that swarm in the winter wind have a queen like the bees. She then tells them the story of the Snow Queen, the biggest of all the snowflakes, who never lies down to rest like the others. Instead, she visits the homes of humans and spreads ice flowers on the windows wherever she goes. Gerda is afraid that the Snow Queen might come to visit their home. But Kay boasts, "Just let her try! . . . I should put her on the warm stove and then she would melt" (p. 232).

That night Kay thinks he sees the Snow Queen outside of his window.

> She was very beautiful and dainty, but she was of ice, dazzling, gleaming ice, all through, and yet she was alive; her eyes shone like two clear stars, but there was no rest nor quiet in them. She nodded

towards the window and beckoned with her hand. The little boy
was terrified and jumped down from the chair; and then it was just
as if a great bird flew past the window outside. (p. 232)

This is the stuff of nightmares and subconscious fears and
desires. The worst actually happens, however, when on a winter
day the Snow Queen captures Kay and takes him to her castle.
Now Kay is physically removed from the presence of those
who love him and who represent goodness and faith in his life.
Andersen comments: "He [Kay] was completely terrified and
wanted to say the Lord's Prayer, but all he could remember were
his multiplication-tables" (p. 236).

Kay's "captivity" in the Snow Queen's ice castle is not so much a
physical incarceration as a spiritual self-subjugation. Kay wants to
stay because his heart is frozen by the Snow Queen's deadly kiss,
and he forgets Gerda and his grandmother. With his heart frozen,
all that Kay is left with is his reason, of which he has grown overly
proud. Remember that he has forgotten the Lord's Prayer but can
recite his multiplication tables.

The Snow Queen uses Kay's pride to control him. She promises
him that if he can spell the word "eternity" out of the thousands of
pieces of ice that lie in a vast frozen lake in the middle of her palace,
he will become his "own master," and she will "present him with
the whole world—and a new pair of skates" (p. 268). Kay spends
his days locked up behind the icy walls of the Snow Queen's castle,
"dragging sharp pieces of ice about, arranging them in all sorts of
ways . . . In his own eyes the patterns were quite remarkable and
of the utmost importance—that was what the grain of glass that
was stuck in his eye did for him!" He lays out his patterns trying to
form words. But he is never quite able to "hit upon the way to lay

out the one word he [wants], the word eternity" (pp. 267–68). Kay acts out of the same kind of hubris that sent the demons up into the heavens with the magic mirror to ridicule God and the angels. He has settled into his own personal hell.

Kay represents us all not just in his lurch toward evil but in his susceptibility to it through his suffering. The twentieth-century Russian religious philosopher Nicholas Berdyaev writes that "the struggle against the Creator is waged not only by those who distort with evil the image of the created world, but also by those who suffer from the evil in it."[6] In "The Snow Queen," Kay is much more a sufferer of evil than an agent of it. Andersen does not rationalize about this or attempt to sort out the difference. Instead, he lets the allegory speak directly with all of its imagistic force. He reports the "facts" of Kay's predicament in rich evocative imagery. The frozen lake that is broken into thousands of pieces all looking the same is an image (or reflection) of the devil's shattered mirror. But it might also be interpreted as a metaphor for our hardened and shattered humanity, of which each one of us is a broken piece.

Andersen does not propose a theodicy that resolves the big problem of why there is evil and suffering. Nor does he address the more particular questions that his story is bound to raise, such as: "Why did a splinter of the devil's mirror enter Kay's eye and heart and not those of someone more deserving of such a fate?" Instead, Andersen turns his attention to how our separated and splintered lives might be made whole again and brought into harmony with one another. As God sent his only begotten Son to rescue humanity, Gerda is sent to rescue Kay. Isn't this how evil is answered and remedied in the course of real living—by love on a mission to reclaim the beloved and restore complete communion?

Gerda's Quest and the Redemptive Power of Love

Gerda searches for Kay all over the world and at every turn resists tempters and temptations that would make her forget Kay and abandon her search. When Gerda finally finds the Snow Queen's palace and readies to enter it, she remembers the Lord's Prayer that Kay forgot, and the breath of her speech forms "itself into bright little angels that grew bigger and bigger as they touched the ground. They all had helmets on their heads and spears and shields in their hands . . . [and] there was a whole legion of them round her" (pp. 265–66). Under this protection, Gerda enters the castle and finds her way to Kay. When she sees him she cries warm tears and recites a hymn of praise that the two of them used to sing in their parents' garden: "In the valley grew roses wild. / And there we spoke with the Holy Child!" (p. 269).

Gerda's words and tears penetrate Kay's heart and thaw it, and Kay himself weeps so bitterly that the grain of glass washes out of his eye. Andersen seems to have believed that the good memories of childhood possess profound redemptive power and are capable of opening our hearts to goodness and love for the rest of our lives. I do not think this is mere sentimentality. A similar thought is expressed by Dostoevsky in *The Brothers Karamazov*. In the closing scene, which I recalled many times when raising my own children and continue to recall when I am with my grandchildren, Alyosha Karamazov, the youngest brother, addresses a group of boys for whom he has become a mentor and role model. He makes his speech after the funeral of one of their young comrades whom the boys had once taunted and persecuted but later were reconciled with and grew to love.:

You must know[Alyosha states] that there is nothing higher, or stronger, or sounder, or more useful afterwards in life, than some good memory, especially a memory from childhood, from the parental home. You hear a lot said about your education, yet some such beautiful, sacred memory, preserved from childhood, is perhaps the best education. If a man stores up such memories to take into life, then he is saved for his whole life. And even if only one good memory remains with us in our hearts, that alone may serve one day for our salvation.[7]

A Message for Our Times

I began this discussion of "The Snow Queen" with some comparisons to the biblical story of the Creation and the Fall. I conclude by returning to it. Like that story, Andersen illumines one of the most fundamental forms of division and alienation in human experience—the alienation of man and woman from each other. In the Bible's terms, the two, whom God intended to be intimate companions in communion with each other, became divided into two opposing sexes. The complementarity of gender was corrupted; the communion was replaced by brokenness and separation, love by lust. And henceforth the sexes play out a deadly and demeaning game of lure and pursuit.

Most of the stories with which our children become acquainted through the popular culture reinforce these distorted and corrupted images of male and female and their relations. Movies and television sitcoms humorously objectivize the body as a specimen for sexual browsing and fantasy. Sexual love is depicted as a sport in which the game includes rules made up as you go along.

This is the rotten fruit of a decadent romantic love. The culture's already depraved vision of the romantic lover is now being transmuted into the image of the sexual user. Baseness, selfishness, and even ruthlessness are often presented humorously so as to seem like desirable traits of character.

"The Snow Queen" answers this twisted message of the contemporary stories of our lives that are scripted by the new mythmakers of television and the screen. Near the end of her journey, Gerda finds the home of a Finnish woman, an archetypal wise woman who possesses great magical powers. She sees what is at stake in the success or failure of Gerda's quest: Kay's humanity and Gerda's own completeness. As she tells the reindeer whom she enlists to lead Gerda to the palace of the Snow Queen, "They [the splinters] must be got out [of his eye and heart] first, otherwise *he'll never be human again*" (p. 264, my emphasis). The reindeer pleads with her to give Gerda "'the power to put everything right." But the old woman answers with perhaps the most significant statement of any character in the story: "I can't give her greater power than she has already!" She declares, "Can't you see how great that is? Can't you see how she makes man and beast serve her, and how well she's made her way in the world on her own bare feet? She mustn't know of her power from us—it comes from her heart" (p. 264).

I find myself mostly at odds with Wolfgang Lederer's book on "The Snow Queen" because of its psychological analysis. Lederer, however, makes a very important point. He comments, "If Kay were not rescued, were not redeemed by Gerda, he could continue his frigid intellectual games amid the vacuous light show of the aurora borealis forever—and he would never *come alive*." Lederer claims that Gerda, taking the initiative, brings Kay alive again by restoring between them the communion of love. "The most moving passages of the story," Lederer maintains, "are those relating the reunion of Gerda and Kay. . . . [T]hey remind us how lonely we are or have been; how, if we are men, we need the validation, the confirmation, the redemption by woman; and if we are women, how the redemption of such a lonely man is one of the magic feats, one of the miracles a woman can perform."[8] I do not agree entirely with Lederer. There may be a distinctively womanly way in which Gerda sets out to save Kay. And we must discuss whether this is or is not gender-specific. But Lederer generalizes from this story in such a way that he seems to suggest that the role of redemptor belongs solely to woman. I want to say that the roles are interchangeable—and I think Andersen would agree with me. The wholeness of man and woman depends upon a relationship of complete mutuality.

But Lederer is right that the heart of evil is the cold heart of a self in isolation vainly imagining that by being autonomous it is free and complete. Some of the ways in which the differences between men and women are described by contemporary critics unfortunately only contribute suspicion, separation, and loneliness. Andersen's story is a healthy reminder that communion and love are the highest goals of human association. "As he [Kay] clung to her [Gerda]," writes Andersen, "the pieces of ice" that Kay had struggled with for all his time in captive isolation "danced for joy all round them, and where they grew tired lay down . . . [and] formed the very letters the Snow Queen had told him he must find out if he were to be his own master and she were to give him the whole world and a new pair of skates" (p. 269). The good that the Snow Queen abhors is not an abstract principle but the communion of love that heals the primal rift forced by Adam and Eve when they succumbed to the promise of an impossible twisted autonomy and immortality. In Hans Christian Andersen's "The Snow Queen," goodness and immortality are rightly considered in relation to the communion in love that ought to exist between man and woman.

The Lion, the Witch and the Wardrobe: Diabolic Enchantment and the Liberation of Forgiveness

Like Hans Christian Andersen, C. S. Lewis explores the dynamism of evil that immobilizes and destroys our humanity and forcefully depicts the struggle between good and evil that is waged within the human heart. His story *The Lion, the Witch and the Wardrobe,* the first of the Narnia series, embraces the great themes of sin, repentance, and forgiveness in the Christian story of salvation.

Like Kay, Edmund Pevensie, the youngest of the four brothers and sisters who visit Narnia, does not consciously set out to be evil. Youthful pride, sibling rivalry, and jealousy are the only imperfections that evil needs in order to capture his youthful imagination, twist his mind, and set him on a disastrous course from which he will need to be rescued by another. The rescuer, in this case, is Aslan, the great lion, the son of the Emperor-Beyond-the-Sea. Aslan is the long-looked-for Messiah of Narnian faith who will come to redeem the land from its captivity in a perpetual winter under the rule of the White Witch, who is Queen of Narnia.

Kathryn Lindskoog helps to confirm my own long-held suspicion that there is a connection between Andersen's story and Lewis's. In a book entitled *The Lion of Judah in Never-Never Land,* she astutely observes:

Edmund's encounter with the witch, which leads to his enchantment, is parallel to the story of little Kay meeting the evil snow
queen.... Both of these witches appear in great sledges, dressed in
white fur. Both are tall and beautiful and seem always perfect to the
eyes of their little victims; but both are as cold and pale as white ice.
As soon as the boys are enchanted, they are no longer afraid. They
feel very important, try to show off, and indiscreetly tell anything
that is asked of them.[9]

Lindskoog concludes that in both stories an evil temptress
appeals to a young boy's self-centeredness, pride, and inordinate
desire for some *thing,* and gains a demonic control over him.

The Story and Edmund's Place in It

The Lion, the Witch and the Wardrobe is a fantasy and a morality play
that captures the imaginations of children because it so closely
reflects their own experiences of and feelings about belonging to a
family, sharing a life with siblings, and the difficulty of controlling
passions and appetites. At the start, Lewis introduces his reader to
the four Pevensie children, who in this and other books journey
into the parallel world of Narnia. A dramatic struggle between
good and evil is being played out in Narnia, a struggle much like
that described in the Christian saga of Creation, Fall, and redemption. Upon their arrival in Narnia, the four children are told by
Mr. and Mrs. Beaver that when four sons and daughters of Adam
enter Narnia this is the sign that Aslan is returning to reclaim his
kingdom. Then he will hand over his reign to them, making them
kings and queens of Narnia, who will rule from the thrones that
await them at the ancient castle of Cair Paravel.

Lucy, the youngest of the children, enters Narnia before the others. She is a child of uncommon innocence and also deep intuition, who seems especially drawn to mystery. Susan, the second-oldest, is tenderhearted but timid and normally falters when faced with the unknown. Peter is the oldest of the Pevensie children. He is courageous and rises to become the High King of Narnia, sharing his reign with his three younger siblings.

But Edmund's role in this story is special and is the focal point of the story, apart from the character of Aslan himself. For Edmund is "the prodigal" and the "most important of the children to the theme of redemption." Like Kay in "The Snow Queen," Edmund is not what we would call a great sinner. Rather, "he is just a small boy whose tendency to selfishness and bullying needs to be checked before it colors his whole life."[10] Like Kay, he is everyman or, to be more exact, everychild. Edmund has too much pride, and this pride gets in the way of his better judgment. On Lucy's second journey into Narnia, Edmund follows her through the mysterious wardrobe. When he encounters the White Witch for the first time, he does "not like the way she looked at him."[11] But he does not follow his better judgment and turn away from her. Instead, he lets down his guard and submits to her charm. He takes the deadly bait she dangles in front of him and falls entirely under her spell. Edmund (like Kay) becomes mentally confused: his mind becomes the captive of its own prison of "fallacious rationalization."[12]

Edmund's pride and desire to shine above his siblings aid and abet his desire to believe the White Witch's promise that if he brings his brother and sisters to her, she, in turn, will make him the Prince and—later on—the King of all Narnia. We do not know whether the witch has ever before encountered a human child, but she certainly figures out quickly how to hold Edmund's attention, capture his will, and pry into his mind. Hunger is perhaps the most powerful bodily and emotional force that can influence and change the behavior of a small child. Physical appetite, combined with a strong sense of taste, can literally overwhelm a child with dizzying desire. When Edmund comes upon the White Witch for the first time, he is disoriented, cold, and *hungry*. The witch magically produces a hot drink in a cup and then asks Edmund what he would like to eat. He answers, "Turkish Delight, please, your Majesty." Then the Queen produces a box "tied with a green silk ribbon . . . [that] contain[s] several pounds of" the candy (p. 38). Edmund hurriedly consumes all of it as he becomes entirely fixated on this source of such a strong pleasure in the midst of a very unpleasant and frightening situation. He no longer is cold or afraid. This enables the Queen to pry from him all the information she needs to make her plans to thwart the prophecy of the end of her power over Narnia. Lewis writes:

> At first Edmund tried to remember that it is rude to speak with one's mouth full, but he soon forgot about this and thought only of trying to shovel down as much Turkish Delight as he could, and the more he ate the more he wanted to eat, and he never asked himself why the Queen should be so inquisitive. (p. 38)

Lewis accurately portrays a common childhood experience of aching hunger and the insatiable and uncontrollable need to "fill the stomach" and satisfy taste. Edmund's behavior is wholly believable and existentially compelling for young people. They can relate to the vortexlike inner force that swallows him up into his dark night and descent into a personal hell. Edmund's hunger is also a metaphor for a deeper form of desire that draws not only children but adults into sin and evil.

Gilbert Meilaender identifies the source of Edmund's religious and moral crisis: "The key [to the understanding of evil in Lewis's story] is given us right there: 'the more he ate the more he wanted to eat.' At that moment Edmund wants nothing more than he wants Turkish Delight; and his inordinate love makes a god of Turkish Delight, a god that leads him on and controls him."[13] All of the White Witch's future power over Edmund is predicated on this inordinate love. Edmund's defiance leads to a self-imposed alienation from his own siblings. And this encounter with the White Witch and the taste of her forbidden food marks the start of his long, lonely journey into the darkness. In his twisted and confused mind, his brother and sisters grow ugly and insignificant, and he cannot even understand why the Queen would want to bother with them. Nevertheless, Edmund decides that he will bring his brother and sisters back to the witch as she demands. Thus, evil takes a foothold in Edmund's will and imagination, much like the rot that attacks the soft spot of a fruit and spreads through the entire flesh. Whatever else Edmund does, even to hurt his brother and sisters, he rationalizes in terms of some greater good that he persuades himself he sees better than they can. He convinces himself that all the bad things said about the White Witch are untrue. Later he says to himself, "All these people who say nasty things about her are her enemies and probably half of it isn't true. She was jolly nice to me, anyway, much nicer than they are. I expect she is the rightful Queen really" (pp. 96–97).

After the Queen leaves him, Edmund and Lucy are reunited. She straightforwardly tells Edmund that she has learned of an evil White Witch who is holding Narnia in her thrall. Edmund realizes that his sister is referring to the person he has met, but he keeps his encounter with the Queen secret so as not to have to face the truth about his own treacherous heart or admit that Lucy is right. Even small children can relate to this manner of self-deception. They know just what Edmund is up to.

Following their return to the everyday world, Edmund denies to the others that he was ever with Lucy in Narnia. But he cannot get his mind off the Turkish Delight. Lewis wants us to think of sin as a kind of addiction. Some adults in continuing education courses that I have taught, who have had spouses with substance addictions or worked with alcoholics and drug addicts, have remarked that Edmund shows all the signs of the addict. In any case, Edmund's temptation becomes an uncontrolled obsession and he is no longer able to enjoy good and legitimate pleasures; much as with Kay, everything that is truly beautiful looks ugly.

Edmund's act of complete treachery follows. When all four of the children enter Narnia together they are led to the home of the good Beavers. The Beavers are among the remnant of Narnians who still believe in the ancient prophecy that Narnia will be liberated. At dinner Edmund's desire for the poisonous food of the White Witch overwhelms him.

> He had eaten his share of the dinner, but he hadn't really enjoyed it because he was thinking all the time about Turkish Delight—and there's nothing that spoils the taste of good ordinary food half so much as the memory of bad magic food. (p. 95)

The Beavers relate the history of Narnia. But when Mr. Beaver gets to the part about Aslan and the plan to meet him in the appointed place in order to fulfill the ancient prophecies, Edmund makes up his mind to slip away and go to the witch's castle with the information, "for the mention of Aslan gave him a mysterious and horrible feeling just as it gave the others a mysterious and lovely feeling." Edmund makes a bad decision. Nevertheless, admonishes Lewis, "You mustn't think that even now Edmund was quite so bad that he actually wanted his brother and sisters to be turned into stone. . . . [H]e managed to believe, or to pretend he believed, that she wouldn't do anything very bad to them" (p. 96). Edmund may be getting himself and the others into serious trouble, but he is still redeemable.

The Way to Goodness After the Fall: Repentance and Forgiveness

Evan Gibson observes that the story of *The Lion, the Witch and the Wardrobe* centers on Aslan: he is the "unifying character of the entire [Narnia] series."[14] The expectation of the lion's re-appearance, his arrival, his sacrificial act that saves the life of Edmund, and his resurrection that seals the liberation of Narnia are the dramatic heart of the story. The scene when Aslan willingly submits to being bound and permits his great mane to be shorn, followed by his voluntary death, is a moving depiction of self-donative love. In order to save Edmund, Aslan must offer his own life in the boy's stead, since blood is the currency of sacrifice and salvation.

If we concentrate too much on these memorable moments, however, we risk overlooking the vital struggle between good and evil that is waged in Edmund's heart and reaches a conclusion even before this occurrence at the story's close. Edmund's inner struggle and its final outcome speak powerfully to children. Children see that admitting one's mistakes and errors, while difficult, is the right thing to do and may lead to forgiveness and true happiness.

Edmund comes to regret his decision to seek out the White Witch. But at the start, his plunge into darkness and ignominy seems irreversible. Propelled by his insatiable appetite for the witch's poisonous food and driven by his pride and spitefulness, Edmund is in a free fall into darkness and void. "The silence and the loneliness were dreadful," Lewis comments in his narrator's voice. "In fact I really think he might have given up the whole plan and gone back and owned up and made friends with the others, if he hadn't happened to say to himself, 'When I'm King of Narnia the first thing I shall do will be to make some decent roads.'" The diabolical imagination has some things in common with the moral imagination. It too has its alluring landscapes and objects of delight. And so Edmund begins to imagine how as king he would make laws "against beavers and dams" and come up with "schemes for keeping Peter in his place" (p. 98).

When he arrives at the gates of the Queen's castle, Edmund even manages to overcome fear that might ordinarily have turned him around. Initially, he is terrorized by the sight of a stone lion that he thinks is Aslan. But he quickly realizes that the lion is a statue and decides that the White Witch has transformed Aslan into stone, as she does with all of her enemies that she takes prisoner. In a spiteful act of feigned courage, he defaces the lion by penciling in a mustache over its lips and drawing a pair of spectacles around its eyes. But the beast, writes Lewis, still looked "so terrible, and sad, and noble, staring up in the moonlight that Edmund didn't really get any fun out of jeering" (p. 103). Once again Lewis hints that Edmund's heart is not entirely hardened. Kay's transformation back to his better self is virtually instantaneous, once his heart is warmed and awakened by the tears and tender embrace of Gerda. Perhaps in these moments of fear and isolation the same is possible for Edmund, but he is not visited by such an angel. Edmund's dark journey has only begun, and he will travel it alone until the appointed hour.

Finally, after encountering countless stone statues of every kind of Narnian creature, Edmund is greeted by the White Witch. Her displeasure that he has not brought his siblings with him and her alarm at the news that Aslan may be on the move spell misery for Edmund. She refuses to give him more Turkish Delight. Instead he gets a bowl of water and a plate of dry bread. Then he is loaded onto the witch's sledge as they race to cut off Aslan at the sacred Stone Table. Lewis describes Edmund's dreadful situation:

> This was a terrible journey for Edmund who had no coat. Before they had been going a quarter of an hour all the front of him was covered with snow. . . . Soon he was wet to the skin. And oh, how miserable he was! It didn't look now as if the Witch intended to make him a King! All the things he had said to make himself believe that she was good and kind and that her side was really the right side sounded to him silly now. (p. 124)

The nightmare gets worse still. After what seems like an eternity, the sledge comes upon a family of squirrels, some satyrs, a dwarf, and an old dog-fox who are having a picnic party because Father Christmas has returned to Narnia and the perpetual winter without Christmas is ending. The witch knows that this means that her spell is being broken by a power greater than her own. And over Edmund's pleas of "Oh don't, don't, please don't" (p. 127), she waves her wand and turns them all into statues. Once the terrible deed is done, the witch strikes Edmund hard on the face and says, "Let that teach you to ask favor for spies and traitors" (p. 128). Lewis now interjects, "And Edmund for the first time in this story felt sorry for someone besides himself." Having come so near to being turned into a statue himself, or perhaps even fearing that the same would befall him soon, he now finds empathy and pity shifting his imaginings to the dreadful meaning of such a fate. "It seemed so pitiful to think of those little stone figures sitting there all the silent days and all the dark nights, year after year, till the moss grew on them and at last even their faces crumbled away" (p. 128).

Edmund feels compassion. And compassion is a powerful impulse in the human breast. It has deep, even physiological resonances. It comes from the very guts of our being. It taps a primal sense that we are all bound one to another in a solidarity of flesh and spirit. Compassion binds us especially to the suffering of others so that we share their suffering vicariously and want to do something to alleviate it. No one who is without compassion deserves forgiveness. But he who has compassion is already far along toward repentance. Compassion not only awakens us to the suffering of others but moves us to see how we are responsible for having brought about some of that suffering. This movement of compassion and the dynamic of forgiveness are at the heart of the story of the two thieves crucified beside Jesus. One thief heaps scorn upon the Man: "Are you not the Messiah? Save yourself and us." But the other rebukes him, "Do you not fear God, since you are under the same sentence of condemnation? And indeed we have been condemned justly, for we are getting what we deserve for our deeds, but this man has done nothing wrong." He then says to Jesus, "Remember me when you come into your kingdom." And Jesus replies, "Truly I tell you, today you will be with me in Paradise" (Luke 23:39–43).

Gradually, just as the snow that covers Narnia starts to melt, Edmund's heart turns back to goodness. In traditional religious speech, Edmund is converted. Lewis himself insisted that he did not set out to write an allegory of the Christian gospel of redemption. He preferred to describe *The Lion, the Witch and the Wardrobe* as a story that runs parallel to the gospel, as if in the story it is being asked, "What if the Messiah were to come in another world?" This may be so. Nonetheless, Edmund's story communicates religious and moral truths that are inseparable from the teachings about sin and redemption in the Bible. Evil in Narnia, as in the Bible, is fundamentally a rebellion against the deity. Evil is vanquished in the human soul when the person turns against his own pride and selfishness back toward God. That turn may well begin in the compassionate act of loving the suffering other as one would love oneself.

When Edmund is finally saved from the clutches of the White Witch, he has already undergone an inner transformation. When Aslan takes him aside and presumably reminds him of his wrongdoings and the great trouble his treachery has wrought, Edmund is already penitent. And so everything can be forgiven and forgotten. "There is no need to tell you (and no one ever heard) what Aslan was saying but it was a conversation which Edmund never forgot. As the others drew nearer Aslan turned to meet them bringing Edmund with him. 'Here is your brother,' he said, 'and— there is no need to talk to him about what is past.'" Then Edmund turns to the others and says, "'I'm sorry,' and everyone said 'That's all right'" (pp. 152–53). The circle of sin, repentance, and forgiveness is completed. Later, in the battle that brings about the final victory, Edmund proves his worthiness. "He had become his real old self again and could look you in the face" (p. 197). And in the future Edmund is called "King Edmund the Just" (p. 201).

Conclusion

The stories of Kay in "The Snow Queen" and Edmund in *The Lion, the Witch and the Wardrobe* are similar. And yet there are also important differences. Kay's innocence seems more pristine and his suffering less deserved than Edmund's. Andersen raises difficult questions about the phenomenon of affliction, of being the unsuspecting and undeserving victim of evil. Yet we actually learn very little about Kay's inner state during his imprisonment in the Snow Queen's frozen palace. And Kay's redemption happens almost as suddenly as his capture. Most of the story is about Gerda and her untiring quest to find and be reunited with her beloved Kay. Andersen tells his story primarily from the point of view of the lover and redeemer who will not abandon the beloved in his distress. It is from Gerda's experiences that we come to realize the vicious blow that evil strikes at love and communion in life.

Lewis, on the other hand, takes great pains to describe the evolution of Edmund's inner state of mind and heart as he grows more and more wedded to the evil that he has met. Edmund is young, though perhaps not quite as young as Kay, and like Kay he is also a victim of a temptress. But unlike Kay, Edmund is truly culpable. And so whereas Andersen tells a profound and haunting tale about the genesis of evil, the inscrutable and unpredictable thing that it is, and the brokenness it inflicts upon life, Lewis's story is about what biblical religion calls sin, the willful rejection of goodness and the willing embrace of evil. It is also about repentance, rejection of that very same evil, and thus its disarmament from the human will and imagination. And last of all, *The Lion, the Witch and the Wardrobe* is about redemption—the conversion of the mind and rescue of the heart by the Divine Lover who never gives up on the beloved and forgives the beloved unconditionally.

6

HEROINES OF FAITH AND COURAGE

*Princess Irene in The Princess and the Goblin
and Lucy in Prince Caspian*

George MacDonald's *The Princess and the Goblin* was published in 1872 and was followed some nine years later by a sequel, *The Princess and Curdie*. The protagonists of these fairy-tale romances are two of the most memorable children in Victorian literature—the Princess Irene and the miner's son Curdie.

In this chapter, I will deal only with *The Princess and the Goblin* and the character of the Princess Irene. One other character, aside from the boy Curdie, figures prominently in this discussion. She is the mysterious great-great-grandmother whom Irene discovers one day in the attic rooms of her home. The grandmother is a numinous presence in the story, a type of wise woman or wisdom figure that MacDonald introduced into a number of his better-known fantasies. Through the relationship that develops between the grandmother and Irene, MacDonald builds tissue and membrane into the faith and courage of his young heroine.

Tending the Heart of Virtue. Second Edition. Vigen Guroian, Oxford University Press.
© Vigen Guroian 1998, 2023. DOI: 10.1093/oso/9780195384307.003.0007

The Role of the Moral Imagination in George Macdonald's Storytelling

> I for one can really testify to a book that has made a difference to my whole existence, which helped me to see things in a certain way from the start; a vision of things which even so real a revelation as a change of religious allegiance has substantially only crowned and confirmed. Of all the stories I have read, including even all the novels of the same novelist, it remains the most real, the most life like. It is called *The Princess and the Goblin,* and is by George MacDonald.
>
> —G. K. Chesterton

There are critics who say that George MacDonald wrote over the heads of children. MacDonald himself said that he wrote for "children" of all ages. He endeavored to appeal to the childlike in everyone—not the childish, but the *childlike*—and to feed the moral imagination. MacDonald did not exaggerate the power of the imagination. Imagination is a power of discovery, not a power to create. The latter capacity he reserved to God alone. Nor did MacDonald equate imagination with mere fancy, what we used to call "vain imaginings." Rather, for him, imagination is a power of perception, a light that illumines the mystery that is hidden beneath visible reality; it is a power to help "see" into the very nature of things. Reason alone, MacDonald argued, is not able to recognize mystery or grasp the moral quiddity of the world. As the sensible mind needs eyes to see, so reason needs the imagination in order to behold mystery and to perceive the true quality of things. Imagination takes reason to the threshold of mystery and moral truth and reveals them as such. Reason may then approve or submit. But it remains for the heart of courage with the will to believe and the vision of imagination to embrace the beauty of goodness and the strength of truth as the foundation of virtuous living.

MacDonald advised parents: "Seek not that your sons and your daughters should not see visions, should not dream dreams; seek that they should see true visions, that they should dream noble dreams."[1] But a literature that would awaken the imagination with such effect is bound to outpace the dull-witted adult every bit as much as the child whose mind is the captive of a utilitarian education that teaches nothing but "the facts."

George MacDonald dared to invent a modern genre of fairy tale that even today challenges the positivism and twisted puritanism of our contemporary taste for stories "suited" for children. He eschewed both the popular penchant for so-called practical stories about "real life" and the untrained appetite for sentimental stories suffused with warm feelings. Why shouldn't children's stories arouse deep questionings about the nature of good and evil, about death and what comes after, about faith and doubt? Do we not risk doing much greater harm to our children if we deny them the opportunities and the possibilities to work through their fears, inquire into the meaning of their loves, and. follow the lead of questions about the human lot that begin to percolate to consciousness quite early in life?

The Princess and the Goblin is a story that breathes with this freedom and risk. It is a story about a young girl of just eight years who, although she is a real princess, "grows up" very fast to become a *real* woman. And it begins when, as I have mentioned, Irene discovers in the attic of the house in which she lives a mysterious woman who is both old and young, beautiful and frightening, and whose love, as Irene also learns, spares not pain.

How Faith and Courage Need Each Other
in *The Princess and the Goblin*

> We teach everyone and instruct everyone in all the
> ways of wisdom, so as to present each one of you as a
> mature member of Christ's body.
>
> —Colossians 1:28

> But you are a chosen race, a royal priesthood, a
> dedicated nation, a people claimed by God for
> his own . . . called . . . out of darkness into his
> marvellous light.
>
> —1 Peter 2:9

"The princess was a sweet little creature, and at the time my story begins, was about eight years old, I think, *but she got older very fast*" (p. 5, my emphasis). This is how George MacDonald introduces his reader to the young heroine, Princess Irene, and with the simple and easily overlooked phrase "but she got older very fast" he plants the first and most significant clue about the meaning and nature of Irene's relationship with her mysterious grandmother.

At the start of the story, we are told that the Princess Irene does not live with her father, the king, in his palace. Instead, she lives in "a large house, half castle, half farmhouse," in the countryside on the side of a mountain (p. 5). This is because her mother was not strong when Irene was born, and we are also given to suspect that the mother is deceased at the time the story begins. But danger lurks beneath the mountain on which the house rests. Inside the mountain resides a race of goblins who hold an ancient grudge against the king and his family and are set on a plan to capture Irene and marry her to Harelip, the goblin crown prince.

The king is aware of the presence of these creatures, and so Irene is watched carefully. She is not permitted to go out after dark because the goblins sometimes venture to the surface at night and cause mischief. The king is unaware, however, of the goblins' scheme to take his daughter prisoner. It remains for a boy named Curdie, who works with his father in the mines, to discover the goblin plan and finally to foil it. Meanwhile, the story's main action shifts back and forth from "the universal and constant darkness" (p. 100) of the goblin dwellings below, where Curdie pursues his mission, to the grandmother's moon- and starlit garret rooms that Irene visits.

But let us start at the beginning. One dreary day when she is unhappily closed up in her nursery, Irene slips into a deep slumber. When she awakens, she falls from her chair hard onto the floor. Then, for no apparent reason at all, the little princess races out of the nursery, dashes in a direction she has not gone before, and scampers up "a curious old stair" (p. 9), which leads to she knows not where.[2] A child (even an adult reader) might wonder whether Irene is really quite awake or whether she is in a dream, and later Irene herself wonders the same. Irene's inexhaustible curiosity (signified by the play on words "curious stairs") sends her upstairs until she reaches a landing, where she follows a narrow hall lined with doors, all of which are shut. The rapping of the rain on the roof disturbs Irene, and she hurries to find the stairs to the safety of her nursery. She is unsuccessful and runs crying down the labyrinthine corridors. But Irene does not cry for long, MacDonald interjects, because she is "brave as could be expected of a princess of her age" (p. 9).

Irene collects herself and resolves once more to find her way back to her nursery. But she only gets more lost and now becomes quite frightened. She reaches another flight of stairs that leads up only. With no other choice left to her, Irene scrambles up these stairs until, at last, she arrives at a small square landing with three doors, one to either side and a third facing her. She hesitates at first, not sure "what to do next." Then all of a sudden, she hears "a curious humming sound . . . It was . . . like the hum of a very happy bee that had found a rich well of honey in some globular flower." The sound is coming from behind the door in front of her. Irene opens it, and there in full view is "a very old lady" seated at a spinning wheel (p. 11).

This is a suspenseful moment. The first time I read *The Princess and the Goblin* to my son, Rafi, he was about Irene's age, and he stopped me and asked nervously: "Is the old lady good or bad?" Only with great hesitancy did he let me continue. My daughter, Victoria, asked the same question when I read the story to her, but she would not even permit me to read further unless I assured her that the lady would do no harm to Irene. Perhaps because of his extraordinary oral storytelling powers, which he practiced on his own children, MacDonald was remarkably good at creating a voice in his writing that stirs the emotions and arouses a sense of awe. Yet sometimes fear and awe are not so easily disentangled, as testified by the responses of my son and daughter.

I think that MacDonald makes Irene's first adventure up the stairs into a metaphor for a process wherein the self (in this case Irene, but really any child) is challenged by its most primal fears to risk safety in order to learn more and be in command of its own powers. When Irene runs down the stairs thinking she has found her way back to her "safe nursery," MacDonald adds enigmatically: "So she thought, but she had lost herself long ago. It doesn't follow that she *was* lost, because she had lost herself, though" (p. 9).

In a short space, the reader learns better what this action signifies. Having been magically returned by her grandmother to her nursery room, Irene tells a disbelieving nanny where she has been and whom she has discovered in the garret rooms at the top of the house. She is bothered when her nurse suggests that perhaps she was dreaming, and bursts out: "I didn't dream it. I went upstairs, and I lost myself, and if I hadn't found the beautiful lady, I should never have found myself" (p. 18). Irene couldn't possibly intend the deeper meaning that MacDonald invests in her words. But he is playing deliberately on the biblical theme of losing one's life in order to gain it (Matt. 10:39), of following Christ, even to death, and by so doing becoming a true daughter or son of God. Irene's belief in her grandmother and willingness to obey her launch her on an important journey toward moral and spiritual maturity—a passage by trial that calls on her to risk even her life in order to save the life of another.

MacDonald's careful portrait of the grandmother and her environs also deserves attention. The great-great-grandmother is no ordinary person, and Irene's complete entrustment of herself into the mysterious woman's care and guidance is analogous to a religious act of giving oneself over to something or someone sacred and transcendent. The grandmother is quite beautiful, although in a most unusual way. Her skin is "smooth and white," and her hair, which is "combed back from her forehead and face," hangs loose "far down and all over her back." She would not appear to be old, except that her eyes look "so wise that you could not have helped seeing she must be old." And her hair is "white almost as snow" (p. 11). Moonlight floods the rooms the woman inhabits, and the walls are painted blue, "spangled all over with what looked like stars of silver" (p. 64). On one occasion the woman herself is dressed in "slippers [that] glimmered with the light of the milky way, for they were covered with seed-pearls and opals in one mass" (p. 79).

In every respect, the grandmother is surrounded in mystery, literally clothed with numinous qualities, so some commentators have associated her with the ancient Greek goddess Demeter, the daughter of Cronos and Rhea, sister of Zeus.[3] In my view, the striking symbolism of the blue sky, the moon, and the stars suggests more strongly Christian meaning—namely, the person of the Virgin Mary. Traditionally, it is with just such symbolism that Mary is represented in Christian art and poetry as the Queen of Heaven.[4]

MacDonald leads the reader still more deeply into the mystery of the grandmother's identity and Irene's relationship to her. Yes, the old woman tells Irene that she is her great-great-grandmother, that she is a queen herself, that her name is Irene also, and that, indeed, Irene is named after her (pp. 13–14). But a spiritual bond unites the two that transcends even the implied biological relationship and family connection. At the start of the story, MacDonald describes Irene's face as "fair and pretty, with eyes [just] like two bits of night sky, each with a star dissolved in the blue ... Those eyes you would have thought must have known they came from [the sky], so often were they turned up in that direction" (p. 5). And Irene's own bedroom nursery ceiling is painted "blue, with stars in it" (p. 5), just like the walls of the grandmother's bedroom.

Thus, it seems that when Irene discovers the grandmother and entrusts herself to the woman, she is finding her own deepest identity and destiny. Contemporary interpreters have interpreted this process in purely psychological terms.[5] They point not only to the correspondences of imagery in the descriptions of Irene and the grandmother and their surroundings but to several other scenes in order to argue that this is a story about a young girl's passage from childhood to puberty, individuation, and psychological self-integration.

One such scene occurs in Irene's nursery the evening she visits the grandmother for a second time. Irene pricks her thumb on a brooch and her thumb bleeds a drop of blood. Irene falls asleep, but the swelling and pain eventually awaken her and she follows the bright moonlight that is streaming through the windows up the old oak stairs to the grandmother's rooms. The spot of blood and the lunar imagery have been interpreted as alluding to the female menstrual cycle, and so the phrase "she got older very fast" means that Irene was about to make her passage into adolescence.

I disagree. I do not think that this is what MacDonald had in mind at all. We live in an age that is obsessed with supposed psychological and sexual connotations of words and actions, whereas MacDonald's "obsession" was over spiritual matters. This means his theological convictions need to be taken seriously. (And, after all, eight years old does seem a bit young for the onset of puberty.) MacDonald stations a strong metaphor at the heart of this story, as witnessed by the title itself. "Princess" is the root metaphor in his story, and I believe it is the key to the meaning in the images and events that have been mentioned. Furthermore, it explains the primary significance of Irene's relationship to the grandmother.

In biblical faith, the status of princess, like that of king or queen, has sacral and sacramental connotations: it signifies a divine calling to moral responsibility and spiritual leadership. Irene's spiritual "rite of passage" under the direction and care of the mysterious and numinous grandmother carries this kind of sacral and sacramental meaning. In the magazine version of the story, MacDonald interrupts the narrative with this revealing dialogue between the "Editor" and an imaginary reader:

> "But Mr. Editor, why do you always write about princesses?"
> "Because every little girl is a princess."
> "You will make them vain if you tell them that."
> "Not if they understand what I mean."
> "Then what do you mean?"
> "What do you mean by a princess?"
> "The daughter of a king."
> "Very well; then every little girl is a princess, and there would be no need to say anything about it except that she is always in danger of forgetting her rank."[6]

So MacDonald is quite clear about this. He reminds us of the several levels of meaning of "princess." But he wants us to ponder especially its religious meaning, for which the earthly political and social title is only a metaphor. To be a princess means ultimately to claim a status as a child of God the Father (and perhaps also Mary, the Queen of Heaven, if I have read MacDonald accurately) and to become a full member of the household of God. How one achieves this status is what his story is really about. And faith and courage are strongly associated with this special identity and calling. Together they are virtues that have the power to open our lives onto the mystery of our relationship as sons and daughters of God.

The Trial and Transformation of Princess Irene

> There is no fear in love, but perfect love casts out fear ... and whoever fears has not reached perfection in love.
>
> —1 John 4:18

Courage is one of the cardinal virtues named by the great classical and Christian thinkers of Western culture. Plato, Aristotle, Cicero, and Thomas Aquinas all agree that courage is the moral and spiritual capacity to risk harm or danger to oneself for the sake of something good. And yet not one of these writers maintains that courage banishes fear entirely—although it certainly is the opposite of cowardice. If these authorities are right about courage, then our modern dictionaries can be misleading.

For example, a widely used school dictionary, which I purchased for my son and daughter when they were in grade school, defines courage as "a quality that makes it possible for a person to face danger or difficulties *without fear*" (my emphasis).[7] In *The Princess and the Goblin*, MacDonald agrees with the ancient authorities and dissents from the modern dictionary. We cannot completely understand the process of Irene's maturation into the full status of a princess unless we see how courage and fear are related in her character and how, in the end, her faith fortifies her courage, enabling her to conquer her fear and make her a strong daughter of the King.

On her second visit with her great-great-grandmother, Irene exclaims: "I don't think you are ever afraid of anything." And the woman replies: "Not for long, at least, my child. Perhaps by the time I am two thousand years of age, I shall, indeed, never be afraid of anything. But I confess I have sometimes been afraid about my children—sometimes about you, Irene" (p. 86). A fear for one's own safety and the well-being of others that arises from the rich soil of our humanity and the relationships we forge in life is perfectly natural, says MacDonald. It is the reasonable response of a rational being to something that endangers those relationships. It is like a pain in the body, which signifies that a limb or an organ might come to harm. Fear, like physical pain, signals the need for preventive measures and a remedy. Courage may be that remedy.

MacDonald also demonstrates that courage and fear are paradoxically related. They have fundamental things in common and yet they point to very different outcomes. Both arise from the same deep wellsprings of our human condition. Both originate in our creaturely finiteness and our mortal nature as well as from our capacity and our need to love and be loved. Both are psychologically and spiritually counterpoised to death. Unlike fear, however, courage enables us to stand fast in the face of danger, not to waver or flee from it, but instead to thwart danger before it brings harm to us or to others.

Nevertheless, Irene's suspicion that her grandmother knows no fear is not entirely groundless. The difference that Irene sees in her grandmother is that while the mysterious woman may experience moments of fear for others, she no longer fears for herself. The grandmother's fear for her "children" is connected to love like muscle is to tendon. Fear and love work together within her so that love sublimates fear into the courage to be and to act for the good of her children.

Indeed, MacDonald believed that fear is a precondition of as well as a force that drives toward moral and spiritual perfection. The grandmother alludes to this perfection when she says to Irene that maybe in two thousand years even she, who is so fearless and beautiful in Irene's eyes, will outgrow fear entirely—much as the saints "outgrow" sin in their constant struggle to become holy. In a sermon, MacDonald explained this concept:

> Fear is natural, and has a part to perform nothing but itself could perform in the birth of the true humanity. Until love, which is the

truth towards God, is able to cast out fear, it is well that fear should hold; it is a bond, however poor, between that which is and that which creates, a bond that must be broken only by the tightening of an infinitely closer bond.[8]

MacDonald believed that the height of fear is also its transcendent focal point. Biblical religion speaks of this fear as the "fear of God." And when all of our common fears are successfully referred to this one "fear," then all that remains is love and obedience to God. Thus, MacDonald distinguished between our common fears and the fear of the Holy. The former challenges the self to face and overcome the existential reasons that give rise to fear, the possibilities of personal diminishment and death. The latter perfects the courage that the common variety of fear demands of the self. And it transforms this fear into a bridge to complete obedience to God. "Obedience is but the other side of the creative will. Will is God's will, obedience is man's will: the two make one," MacDonald observed.[9] He went on to make this significant religious statement:

> The root-life, knowing well the thousand troubles it would bring upon Him, has created, and goes on creating other lives, that, though incapable of self-being, they may, by willed obedience, share in the bliss of his essential self-ordained being. If we do the will of God, eternal life is ours—no mere continuity of existence, for that in itself is worthless as hell, but a being that is one with essential Life, and so within his reach to fill with the abundant and endless outgoing of his love.[10]

Courage, therefore, is an important natural virtue that helps us navigate a course to the supernatural end of perfection through obedience to God. All of the so-called natural virtues, including courage, are profoundly related to the cardinal theological virtues of faith, hope, and love through a ceaseless and heightening process of participation in the goodness and immortality of the Divine Life.

Irene's maturation takes this course as she learns to trust in her grandmother and follow her instructions. Irene's courage, like all natural courage, comes from the struggle with fear. But courage also needs the ground of ultimate trust on which to stand and act—something or someone who embodies goodness and truth wholly and unqualifiedly. Then it may deepen into a courage to be wholly for others and to risk the self in their behalf. Authentic courage, therefore, makes use of faith and love—or, rather, it fulfills itself in faith and love through selfless and unselfish acts of being for others. True to this conviction, MacDonald in *The Princess and the Goblin* shows us how courage gets joined with the theological virtues, especially faith and love.

Irene's Final Test

As I have said, the main action of *The Princess and the Goblin* shifts back and forth (or should I say up and down) from the luminous garret rooms, where Irene visits her grandmother, to the dark mine shafts and dwellings of the goblins beneath the mountain, where Curdie unravels their plans to kidnap the princess. Irene journeys just once into the dark underworld inside the mountain. It is, however, the turning point of the story.

Her journey begins early one morning when she is awakened by the hideous noise of goblins outside her nursery window. Irene remembers the instructions her grandmother gave her: if she ever thinks she is in grave danger, she must immediately remove her grandmother's ring from her finger and place it under her pillow.

With the same ring finger she must feel for the gossamer thread spun for her by her grandmother that is attached to the ring. She then must follow the thread wherever it leads her, even if that be to the most unexpected places.

So Irene does just what her grandmother has told her. She follows the thread, even when it takes her straight into the mountain through narrow and winding passages. All this time Irene does not know that Curdie is being held prisoner and that the thread is leading her to him. So as the passages become narrower and darker, Irene grows more frightened and nearly despairs. Her trust in her grandmother wins out, however. "She kept thinking more and more about her grandmother, and all that she had said," writes MacDonald (p. 107). Her grandmother had said that she must never "doubt the thread" (p. 84) and to trust that it would return her to safety.

The thread eventually brings Irene to Curdie and, after a tussle with some goblins, both children are delivered from the mountain as the thread leads them to the grandmother's bedroom. However, the physical danger that Irene has faced is only the prelude to one final difficult lesson. Curdie has refused to believe Irene's story about the thread, since he can neither see nor feel it. When they arrive at the garret, Curdie is also unable to see the grandmother or the beautiful furnishings of her bedroom. By his own testimony, all that he can see is "a big, bare, garret-room—like the one in mother's cottage" (p. 121). Worse still for Irene, he is angry with her because he thinks she has lied to him and has deliberately humiliated him.

The child in each one of us expects to be able to share with friends our greatest joy. In her childlike innocence, Irene quite simply assumes that Curdie will see her grandmother and believe everything she has told him. Instead, she learns the hard truth that we cannot make even those whom we love most believe as we believe, and that, if we truly love them, we must permit them to come freely to that belief.[11]

How Irene "Got Older Very Fast"

> Then she carried her to the side of the room. Irene wondered what she was going to do with her, but she asked no questions—only starting a little when she found that she was going to lay her in the large silver bath; for as she looked into it, again she saw no bottom, but the stars shining miles away, as it seemed, in a great blue gulf. Her hands closed involuntarily on the beautiful arms that held her, and that was all.
> —George MacDonald, *The Princess and the Goblin*

When a disconcerted Curdie leaves the grandmother's room, Irene bursts into tears. She beseeches her: "What does it all mean, grandmother?" And the woman answers as only Wisdom can: "It means, my love, that I did not mean to show myself. Curdie is not yet able to believe some things. . . . Seeing is not believing—it is only seeing" (pp. 122–23).

Patience is the practical fruit of faith and is a natural ally of courage. For the time being, Irene must endure being alone in her faith and wait patiently for Curdie. "I see," she says to her grandmother. "So as Curdie can't help it, I will not be vexed with him, but just wait" (p. 123). When Irene "lets go" of Curdie, her trust in the grandmother gives life to a new form of courage within her. The philosopher Josef Pieper has called this "'mystic' fortitude."[12]

Irene ceases fearing for Curdie, not because she no longer cares for him but because she believes in someone who cares for him even more. Mystic fortitude is an attribute of the faithful self that abandons itself for the sake of the other, letting go of earthly fear and natural desire. Mystic fortitude is entrustment of oneself and those one loves entirely to God. "The self is given to us that we may sacrifice it," wrote MacDonald. "It is ours, that we, like Christ, may have somewhat to offer—not that we should torment it, but that we should deny it; not that we should cross it, but that we should abandon it utterly: then it can no more be vexed."[13]

In his fantasy stories, George MacDonald brilliantly uncovered and explored the vital pre-moral roots of the virtues and the vices. However, he also found metaphors and invented allegories to illuminate the transcendent fulfillment of the virtues in mystic love and communion with God. According to MacDonald, the process by which a human being attains full maturity includes not only psychological development and moral growth but religious conversion, and, finally, mystical participation in the Divine Life. Pieper connects mystic fortitude and the self's self-sacrifice to God with baptism. He writes: "The more strictly moral fortitude ... reaches essentially beyond itself [in self-abandonment, the more it reaches] into the mystic order, which ... is nothing other than the more perfect unfolding of the supernatural life that every Christian receives in baptism."[14]

In *The Princess and the Goblin*, MacDonald too turns to the symbolism of baptism in order to convey this meaning. I think that Irene's descent into the mountain and ascent to the surface and up to the grandmother's rooms anticipates a "baptismal" event that she now experiences. Earlier, Irene literally disappeared beneath the earth and then arose from this "grave" because she did not lose faith. This symbolic journey of death, descent into Hades, and rebirth is completed in the grandmother's apartment. Dirty, exhausted, and downcast, Irene collapses into the arms of her grandmother and permits the woman to immerse her in the large silver basin. Irene has looked into that basin's bottomless depths before, and seen in them "the sky and the moon and the stars" (p. 81), infinity itself. We are invited to consider what it would take for a child of Irene's age to overcome the natural fear of being plunged into such bottomless depths.

> The lady pressed her once more to her bosom, saying—
> "Do not be afraid, my child."
> "No, grandmother," answered the princess, with a little gasp; and the next instant she sank in the clear cool water.
> When she opened her eyes, she saw nothing but a strange lovely blue over and beneath and all about her. The lady and the beautiful room had vanished from her sight, and she seemed utterly alone. But instead of *being afraid, she felt more than happy—perfectly blissful.* (p. 124, my emphasis)

The paradoxical relationships of fear and faith and fear and courage are never wholly resolved in our temporal lives. Indeed, "fear is better than no God," wrote MacDonald, "better than a god made with hands. [At least in] fear [lies] deep hidden the sense of the infinite."[15] While fear may sweep us into nothingness, it is also the condition under which a finite and sinful human being finds the faith and courage to yield herself up entirely to God. Baptism is an initiation into and the beginning of a whole new way of being, a way of being whose ultimate end is life unspoiled by fear and ripened instead by Love. Irene will no doubt fear again. But she has also embarked on a new life. Fear will never be quite the same. Love will see to that.

After she is drawn out of the water, Irene immediately catches the sweet scent of the burning roses in her grandmother's fireplace. Then the woman dresses Irene in her nightgown, which she has cleansed in that fire so that it is now "as white as snow." When Irene stands up, she feels "as if she had been made over again. Every bruise and all weariness were gone, and her hands were soft and whole as ever" (p. 125). The "death" of her old (childish) self is completed in the grandmother's font. Irene arises a new being possessing faith and courage, a true princess and daughter of the King. She *has* grown up very fast, as we have been told she would. On the very next day she takes command of the household. And the royal attendants quickly realize that Irene is changed and has grown into the stature of her royal title. "Up to this moment, they had all regarded her as little more than a baby" (p. 135). Irene's nurse, however, saw that "she was no longer a mere child, but wiser than her age would account for" (p. 137).

George MacDonald's religious imagination took over where his moral imagination left off. Or more precisely, his moral imagination was thoroughly interpenetrated by his religious vision. The Greek and Stoic ideals of virtue for virtue's sake did not suffice for him. That is why he made a "baptismal event" the penultimate event of this story. Beatitude transcends not only fear but the death that we fear and the courage that helps us to face it. Immortality, the permanent home of the grandmother—the Queen of Heaven—is the reward and the achievement of a life lived faithfully and courageously. This, it seems to me, is the crowning meaning of George MacDonald's marvelous story.

How Lucy Saw: The Power of Faith in C. S. Lewis's *Prince Caspian*

> Jesus said, "It is for judgment that I have come into this world—to give sight to the sightless and to make blind those who see."
>
> —John 9:39

In *The Princess and the Goblin,* George MacDonald defines the heart of the relationship of faith and courage and depicts how together they are able to bring the self to moral maturity and, ultimately, mystical participation in the life of the Spirit. In *Prince Caspian,* of Lewis's Narnia series, Lewis likewise attends to this theme of moral and spiritual maturation through faith and courage. Furthermore, he expands on several closely related subjects—namely, faith as a power of memory and perception, and courage as a virtue that enacts faith.

My pairing of MacDonald and Lewis is neither accidental nor incidental. George MacDonald was a strong religious and literary influence on C. S. Lewis. He readily acknowledged that MacDonald's fantasy literature made an indelible impression on his artistic and religious imagination. Lewis credited the Victorian writer with not only "convert[ing]" but even "baptiz[ing]" his "imagination." This, he said, did not happen at the first meeting. But there came a time in Lewis's journey from atheism to faith when he was "ready to hear from him [MacDonald] much that he could not have told me at the first meeting."[16] Lewis had searched for the essential truth in religion that, he thought, could be held on to after the mythic wrappings are removed. MacDonald's fantasy works persuaded him, however, that the moral and spiritual truth of religion is inextricably interwoven with myth and story, such that it cannot be removed like the kernel from the husk. Lewis also realized that that quality in MacDonald's imaginative works that had always enchanted him "turned out to be the [actual] quality of the real universe, the divine, magical, terrifying, and ecstatic reality in which we live."[17]

In the end, MacDonald inspired Lewis to make his own attempts at writing fairy tales and fantasy stories. These endeavors bore fruit in the seven books of Narnia and in his Space Trilogy. Thus, while I cannot prove conclusively that MacDonald's Princess Irene was the inspiration for Lewis's Lucy Pevensie, I am personally persuaded of a strong connection. The length of time that separates the publication of the books in which Irene and Lucy appear spans nearly a century. Yet it is possible, nay appropriate, to say that these two young girls are sisters in faith and courage, much as their respective authors were brothers in spirit.

Lucy's Spiritual Lineage

In one of his sermons, George MacDonald argues that "the highest condition of the human will is in sight. . . . I say not the highest condition of the Human Being," he continues, "that surely lies in the Beatific Vision, in the sight of God. But the highest condition of the Human Will . . . is when, not seeing God, not seeming it-self to grasp Him, at all, it yet holds Him fast."[18] Thus, when the grandmother says to Irene that "seeing is not believing—it is only seeing" (p. 123), she sounds a theme that resonates not only with the biblical irony in the passage I have cited from the Gospel of John but also with MacDonald's own truest thoughts about the na-ture and power of faith.

When we trust in our bodily eyes we see what we desire, and normally (in our sinful and spiritually immature condition) what we immediately desire is not God. MacDonald agreed with the great medieval doctors of faith who diagnosed the human condition as afflicted with what they called the "concupiscence of the eyes," lustful eyes of sinful flesh. In the preceding chapter, we saw how Hans Christian Andersen depicted this condition through the powerful allegory of the devil's splintered mirror. Without people even knowing it, fragments of the mirror get lodged in their eyes and hearts, distorting their feelings and perceptions. They may even regard that which is ugly as beautiful and be drawn to wickedness rather than to goodness.

Nevertheless, while not all seeing is believing, believing is still a form of "seeing." Or, putting the matter somewhat differently, one *truly* "sees" when one believes. When one believes, then the scales fall from one's eyes and one "sees" into the deeper reality of things. One may then enter across the threshold of Mystery. In *Prince Caspian*, especially in his beloved character Lucy Pevensie, C. S. Lewis turns quite deliberately to this sacramental metaphor of faith as seeing and the mystery that faith alone is able to apprehend.[19] Indeed, Lucy's name is the first clue about her character.

In Christian hagiography, St. Lucy is the patron saint for those afflicted in the eyes. "Lucy" is etymologically derived from the Latin root *lucer*, which means to shine. Christian tradition reports that the pagan nobleman who pursued St. Lucy loved her eyes so much that she tore them out, saying, "Now let me live to God alone." St. Lucy's sight was miraculously restored, but her greater glory was in becoming a martyr, dying by the sword for refusing to renounce her faith in Christ.[20]

Memory and the Vision of Faith

Remembering (or memory) is a prominent theme in biblical religion that relates to faith's power to apprehend and to perceive. In Judaism and Christianity, faith (in its "seeing" and "grasping" modes) belongs within the context of a history of salvation. Remembrance of what God has done for us is an essential portion of the whole ongoing process of faith, that is, of perceiving, understanding, and responding with obedience to the will of God. Memory not only captures and keeps our experience of God but illumines that experience, gives birth to spiritual vision.

We will not grasp wholly the meaning of faith as "seeing" and of how our heroine Lucy "saw" unless we understand this role of memory in relation to faith. Lewis sheds light on the matter in *Prince Caspian,* the story of how under the terribly adverse conditions of tyranny a band of faithful Narnians continue to hold on to the memory of the central redemptive events in Narnia's past. This is when the great lion Aslan, assisted by four sons and daughters of Adam, liberated Narnia from the wicked servitude of the White Witch. This memory is also the touchstone of hope for a future in which Narnia will be liberated from the present tyranny.

Lewis introduces the theme of remembering right at the start of the story. The four Pevensie children are waiting at a train station as they return to school from summer holiday. All at once they feel a strange pulling sensation. Edmund, the second-youngest, exclaims: "Look sharp! ... All catch hands together. This is magic—I can tell by the feeling. Quick!"[21] Then, suddenly, they are transported out of this world into a dense thicket in Narnia. At first the children do not recognize their surroundings. But they are hungry and thirsty, so they set out in search of food and water. Their searching leads them to the ancient ruins of Cair Paravel, the castle in which they once reigned as kings and queens of Narnia. But they do not recognize it. Gradually, however, their hunger and the peculiar atmosphere of the surroundings help them to recall memories of long ago Narnian adventures.[22] Peter exclaims: "'Have none of you guessed where we are?' 'Go on, go on,' said Lucy. 'I've felt for hours that there was some wonderful mystery hanging over this place.' . . . 'We are in the ruins of Cair Paravel itself,' said Peter. . . . 'Don't you *remember*?' . . . 'I do! I do!' said Lucy, and clapped her hands" (pp. 18–19, my emphasis here and in the following). The children muster the courage to explore further. They uncover their coronation rings, jewelry, and armor. "'Oh look! Our coronation rings—do you *remember* first wearing this?—Why, this is the little brooch we all thought was lost—I say, isn't this the armour you wore in the great tournament in the Lone Islands?—Do you *remember* the Dwarf making that for me?—Do you *remember* drinking out of that horn?—Do you *remember*, do you *remember*?'" (p. 25).

Remembrance in Jewish and Christian faith often is expressed liturgically. I believe that these first scenes are liturgical and eucharistic. The dialogue rings with the musicality and rhythm of the ancient anaphoras (thanksgiving prayers) of Jewish and Christian worship. The purpose of these prayers is to call to memory God and his gifts to the people and to offer thanksgiving (Greek *eucharistia*). I do not think it is stretching things too far to say that even the hunger and the thirst that the children experience fit into a eucharistic scheme. The Christian eucharist takes place around a meal; in the book, the children satisfy their hunger and thirst with repast and refreshment that sets them on a mission of salvation.

Seeing and the Gift of Presence

One doesn't read very far in *Prince Caspian* before it is evident that there are two principal heroes: Prince Caspian himself and little Lucy Pevensie. Each, in his or her own way, stands out as a character whose faith in the numinous figure of Aslan is severely tested. Each rises courageously to the occasion and as a result serves well all of Narnia. The twentieth-century Protestant theologian Paul Tillich describes courage as "the self-affirmation of being in spite of non-being. The power of this self-affirmation," Tillich adds, "is the power of being which is effective in every act of courage." Thus faith may also be defined as "the experience of this power."[23] Both Prince Caspian and Lucy prove that they possess this power of faith and courage. It is with Lucy, however, that we will be concerned, and especially her gift of faith as "seeing" and how that contributes to the happy outcome of the story.

Lucy is the one who *sees*, as her name implies. She sees the freshwater stream and the apple trees near the castle ruins of Cair Paravel. She is the first to see the walls of the ruins. And as we've seen, when Peter challenges the children to guess where they are, Lucy responds: "Go on, go on . . . I've felt for hours that there was some wonderful mystery hanging over this place" (pp. 18–19). But her physical sight and memory signify a more profound power of believing and seeing with the eyes of faith.

Nowhere is this power more dramatically portrayed than in two remarkably beautiful chapters: chapter 9, "What Lucy Saw," and chapter 10, "The Return of the Lion." In chapter 9, the children and the dwarf Trumpkin (sent by Prince Caspian to try to locate the children) come ashore at evening onto the mainland, having cast off in a boat that morning from the island ruins of Cair Paravel. After dinner the entire party falls asleep, all, that is, except Lucy, whose wakefulness has a dreamlike quality under the moon and stars that bathe the water and the woods with the purest light. A nightingale sings, and as Lucy gazes up at the Narnian night sky, her memory is stirred. When Lucy's eyes have grown "accustomed to the light," she sees the trees "nearest her more distinctly," and a "great longing" washes over her "for the old days when the trees could talk in Narnia" (p. 122).

This scene is strongly reminiscent of Irene's journeys up to her grandmother's rooms. Lewis and MacDonald describe similar atmospheres as their respective heroines' consciousnesses are heightened and sharpened to the sense of a holy and numinous presence. Lewis probably reflects MacDonald's persuasion that when our "memory" of the numinous is awakened, eros will move the soul toward the object of its true desire. The "eyes" of the soul see even more deeply and clearly than the eyes of the body. Whereas our physical eyes may provide us with sensual delight, the soul's eyes are the receptors of real joy. In *Surprised by Joy*, his autobiographical essay, Lewis comments that this sort of joy breaks in upon the self like a wave of "unsatisfied desire which is itself more desirable than any other satisfaction . . . [and] anyone who has experienced it will want it again."[24]

At the start of *Prince Caspian*, after the children have quenched their thirst in the stream, Lucy remarks: "I do wish . . . , now that we're not thirsty, we could go on feeling as not-hungry as we did when we *were* thirsty" (p. 8). Lucy's hunger signifies a deeper desire to behold the transcendent. Although she does not yet realize it, Aslan is the true object of her desire. Joy is "a desire turned not to itself but to its object. Not only that, but it owes all its character to its object," writes Lewis.[25] Being awakened by joy is not the end of joy. Joy is "a road right out of the self" to its own object, he continues. This means not clinging to or identifying "with any object of the senses" but journeying to that which is "sheerly objective."[26] Nonetheless, we begin with the senses. So on that night Lucy turns to the trees and says, "'Oh Trees, Trees, Trees'... (though she had not been intending to speak at all). 'Oh Trees, wake, wake, wake. Don't you remember it? Don't you remember *me*? Dryads and Hamadryads, come out, come to me'" (p. 123). For a moment it seems that the trees are going to come to life. "Though there was not a breath of wind they all stirred about her. . . . The nightingale stopped singing as if to listen to it. Lucy felt that at any moment she would begin to understand what the trees were trying to say. But the moment did not come. The rustling died away. The nightingale resumed its song. Even in the moonlight the wood looked more ordinary again" (p. 123).

At this exact moment, Lucy experiences "a feeling (as you sometimes have when you are trying to remember a name or a date and almost get it, but it vanishes before you really do) that she had missed something: as if she had ... used all the right words except one, or put in one word that was just wrong" (pp. 123–24). "Me" is the word misspoken ("Don't you remember *me*? . . . come to me"), and the word not spoken, the thought not thought, is Aslan. Aslan must try twice more before he is able to put Lucy on the right road out of herself.

The following day the lion draws nearer. This is when the rescue party gets lost and is in danger of not reaching Prince Caspian in time to help. The children and Trumpkin arrive at a river gorge. They have been looking for the river Rush, which they intend to follow to the Great River and the Fords of Beruna and straight on to Aslan's How (the ancient spot on which the great Stone Table once stood, where Aslan was killed and was resurrected). The question is whether *this* river is the Rush, since in bygone days it did not run through a gorge. In which direction shall they go? Peter decides downstream. Then Lucy exclaims, "'Look! Look! Look! . . . The Lion . . . Aslan himself. Didn't you see?' Her face had changed completely and *her eyes shone*" (my emphasis) (p. 131). The others see nothing, however. They are all skeptical, all except Edmund, who betrayed Lucy in *The Lion, the Witch and Wardrobe* but was changed by his experiences in Narnia and the mercy that Aslan showed toward him. In desperation, Lucy insists that she has seen the lion and that he wants them to go up the gorge rather than downstream. But her pleas do not persuade Peter and the others to change their direction. "So they set off to their right along the edge, downstream. And Lucy came last of the party, crying bitterly" (p. 134).

The decision to head downstream leads the party into an ambush by one of Miraz's scouting parties. They are forced now to turn around and retrace their steps back up the gorge. That evening they all enjoy a meal of freshly killed bear and apples. "It was a truly glorious meal. . . . Everyone felt quite hopeful now about finding King; Caspian tomorrow and defeating Miraz in a few days" (p. 143). Afterward, everyone falls asleep and is not awakened, except Lucy. She wakes up "with the feeling that the voice she liked best in the world had been calling her name." And while Lucy cannot remember whose voice it is, nevertheless, "she was wonderfully rested and all the aches had gone from her bones—but because she felt so extremely happy and comfortable" (p. 144) she did not want to get up.

This scene is reminiscent of the scene in *The Princess and the Goblin* when Irene is bathed by her grandmother in the bottomless water of the mysterious silver basin. Like Irene in that scene, Lucy feels remarkably refreshed and spiritually regenerated. MacDonald uses the baptismal symbolism of water and light to mark an important change in Irene's character, whereas Lewis returns to the eucharistic motifs of food and refreshment to signify an important change in Lucy.

"Awake, wider than anyone usually is" (p. 146), Lucy arises and walks among the trees. "And now there was no doubt that the trees were really moving—moving in and out through one another as if in a complicated country dance.... She went *fearlessly* in among them, dancing herself," Lewis continues. "But she was only half interested in them. She wanted to get beyond them to something else; it was from beyond them that the dear voice had called." And in the midst of this dancing, "Oh, joy! For *he* was there: the huge Lion, shining white in the moonlight" (pp. 145–46, my emphasis). The mystery is fulfilled in the real presence of the One who in Narnia is the object of every true and pure desire.

In a sermon, George MacDonald raises the following: "Do you ask, 'What is faith in him?' I answer, the leaving of your way, your objects, your self, and the taking of his and him ... *and doing as he tells you.* I can find no words strong enough to serve for the weight of this necessity—this obedience."[27] C. S. Lewis included this passage among the 365 selections in his MacDonald anthology, and no doubt it left an impression on him, so much so that it undoubtedly became the inspiration for this scene.

Vision and Obedience: Lucy's True Test

Whatever the case, this appearance of Aslan in the moonlit forest is a stunning objective correlative of the gospel accounts of the Transfiguration of Jesus. The Reformed theologian Samuel Terrien describes the Transfiguration as an expression of the truth that "the vision of the glory [of God] cannot be divorced from the hearing of the voice."[28] What Lucy saw, soon the others would see as well. What Lucy heard, soon they would hear. They would see and they would hear because they too would be obedient. As MacDonald said elsewhere, "Obedience is the opener of the eyes."[29]

But the great lion puts Lucy to her hardest test yet. She tries to excuse herself for failing the day before to persuade the others to follow him. How, she asks, was she to have followed him even if the others were unwilling? What would have been the outcome? Aslan's eyes tell Lucy he wants more from her. Then he speaks. "If you go back to the others now, and wake them up; and tell them you have seen me again; and that you must all get up at once and follow me—what will happen? There is only one way to find out" (p. 137). "A time comes to every man," wrote MacDonald, "when he must obey, or make such *refusal—and know it.*"[30] For Lucy that moment comes on this luminescent night.

> "Do you mean that is what you want me to do?" gasped Lucy.
> "Yes, little one," said Aslan.
> "Will the others see you too?" asked Lucy.
> "Certainly not at first," said Aslan. "Later on, it depends."
> "But they won't believe me!" said Lucy.
> "It doesn't matter," said Aslan.
> "Oh dear, oh dear," said Lucy. "And I was so pleased at finding you again. And I thought you'd let me stay. And I thought you'd

come roaring in and frighten all the enemies away—like last time.
And now everything is going to be horrid."

"It is hard for you, little one," said Aslan. "But things never
happen the same way twice."

Lucy buried her head in his mane to hide from his face. But there
must have been magic in his mane. She could feel lion-strength
going into her. Quite suddenly she sat up.

"I'm sorry, Aslan," she said. "I'm ready now."

"Now you are a lioness," said Aslan. "And now all Narnia will be
renewed." (p. 150)

This haunting scene and the accompanying dialogue do not require any further commentary. Lucy is no longer the child she once
was. In a very short time she has grown up to achieve the moral
and spiritual stature of a genuine heroine of faith and courage. She
is the first to see and hear Aslan because her yearning for him is the
strongest and the purest. Terrien explains: "In biblical faith, presence eludes but does not delude. The hearing of the name, which is
obedience to the will and the decision to live now for an eternal future, becomes the proleptic vision of the glory."[31] What Lucy failed
to do in the first instance she does not fail to do this time. This time
she obeys completely and follows the great lion. And the others
follow her, even though at first they do not see or hear Aslan. "She
fixed her eyes on Aslan. He turned and walked at a slow pace about
thirty yards ahead of them. The others had only Lucy's direction to
guide them, for Aslan was not only invisible to them but silent as
well" (pp. 157–58).

John Henry Newman says in one of his Oxford sermons: "Every
act of obedience is an approach—an approach to Him who is not
far off, though He seems so, but close behind this visible screen
of things which hides Him from us." And, Newman writes, "you

have to seek his face; obedience is the only way of seeing Him."[32]
Through obedience, Peter, Susan, and Edmund, and even the
skeptic Trumpkin, eventually catch sight of Aslan and hear his
roar. And with that roar Aslan awakens all of the sleeping land and
seals the triumph of goodness over evil in Narnia.

The Vision of God and the Kingdom

C. S. Lewis's sensibilities, no doubt, were less mystical than George
MacDonald's. But he too draws the important connections between faith and courage enacted as moral character and faith
and courage fulfilled in the vision of God. Lewis depicts this final
fulfillment of faith and courage with moving effect in the seventh, concluding book of the Narnia series. The story of *The Last
Battle* recounts the final days of the Narnian world when wickedness conspires against goodness and wins the temporal struggle.
Nevertheless, even in these latter days as evil stalks the land, Narnia
is not without noble and courageous defenders who are faithful
to the ancient truth and the good name of Aslan. Nor does Aslan
abandon this faithful remnant.

As King Tirian, the last, noble king of Narnia, is taken down in
battle, a miraculous event occurs behind the doorway of a mysterious stable. In the final moment of his life, Tirian is forced through
the doorway of that stable and beholds within not the interior of a
stable but a whole fresh new world. Now standing before him are
fourteen kings and queens, those heroes and heroines from our
world who had been transported to Narnia at critical moments
in its history and by their noble deeds ensured that goodness and
right reigned there—all friends of Aslan, and Lucy is among them.

It would take too long to explain the exact circumstances of this occurrence. I leave that for the reader to discover. What is of immediate importance is the fact that every one of these heroes and heroines of Narnia is now on the other side of death. All have met their temporal end, whether in Narnia or in England.—Three of the Pevensie children are included among these, excluding Susan. As Aslan says, they are now in the "Shadow lands—dead. The term is over: the holidays have begun. The dream is ended: this is the morning."[33] In the conversations that follow, Lucy is given to speak and raise questions and make observations much as she always has. But I think that in her speech Lewis also supplies the last important key that unlocks the lineage and legacy of her remarkable character.

Lucy utters a litany of observations that clarify just where everyone is. With the help of her sharp eyes and extraordinary powers of perception, the whole company is able to identify the familiar and yet transformed landscape that surrounds them. They realize that they are in a new Narnia, an archetype and perfection of that world whose ending they just witnessed. And they are drawn in (or is it out?) toward the places of their deepest love and desire, only these places are more beautiful now than they ever were before. Finally, everyone arrives at the walls of a garden, a place familiar to some among the party who once upon a time visited a garden very much like this one when Narnia was fresh in creation. They see before them a panorama within the garden walls that is somehow even larger and greater than the country outside.

Lucy speaks once again:

> "I see," she said at last, thoughtfully. "I see now. This garden is like the Stable. It is far bigger inside than outside." . . .

Lucy looked hard at the garden and *saw* that it was not really a garden at all but a whole world, with its own rivers and woods and sea and mountains. But they were not strange: she knew them all.

"I *see*," she said. "This is still Narnia, and more real and more beautiful than the Narnia down below, just as *it* was more real and more beautiful than the Narnia outside the Stable door! I *see* . . . world within world, Narnia within Narnia." (pp. 224–25, my emphasis)

We should take note especially of the repetitive and responsive quality of Lucy's speech. The whole of it is musical, liturgical, and celebratory. She ends her speech with this exclamatory phrasing: "I see . . . world within world, Narnia within Narnia," which I take to be a deliberate variation on the ancient liturgical formula "Now and forever and to the ages of ages. Amen."

Through Lucy's special eyes we see the new and eternal Narnia. "Lucy looked this way and that and soon found that a new beautiful thing had happened to her. Whatever she looked at, however far away it might be, once she had fixed her eyes steadily on it, it became quite clear and close as if she were looking through a telescope." Lucy's eyes see so far and with such sharpness that she makes out in the far distance something that, although it first appears to be "a brightly-colored cloud," is "a real land." She points this out to Edmund and Peter, and together they recognize that the land that lies in front of them is England. Then they catch sight of "Professor Kirke's old home in the country," where, through the mysterious wardrobe, their journeys to Narnia began, and they are puzzled. This is because the home had been destroyed some years ago. However, their old Narnian friend Mr. Tumnus, the faun, tells them that what they are seeing is "the England within England, the real England just as real as the real Narnia. And in that inner England no good thing is destroyed" (p. 226).

And if you or I ask how come the others are now able to see what Lucy sees, the answer is that "their eyes also had become like hers" (p. 226). Eyes of true faith are rewarded with the vision of God. Then fear is also ended, courage is completed, and every worthy desire is joyfully fulfilled. "Aslan turned to them and said: 'You do not yet look so happy as I mean you to be.' Lucy said, 'We're so afraid of being sent away, Aslan. And you have sent us back in our own world so often.' 'No fear of that,' said Aslan. 'Have you not guessed?' Their hearts leaped and a wild hope rose within them" (pp. 227–28).

Aslan tells Lucy, Edmund, Peter, and the others who were with them at the train station from which they had been transported into Narnia, what they have already suspected: that they were killed in a real railway accident. But now they have passed beyond the "Shadow-lands" to a place where it is always "the morning." As Aslan explained these things, they all *saw* more than they had ever seen before. And Aslan "no longer looked to them like a lion; but the things that began to happen after that," says Lewis, "were so great and beautiful that I cannot write them" (p. 228).

THE TRIUMPH OF BEAUTY IN "THE NIGHTINGALE" AND "THE UGLY DUCKLING"

Never is a good story merely about one thing. This is certainly true of Hans Christian Andersen's "The Nightingale" and "The Ugly Duckling." Many regard "The Nightingale" as among Hans Christian Andersen's very finest achievements. In her delightful biography of Andersen, Jackie Wullschlager argues that "The Nightingale" "is one of Andersen's aesthetic manifestos, setting out in fairy tale form his ideal of naturalness and simplicity battling the demons of artifice and reason."[1] Nevertheless, "The Nightingale" has much more to offer. For it is also a story about love, death, immortality, and beauty—in my view, beauty above all else.

Why, however, pair "The Ugly Duckling" with "The Nightingale"? After all, the view of experts and common folk alike has been that "The Ugly Duckling" is about the suffering and triumph of the disinherited or the harm of bullying. And these themes do certainly belong to the story. Yet here again, I wish to say that "The Ugly Duckling" is also about beauty, in this case the transformative power of the love of beauty.

Tending the Heart of Virtue. Second Edition. Vigen Guroian, Oxford University Press.
© Vigen Guroian 1998, 2023. DOI: 10.1093/oso/9780195384307.003.0008

The Beauty of the Nightingale's Song

Sister Joan Chittister, while reflecting on monastic wisdom, speaks of the imperiled state of beauty in the modern world. Her description of how in our time beauty is in jeopardy is sympatico with Hans Christian Andersen's viewpoint in "The Nightingale." She argues that what "may be most missing in this highly technological world of ours is beauty." "Even when what is presented to us is called art," we desire functionalism and efficiency over beauty. "We prefer plastic flowers to wild flowers. . . . We forgo the natural and the real for the gaudy and the pretentious."[2] We mistake the dazzling for beauty and are awash in the banal. And when genuinely beautiful things give us pleasure, that pleasure very often sinks to smugness or ostentation.

In "The Nightingale" Andersen introduces us to two birds. The first is a living, breathing creature whose drab appearance and humble demeanor yield no hint of how beautifully it sings. This Nightingale is a retiring sort. It seeks neither audience nor applause for its music, though when he hears the Nightingale's song, a fisherman is moved to exclaim: "Blessed God, how beautifully it sings!"[3] The second bird is a mechanical invention. Although this mechanical bird is fashioned in the shape of a nightingale, its body is bejeweled with sapphires and rubies, its insides are made of wheels and springs, and it has a cylinder in place of a heart. It boasts but one song, a perfect imitation of one of the real Nightingale's songs. Whereas the real Nightingale is humble and unassuming, the imitation nightingale has been created to be displayed as an object of pride and vanity—thus it arrives at the Chinese emperor's palace with a ribbon around its neck that says,

"The Emperor of Japan's nightingale is inferior to the Emperor of China's" (p. 207).

The Humor That Delights Children

Andersen's humor is playful and beguiling. As with most humor, however, the titillation of incongruity and absurdity slips through the fingers when analyzed. That is why in my narration of "The Nightingale," I rarely stop to point it out. It is best to let the humor speak for itself. Still, something must be said about it. Children enjoy this humor. It draws them into the story. For instance, "The Nightingale" begins with this declaration: "In China, as you know, the emperor is Chinese, and so"—as if it should surprise us!—"are his court and all his people." Andersen adds for good measure: "This story happened a long, long time ago; and that is just the reason why you should hear it now, before it is forgotten" (p. 203).

This kind of folk humor often is satirical and exposes the misshapen character of the inhabitants of the royal palace. For example, we are told that the emperor's palace is "the most beautiful in the whole world" (p. 203). We needn't doubt that this is so. The trouble is that the emperor and his court boastfully claim ownership of this beauty. In so doing, they inflate their own self-image and self-importance. Pride and ostentation spoil the pristine pleasure that may naturally attend the experience of beauty. For example, the beautiful flowers in the palace gardens are described as "the loveliest flowers; the most beautiful of them had little silver bells that tinkled so you wouldn't pass by without noticing them" (p. 203). They represent the hubris and conceit of the entire court.

How the Nightingale Became Known

Andersen contrasts the pretentious beauty of the palace with the pure and exquisite music of the Nightingale. The Nightingale's song refreshes and renews a kitchen maid when she listens to it on her journeys to and from her mother's cottage. The poor and hardworking common folk, who live far from the palace, are blessed by the Nightingale's song. Meanwhile, the imperial court is ignorant of the Nightingale's existence. Even the emperor is unaware of the bird. Nonetheless, foreign visitors have heard the Nightingale. Indeed, they have praised its music in books and have written "long odes about the nightingale" (p. 204).[4]

One day the emperor reads about the Nightingale in one of these books. Its author maintains that the Nightingale's song is the most beautiful thing in all of the emperor's kingdom. The emperor is outraged that no one has told him of the bird's existence. " 'What!' said the emperor. 'The nightingale? I don't know it, I have never heard of it; and yet it lives not only in my empire but in my very garden. That is the sort of thing one can only find out by reading books,'" he adds (p. 204). Yet the emperor needn't have waited to discover the existence of the Nightingale in a book. True, no one in the court has seen or heard the Nightingale. However, had he and his court not been so self-consumed, so fixated on themselves, they might have ventured out beyond the immediate environs of the palace into the forest at the sea's edge where the Nightingale lives. The Nightingale's song is not a commodity but a gift given to those who open themselves to it.

The emperor demands that the Nightingale be found and brought to him immediately. If there is a creature with such a beautiful song, it ought to belong to him. He exclaims: "The whole world knows of it and I do not" (p. 204). The chief courtier frantically searches for someone who knows of the Nightingale's whereabouts. At last, a young kitchen maid is found, the same who listens to the Nightingale on her trips to and from her mother's home. She explains that when she hears the Nightingale sing, it is as if her mother were embracing her.

The chief courtier orders the maid to take him and his entourage to the Nightingale. This sets in motion the drama and comedy that unfold in the search for the Nightingale, its appearance at the court, the honors bestowed upon it, and its escape back to the forest. Throughout all of this action the humble and noble character of the bird is revealed and contrasted with the court's pride and pomposity. The search party, which comprises fully half the court, exhibits a conspicuous inability to identify natural beauty until it is pointed out to them. When they hear a cow bellow, they call out: "There it is. What a marvelously powerful voice the little animal has; we heard it before." They hear a frog, and the Chinese imperial dean exclaims: "Lovely . . . I can hear her, she sounds like little church bells ringing." When at last the Nightingale is heard and seen, the chief courtier exclaims, "I had not imagined it would look like that. It looks so common! I think it has lost its color from shyness and out of embarrassment at seeing so many noble people at one time" (p. 205).

When the Nightingale is informed that the emperor has asked to hear him sing, he displays no bravado or self-congratulation; he merely answers, "With pleasure." Indeed, since he believes that the emperor is in the party, the bird immediately begins to sing. He pleads that his song sounds best "in the green woods." But when he is instructed that he must appear at court, the Nightingale complies without complaint or concern over appearances. When his song brings tears to the emperor's eyes, the Nightingale looks for no favor or reward, and when offered the emperor's golden slipper to be hung around his neck, he demurs: "I have seen tears in the eyes of an emperor, and that is a great enough treasure for me" (p. 206). In spite of his unassuming deportment, the Nightingale swiftly becomes a celebrity. He is given "his own cage at court and permission to take a walk twice a day and once during the night." He is the talk of the town. "Whenever two people met in the street they would sigh; one would say, 'night,' and the other, 'gale'; and then they would understand each other perfectly" (p. 207).

One day, however, a gift mysteriously arrives at court. It is a mechanical nightingale, "made of silver and gold, and studded with sapphires, diamonds, and rubies" (p. 207). It not only sings beautifully but is much more pleasant to look at than the real Nightingale. Someone proposes that the two birds perform a duet. This is not a success. "The real bird sang in his own manner," with inspiration as the moment moved it. The mechanical bird, which could sing but a single song—because it had just "one cylinder in its chest instead of a heart"—sings its song without variation or improvisation, although in "perfect time" (p. 207). The mechanical nightingale wins over the emperor and his entire court, and as everyone's attention turns to the newcomer, the real Nightingale quietly flees the palace and returns to his beloved forest home.

The Beauty of the Mechanical Nightingale Versus Beauty That Opens the Heart

The beauty of the mechanical bird is showy, like all the rest of the beautiful things of the palace. So it is not surprising that everyone prefers the mechanical bird. The imperial music master proudly proclaims that the mechanical nightingale's singing "belongs to his school of music" (pp. 207–8). His school of music follows what we today call logarithms, mathematically precise formulas that leave no room for the heart or inspiration, nor for beauty that speaks to the heart.

On the basis of his "scientific" criteria, the music master pronounces the artificial bird "better than the real nightingale, not only on the outside where the diamonds glisten, but also inside." He explains that "the real nightingale cannot be depended upon. One never knows what he will sing; whereas, in the mechanical bird everything is determined." The mechanical bird may have but a single song, but the beauty of this is that "one can explain everything. We can open it up to examine and appreciate how human thought has fashioned the wheels and the cylinder, and put them where they are, to turn just as they should" (p. 208).

In remote China, the fairyland of Andersen's story, much as in our society, science and technology rule over the minds and imaginations of the people, machines and devices have become small gods, while efficiency trumps creativity. Faith and pride in humanity's rational powers expel mystery from life. Pride in what humans have made and can understand supplants reverence for what God and his nature have given. When it is discovered that the real Nightingale has fled, this is all the justification needed to officially banish it and its music from the kingdom.

Meanwhile, the imperial music master writes "a work in twenty-five volumes about the mechanical nightingale," replete with "the most difficult Chinese words." And everyone, of course, who purchases the music master's writings says that they have read and understood them, "for otherwise they would have been considered stupid" (p. 209). The entire Chinese people join in this cult of celebrity. They become enamored of the artificial bird's song because once memorized it is easy to sing. "The street urchins sang 'Zi-zi-zizzi, cluck-cluck-cluck-cluck.' And so did the emperor" (p. 209).

The Emperor's Illness

In a year's time, the mechanical nightingale breaks. Its cylinder and gears have worn out. Henceforth, it may be wound up to sing but once a year, and even then it cannot complete its song. What was thought to be without flaw proves not so perfect after all.

Some five years pass and the emperor grows gravely ill, so ill in fact that the people begin to mourn his imminent death and to prepare for a new emperor. Death, with his empty skull, visits the emperor in his bedroom. He wears the emperor's golden crown and holds the emperor's saber in one hand and his imperial banner in the other. Shades, some ghastly and others kindly, come to haunt the emperor. They are the emperor's evil and good deeds performed throughout his life. Meanwhile, Death sits heavily on the emperor's heart as the shades of his evil deeds stare down at him, taunting him: "'Do you remember?' whispered first one and then the other." This strikes terror in the emperor's heart, yet he continues to deny the judgment he faces. "No, no, I don't re-member! It is not true!" he shouts (p. 210).

Terrified, the emperor begs for music to drown out these accusations and rid him of the dreadful images. He commands that the Chinese gong be sounded, "so that I will not be able to hear what they are saying." Yet there is no escape from the talking apparitions. When he realizes that there is no respite from this terrorizing judgment, the dying man turns to beauty, albeit the inferior sort of the mechanical nightingale and its music. He commands: "Little golden nightingale, sing." But there is no one to wind it up. Like the golden calf the Israelites built during Moses's absence on Mount Sinai, the mechanical nightingale is powerless against death. "Death kept staring at the emperor out of the empty sockets in his skull; and the palace was still, so terrifyingly still" (p. 210).

One day, suddenly, the real Nightingale's song breaks through the dreadful silence of the emperor's dark bedchamber. He has heard of the emperor's illness and suffering and has come to comfort him and to give him hope. He sits at the emperor's window singing freely, without command. The emperor is not the only one who hears the Nightingale's lovely music. The shades hear it as well, and flee. Strangely, Death is enraptured by the music. He begs, "Please, little nightingale, sing on!" (p. 211) and gives up the emperor's saber, imperial banner, and crown, all so that he might hear the Nightingale sing.

The Nightingale sings a song about "the quiet churchyard, where white roses grow, where fragrant elderberry trees are, and where the grass is green from the tears of those who come to mourn" (p. 211). The white rose and the elderberry have a special place in the Christian imagination. White roses signify purity and innocence. And tradition has it that Judas Iscariot hanged himself on an elder tree. Thus, the tree, its flower, and its fruit are emblematic of judgment, but also of penance and healing.

"Death longed so much for his garden that he flew out of the window, like a white cold mist" (p. 211). What is it that moves Death to behave this way? Is he fleeing the life-giving music of the

Nightingale in order to seek refuge where he belongs? Or can it be that Death himself yearns to be transformed into the new life promised by the garden greened by holy tears?

The Nightingale's return is a pivotal moment in the life of the emperor. Penitently, he thanks the Nightingale for his song. He begs to understand why the Nightingale has returned to save him from "the evil phantoms" and "Death himself" even though he had unjustly banished the Nightingale from his realm. "How shall I reward you?" the emperor asks. "You have rewarded me already," the Nightingale responds. "I shall never forget that, the first time I sang for you, you gave me the tears from your eyes; and to a poet's heart, those are jewels. But sleep so you can become well and strong; I shall sing for you" (p. 211).

Elaine Scarry in her little volume titled *On Beauty and Being Just* argues that beauty "is a compact . . . between the beautiful being (a person or thing) and the perceiver." This compact is an act of freedom and love, the gift of one to the other without condition. Within this compact, within this milieu of beauty, fairness and justice may come to be. "Beauty seems to place requirements on us for attending to the aliveness" of others, Scarry continues.[5] The emperor is healed in this milieu of beauty, and the Nightingale knows that this new aliveness in him will open the emperor's heart and train his thoughts on the well-being of his subjects, especially the poorest and least attractive of them. Perhaps now the emperor will view his subjects *in* beauty and value their lives not for their usefulness to him but because in living they share in the beauty and goodness that he too experiences and that give him joy.

From the start, the Nightingale seems to have discerned within the emperor's soul a spirit of piety, goodness, and truth that begs to be freed. No matter that he first caged the Nightingale and then banished him from his empire. Ironically, it was the emperor who was imprisoned in the hermetic confines of his own ego and palace and needed to be liberated. The very beauty that brought tears to the emperor's eyes promises to be the source of his redemption. Unsullied beauty is this way. For it possesses the power to draw us out of our egocentrism, and then gratitude and empathy for others may move us to act justly and mercifully.

After his recovery, the emperor says to the Nightingale, "You must come always," and promises, "I shall only ask you to sing when you want to" (p. 211). Not only does he proclaim the Nightingale's freedom but he also declares his own emancipation. Inspired by the Nightingale's song, he now may commence a new life of service to his realm. "Let me come to visit you when I want to, and I shall sit on the branch outside your window and sing for you," says the Nightingale. "And my song shall make you happy and make you thoughtful. I shall sing not only of those who are happy but also of those who suffer. I shall sing of the good and of the evil that happen around you, and yet are hidden from you. For a little songbird flies far. I visit the poor fishermen's cottages and the peasant's hut, far away from your palace and your court" (p. 211).

The emperor vows to break the mechanical bird "in a thousand pieces." But the Nightingale tells him not to: "The mechanical bird sang as well as it could, keep it" (p. 211). The emperor has found offense in the mechanical bird. If his anger persists, however, there will be for him no catharsis or healing. To destroy the mechanical bird will not go to the heart of the problem. It is not the source of the spiritual sickness that afflicts the emperor and his realm. Rather, the sickness is inside of human beings. They made the mechanical nightingale the vanity of vanities. And they substituted its fixed and programmed song for the living and life-giving music of the Nightingale.

Beauty That Saves the World

> The beauty of the world is Christ's tender smile for us coming through matter. He is really present in the universal beauty.
> —Simone Weil, "Forms of the Implicit Love of God"

In the second canto of the *Purgatorio*, Dante, Virgil, and the Roman philosopher Cato the Younger stop and stand at the foot of the mountain. There they encounter Dante's recently deceased musician friend Casella. After an exchange of greetings, Dante pleads:

> If no new law has stripped you of your art
> > or seized your memory of those songs of love
> > which used to still the yearnings of my heart …
> oh let it please you now awhile
> > to soothe my soul, which has, in coming here,
> > walked with my body many a weary mile.[6]

Casella's song captivates those standing there, as their minds are "touched by nothing else / But the notes of his song." Yet right before them is Mount Purgatory, which beckons them to the encompassing beauty of the beatific vision. No romantic love song can substitute for this or, for that matter, the lovely psalmody of a newly arrived group of pilgrim spirits. They are chanting Psalm 113. It recounts the story of the Exodus and the Israelites' journey to the Promised Land. This is apropos of the journey on which Dante has set forth. Meanwhile, Cato loses patience and exclaims:

What's this, you sluggish souls! Get to the hill!
What lingering, what carelessness down here!
Hurry to scrape away the scales which keep
the Lord from being manifest to you![7]

The mechanical nightingale of Andersen's story reminds us of
the peril of inordinate love and attachment to earthly objects even
the most beautiful of them: Their beauty is relative but if properly
approached can lead us toward that transcendent beauty which is
beatitude itself. St. Augustine writes about this in his *Confessions*,
where he explains: "There is beauty in lovely physical objects, as
in gold and silver, and all such things." Thus "the life that we live in
this world has its attractiveness because of a certain measure in its
beauty and its harmony with all the inferior objects that are beautiful. . . . These inferior goods have their delights," he concedes.
But these goods, these beauties, we must never confuse with
"God who has made them all."[8] Only the transcendent beauty that
belongs to God—or, as Simone Weil puts it, "the universal beauty"
reflected in "the smile of Christ coming through matter"—can
never disappoint.[9]

Sometimes, as in the emperor's case, this lesson is learned
through the agony of loss and loneliness. Our hearts are opened
to the truth we have ignored or denied, as our spiritual eyes are
opened to the beauty to which we have been blind or that we have
banished from our lives. Andersen's story is a reminder that sometimes goodness, truth, and beauty are found in the most modest
and unassuming of presences, such as the Nightingale—small
pearls of great value.

One of the great characters of Dostoevsky's fiction, Prince
Myshkin of the novel *The Idiot*, is credited with having said, "Beauty

will save the world." Routinely, commentators have interpreted this statement as if it invokes an aesthetic concept. But I am certain that Dostoevsky intended the Christ of scripture as its final referent. In Andersen's fairy tale, the Nightingale saves the emperor. And like the Christ of the Gospels, he comes in humility, not in glory: "He had no beauty, no majesty to catch our eyes, no grace to attract us to him" (Is. 53:2).

The Gospel story is resonant here, especially the Gospel of Mark, in which Jesus repeatedly admonishes the recipients and witnesses of his kindness and healing miracles not to boast or make mention of his deeds to others (e.g., Mk. 1:43–45, 8:29–30). Do not reveal "to anyone that you have a little bird that tells you everything, for then you will fare better," says the Nightingale to the emperor (p. 212). The Nightingale has come to the emperor humbly, without demonstration or exercise of power. Yet the words that the Nightingale speaks, nay, the songs that he sings, bring beauty into the world, a beauty that heals and overcomes even death itself. This is a story that can powerfully shape a child's moral imagination.

"The Ugly Duckling": The Transformative Power of the Love for Beauty

I have said that "The Ugly Duckling" and "The Nightingale" are thematically related and that beauty is that theme. Andersen's underlying aesthetic and ethical convictions alone could account for this thematic concurrence. Yet in this instance, events in the author's life help us to better understand his two protagonists and the meaning in their struggles and triumphs.

Andersen composed "The Nightingale" and "The Ugly Duckling" back to back, completing them both during the late summer and fall of 1843. In September 1843, the young Swedish singer Jenny Lind, upon whom the public had already bestowed the adoring title "The Swedish Nightingale," visited Copenhagen for a second time. She and Andersen had met in that city briefly three years before, but without consequence. On this visit, however, Andersen fell in love with Lind. There would be no love affair, as Lind's affections for him were not of the romantic sort. Nonetheless, she became Andersen's inspiration, his muse, one might say, for both stories. Andersen admired and respected Jenny Lind. He thought her musical talent had, like his storytelling, an exceptional capacity to move audiences deeply. In his autobiography, Andersen writes: "No books, no men have had a better or more ennobling influence on me as a poet than Jenny Lind."[10]

Andersen had been working on "The Ugly Duckling" for over a year before he met Lind for the second time in 1843. Yet within two weeks of Lind's departure from Copenhagen, he wrote that he had "finished the tale of the young swan."[11] No doubt, "The Ugly Duckling" began as something of a self-portrait, but there is good reason to believe that Jenny Lind and her personal story of rags to riches, obscurity to fame—which was much like his—kindled Andersen's creative fires.

Once having completed "The Ugly Duckling," Andersen immediately turned to writing "The Nightingale." And if we take his word for it, Andersen finished this masterpiece of his oeuvre in just one day.[12] When the Nightingale speaks of itself as a "poet" (p. 211), Andersen honors Jenny Lind. Yet Lind favored the story of "The Ugly Duckling." "Oh, what a glorious gift to be able to clothe in words one's most lofty thought," she wrote to Andersen, "and by means of a scrap of paper to make men see so cleverly how the noblest often lie most hidden and covered over by wretchedness and rags, until the hour of transformation strikes to show the figure in a divine light."[13] It is telling of Lind's own noble character that she did not write of the Ugly Duckling with reference to herself, her professional success and fame. Rather, she was impressed by the "noble" character of the Ugly Duckling—noble from the beginning, but excelling in such a way that in the end he shines "in a divine light."

Beautiful Beginnings

I already have said that the usual conclusions readers have reached about "The Ugly Duckling" have purchase. For example, the duckling is ostracized and bullied by others because of his physical appearance. Nonetheless, the theme of beauty gives a special force to the story, even a mystical or religious dimension that the critics rarely, if ever, identify or examine.

I am somewhat puzzled by Andersen's decision to tag this moral onto the ending of "The Ugly Duckling": "It does not matter that one has been born in the henyard as long as one has lain in a swan's egg" (p. 224). My best guess is that Andersen wanted his readers to take from his story the perennial truth that whatever one's origins, however humble they may have been, it is what one is made of, the "stuff" that belongs to one's character, that matters above all else.

I, however, do not think that this moral uncovers the much more profound meaning Andersen plants in his story. To begin, the Ugly Duckling is not born in a homely henyard (the literal meaning of the Danish is duck-garden). He is born, rather, in a bucolic countryside, within a magical "forest of burdock" on a narrow strip of land at the edge of a castle moat.[14] Right at the start, Andersen introduces his theme of beauty. "It was so beautiful out in the country," the narrator remarks.

> It was summer. The oats were still green, but the wheat was turning yellow. Down in the meadow the grass had been cut and made into haystacks.... The fields were enclosed by woods, and hidden among them were little lakes and pools. Yes, it certainly was lovely out there in the country!
>
> The old castle, with its deep moat surrounding it, lay bathed in sunshine. Between the heavy walls and the edge of the moat there was a narrow strip of land covered by a whole forest of burdock plants. Their leaves were large and some of the stalks were so tall that a child could stand upright under them and imagine that he was in the middle of the wild and lonesome woods. Here a duck had built her nest. (p. 217)

Just what sort of beauty does Andersen celebrate? It most certainly is not the kind of beauty attributed to the imperial palace of "The Nightingale." Rather, it is a beauty that is found in nature, the kind of beauty Andersen the romantic favored above all. The Ugly Duckling himself is drawn to this kind of beauty. Nor would it be stretching matters to say that the Ugly Duckling is a romantic in Andersen's own image.[15]

But I also want to add that Andersen's romanticism owes a lot to the Christian imagination that his youthful reading of the Bible formed in him. In my discussion of "The Nightingale," I cited Simone Weil's observation that "the beauty of the world is not an attribute of matter in itself" but is, rather, the "beauty ... [of] Christ's tender smile for us coming through matter."[16] The beauty that can transform our lives, transform who and what we are, reveals itself to us when we love God's creation as he loves it. This is a sentiment with which, I am confident, Andersen, however idiosyncratic his Christianity may have been, would have agreed. This vision of beauty belongs to Andersen's story, for the Ugly Duckling never ceases to love beauty in spite of all the abuse and suffering he endures. In the end, this love of beauty is what makes him beautiful.

How the Ugly Duckling Became Ugly

I am so ugly that even the dog doesn't want to bite me.
—Hans Christian Andersen, "The Ugly Duckling"

While the Ugly Duckling is born in a beautiful place, soon afterward he enters a community of domestic fowl who consider him ugly. Whether the duckling is genuinely ugly may depend upon one's point of view; but that he is different from the rest of the domestic birds, different from even his presumptive siblings, is objectively true. *He is not a duck.* Nor is he a domestic fowl of any sort. The residents of the henyard detect this difference almost immediately. When the mother duck becomes discouraged that one of her eggs has not yet hatched, an old duck offers the opinion, presumably based on long experience, that the egg is not a duck egg at all but a turkey egg. After the duckling finally does hatch, the denizens of the henyard quickly judge him to be very ugly. Yet he is not a turkey, and the mother duck observes that he uses his legs beautifully when he swims and holds his neck straight. This moves her to exclaim proudly: "He is my own child and, when you look closely at him, he's quite handsome" (pp. 217–18).[17] For the moment, her attention is given over to the duckling's real abilities and noble comportment.

Nonetheless, the overwhelming opinion of the henyard is that the duckling is ugly, that he is a mistake, that he is different and does not belong. A revered old duck who wears a red rag around one leg—said to signify her Spanish and aristocratic pedigree—offers her opinion that all of the ducklings "are beautiful" except the Ugly Duckling and that she wishes his mother "could make him over again" (p. 218). The poor duckling is harried, chased, and mistreated by all the residents of the henyard, even by his own sisters and brothers, who quack again and again: "'If only the cat would get you, you ugly thing.'. . . The other ducks bit him and the hens pecked at him. The little girl who came to feed the fowls kicked him" (p. 219).

The duckling internalizes what others say about him: "How he grieved over his own ugliness, and how sad he was" (p. 219). In the end, even the mother duck wishes that he would leave the henyard and go "far away'" (p. 219). Finally, the Ugly Duckling flees from his unbearable circumstances. He leaves the henyard for the wild. Still, after he observes that at the sight of him even the wild birds in the bushes take flight, he concludes: "They, too, think I am ugly" (p. 219). Though he has escaped the henyard, the duckling cannot escape the self-image that he is ugly. "Ugly" has become his identity.

During the months that follow, the duckling enters the company of a variety of creatures. Among wild ducks, geese, and a family of an old woman, her chicken, and a cat, the duckling receives neither respect nor acceptance, nor does he feel at home. It seems his fate is to be estranged from himself and everyone he meets. This displacement and suffering, however, draw out of the duckling a significant character trait that betokens the unexpected triumphal outcome of his peregrinations. He perseveres to see the beautiful wide world beyond the henyard, a beauty to which he is passionately attracted. He survives great hardship and lives to see the spring, when he himself will be forever changed.

I will not recite all that the Ugly Duckling encounters on his journey—indeed, his odyssey. In the middle of the story, however, Andersen places an episode that is crucial for our understanding of the nobility of the Ugly Duckling, the nobility that so touched the heart of Jenny Lind. Though this episode is left out of all the picture book versions of the story that I have seen, it is the axis of Andersen's story. For in it the duckling demonstrates a new maturity. He takes control of his life and becomes the agent of his own destiny whether life or death..

A Hut Is Not a Home

One bitterly cold evening the Ugly Duckling comes upon a "poor little hut." The duckling seeks shelter and manages to slip through a crack in the doorway. The inhabitants of this hovel are an old woman and her two house pets, a cat named Sonny and a hen named Cluck Lowlegs. The cat and the hen think of themselves as worldly wise, far above the rank of other ordinary domestic animals. In the morning, they discover the intruder and interrogate him. Their purpose is not to get to know the Ugly Duckling. Rather, it is to prove that they are his superiors. "They always referred to themselves as 'we and the world,' for they thought that they were half the world—and the better half at that" (p. 221).

"Can you lay eggs?" [the hen] demanded.

"No," answered the duckling.

"Then keep your mouth shut."

And the cat asked, "Can you arch your back? Can you purr? Can you make sparks?"

"No."

"Well, in that case, you have no right to have an opinion when sensible people are talking." (p. 221)

The duckling, who is seated in a corner of the room, under-standably turns sullen. The behaviors and animal skills about which the cat and hen test him do not belong to his nature. He is, after all, a swan, a cob, though he does not know this as yet. He hasn't an incisive response to their accusatory questions because he does not yet have a sure idea of what or who he is. Then, suddenly, there comes into the duckling's mind a bright memory of the wide world outside of this suffocating hovel, a world of beauty of which the pompous cat and hen have no knowledge. "How lovely it could be outside in the fresh air when the sun shone," he muses. Then "*a great longing* to be floating in the water came over the duckling, and he could not help talking about it" (p. 221, my emphasis). The cat and the hen dismiss what the duckling says as mere prattle. They haven't the imagination or interest to put themselves in the duckling's place or relate to his deepest yearnings. Rather, they accuse him of putting on airs, trying to elevate himself in their eyes, and being ungrateful for all his Creator "has done for [him]" (p. 222). They taunt him with a counterfeit offer of friendship, an offer they say he does not deserve because he has not been truthful with them.

Faced with this ridicule, the Ugly Duckling decides to leave the hut and seek out what he loves most in life. His decision to flee the henyard was a negative choice—he wanted to escape from the pain and anguish that its inhabitants were inflicting upon him. This new decision, however, is not principally about removing himself from a place in which he is unwelcome. Rather, it is a resolve to *join* something greater than himself that is a source of immense joy. He cannot yet name this something, but he knows it exceeds anything the cat and the hen can claim possession of or are capable of imagining.

The Arrival of the Swans

Autumn stretches to winter. Wind and clouds, hail and snow, and bitter cold come. "Just thinking of how cold it was is enough to make one shiver," Andersen writes. "What a terrible time the duckling must have had." Then one evening as the sun is "setting gloriously, a flock of beautiful birds came out from among the rushes" (p. 222). These beautiful birds are swans. The sight of them and the impact of their entrance will forever change the life of the Ugly Duckling.

> Their feathers were so white that they glistened; and they had long, graceful necks. . . . They made a very loud cry, then they spread their powerful wings. They were flying south to a warmer climate, where the lakes were not frozen in the winter. Higher and higher they circled. (p. 222)

The Ugly Duckling is captivated by the grandeur, the magnificence, the sheer loveliness of these birds. His natural relationship to them, of which he is completely unaware, is emblemized by his movements in the lake. These movements mirror the circling of the swans high above him: "The ugly duckling *turned round and round* in the water like a wheel and *stretched his neck* up toward the sky" (p. 222, my emphasis). In both his movement and his posture the duckling mirrors the swans. It is as if he is imagining himself in flight with them. In this moment, the duckling is overcome "by a strange longing," and he screeches "so piercingly that he frightened himself" (p. 222). This reminds the reader of the "great longing" to float in the water that the duckling experienced in the old woman's hut.

> Oh, he would never forget those beautiful birds, those happy birds. When they were out of sight the duckling dove down under the water to the bottom of the lake; and when he came up again he was beside himself. *He did not know the name of those birds or where they were going, and yet he felt that he loved them as he had never loved any other creatures.* He did not envy them. It did not even occur to him to wish that he were so handsome himself. He would have been happy if the other ducks had let him stay in the henyard. (pp. 222–23, my emphasis)

The Ugly Duckling has demonstrated an attraction to beauty earlier in the story, yet his encounter with the swans stirs within him an overwhelming feeling, a desire, a kind of longing that C. S. Lewis in *Surprised by Joy* names with the German word *Sehnsucht*.

Sehnsucht

> Beauty bids all things to itself . . . and gathers everything into itself. . . . It is the great creating cause which bestirs the world and holds all things in existence by the longing inside of them to have beauty.
> —Pseudo-Dionysius, *The Divine Names*

In *Surprised by Joy*, Lewis tells us that an absence of beauty, or more precisely the absence of a love or desire for beauty, was "characteristic of . . . [his] childhood."[18] No building or garden prompted a love of beauty, let alone even an appreciation of it, until one day Lewis's brother "brought into the nursery the lid of a biscuit tin which he had covered with moss and garnished with twigs and flowers so as to make a toy garden . . . That," Lewis continues, "was the first beauty I ever knew. . . . It made me aware of nature—not, indeed, as a storehouse of forms and colors, but as something cool, dewy, fresh, exuberant."[19]

Lewis insists that this "toy garden" and a panoramic view of the Castlereach Hills from the nursery windows kindled within him this kind of "longing" or *Sehnsucht*. "For good or ill, and before I was six years old," Lewis states, *Sehnsucht* made him "a votary of the Blue Flower," a romantic.[20] *Sehnsucht* is much more complex than a mere attraction to something. It entails a sadness due to the absence of that something, as well as a "remembering" and "recovering" of it. *Sehnsucht*'s "object" is something one deeply desires and wishes to be joined to, and yet from which one feels removed.

St. Augustine speaks of a form of love that he calls *frui*, a Latin word. The value of this love is not in any use to which its object can be put. It is, rather, a love for the sheer pleasure or delight an object brings and the transcendent beauty that reaches one through it. Lewis associates *Sehnsucht* with this kind of love. When *Sehnsucht* grips the individual, initially it prompts both anguish over the absence of something vital and joy in the discovery of something for which one is longing. In the end, however, this love and longing set the individual on a "road right out of the self" toward that which is transcendently true, good, or beautiful.[21] For Lewis, as for St. Augustine, this road leads to God.

Yet what can this have to do with Andersen's fairy tale? God is not present in the story, nor need he be. Andersen has written a fairy tale, not a theological tract. Nonetheless, the concept of *Sehnsucht* helps us to identify and understand the emotion that sweeps through the Ugly Duckling when he sees the flock of swans, hears them trumpeting with their "loud cry" of something like joy, and notices in their "glistening white" appearance a beauty that exceeds all the other manifestations of beauty that the Ugly Duckling has ever experienced.

Lewis argues that the exhilaration of *Sehnsucht* "is [not] a state of one's own mind" that can be conjured within oneself. Rather, the joy that *Sehnsucht* signals springs from some hidden place outside one's self. "Only when all your attention and desiring is fixed on something else, whether a distant mountain, or the past, or the gods of Asgard—does the 'thrill' arise," Lewis writes. Even this thrill, this joy, however, "is a by-product. Its very existence presupposes that you desire not it but something other and outer."[22] I have been saying throughout that the Ugly Duckling is a lover of beauty. This love has always borne the potential to take him out of himself. He is quite naturally drawn to the swans because he is of their kind. Yet the beauty that the swans embody points to something beyond him and them that his longing is for.

The Metamorphosis of the Ugly Duckling

The winter passes. "It would be too horrible," we read, "to tell of all the hardship and suffering the duckling experienced. . . . It is enough to know that he did survive." Then spring comes. "The sun shone warmly and the larks began to sing," and the Ugly Duckling feels alive and strong. "He spread out his wings to fly... [and] before he knew it, he was far from the swamp and flying above a beautiful garden." The imagery is paradisical. "The apple trees were blooming and the lilac bushes stretched their flower-covered branches over the water of a winding canal. Everything was so beautiful: so fresh and green" (p. 223).

Into this scene of blossoming beauty and erupting new life, "out of a forest of rushes," a trinity of swans suddenly takes wing. The Ugly Duckling recognizes them, and once more he is overcome by "that strange sadness" (p. 223) and longing. But by now we suspect that this feeling of sadness and longing is not just for the company of the magnificent birds. Andersen does not turn to analysis. Rather, he poetically evokes a sense of *mysterium tremendum* when the duckling's attention is entirely given over to the swans gliding across the water not very far from him. At this moment, we are more keenly aware than at any other place in the story of the subjectivity, the inner conscious thoughts, of the Ugly Duckling. "I shall fly over to them, those royal birds!" he thinks. "And they can hack me to death because I, who am so ugly, dare to approach them! What difference does it make? It is better to be killed by them than to be bitten by the other ducks, and pecked by the hens, and kicked by the girl who tends the henyard; or to suffer through the winter" (pp. 223–24). That czar of children's literature Jack Zipes concludes that the Ugly Duckling "wants to kill himself."[23] How he arrives at such an interpretation I cannot say. All I can say is that he is abysmally wrong.

The poignancy and pathos of the duckling's thoughts at this moment when he is surrounded by beauty and so near to the vibrant presence of the swans cannot be gainsaid. But these thoughts are not suicidal, no more so than the acts of the martyrs of the ancient church who willingly went to their deaths with the hope that their mutilated bodies would be transfigured in the kingdom of heaven. Behind these utterances of the Ugly Duckling there lies a profound history of ascetical and mystical thought that suggests a much different interpretation of the duckling's desire. Plato, St. Paul, St. Augustine, St. John of the Cross, Julian of Norwich, St. Catherine of Sienna, and, nearer to our time, Charles Peguy and T. S. Eliot all are witnesses to a profound truth in the duckling's thoughts.

God utters the truth of the duckling's quest in Peguy's poem "Abandonment":

> He who abandons himself, I love. He who does not abandon
>   himself, I don't love. That's simple enough.
> He who abandons himself does not abandon himself, and he
>   is the only one who does not abandon himself.
> He who does not abandon himself, abandons himself, and
>   is the only one who does abandon himself.[24]

These lines of poetry echo the words Jesus utters in Matthew's gospel: "For whosoever will save his life shall lose it: and whosoever will lose his life for my sake shall find it" (Matt. 16:25).

By no means is the duckling's first wish to die, as Zipes would have us believe. His unstated but otherwise demonstrated wish is to live as he has never lived before, no longer consumed by a self-disgust for what he imagines himself to be but, instead, in communion with the beauty that is before him. His humility and self-abandonment are precisely what the great ascetics and mystics prescribe for union with God.

So the duckling lights on the water and swims "toward the magnificent swans." When they see him, they move in his direction "to meet him." Then the duckling humbly bends his head and whispers, "Kill me." There is a note of self-hatred in this remark. The Ugly Duckling is bound to compare the beauty of the swans to his own repellant self-image. Yet his surprising reflection in the water quickly changes this disposition. And he is "thankful that he had known so much want, and gone through so much suffering, for it made him appreciate his present happiness and the loveliness of everything around him all the more" (p. 224). In the henyard, the old duck with "Spanish blood" had said it was a shame the duckling's mother could not "make him over again" (p. 218). Now, in both a figurative way and a very concrete way, this has happened.

The story could end here. Children, even grown-ups, look for more, however, some key to a more complete understanding of what has happened. Thus Andersen continues that the garden through which the canal winds is filled with children who have "brought bread with them to feed to the swans." Suddenly the youngest child shouts, "Look, there's a new one!" and all of the others clap their hands and run "to tell their parents" (p. 224).

> Cake and bread were cast on the water for the swans. Everyone agreed that the new swan was the most beautiful of them all. The older swans bowed toward him.
> He felt so shy . . . but not proud, for a kind heart can never be proud. (p. 224)

A Tale of Transformation

"The Ugly Duckling" is a tale of transformation, and so it possesses elements in common with other great and familiar fairy tales, such as "Beauty and the Beast" and "The Frog Prince." Yet the duckling's transformation is distinctly different from those of the Beast and the Frog Prince. The Beast and the Frog Prince are human beings who by a curse have been turned into something else and then are turned back magically into their rightful selves. By contrast, the Ugly Duckling was never a duckling but from the very beginning was a swan. The kind of magic that belongs to these stories is not present in Andersen's tale. Yet this absence does not make it inferior, just different—and, I wish to add, more complex and perhaps more satisfying.

It is easy to say that the Ugly Duckling's transformation is inevitable, that all that is needed is for him to mature, and then his true form will be revealed. We might go so far as to say that his genetics predestine him to be a beautiful swan. This is not magic but biology. However, the genius of Andersen's tale is that even when the Ugly Duckling's true nature is revealed and his real identity is exposed, the magic of the story is not undercut. Rather, Andersen's masterly storytelling enables us to believe that something much more wonderful than a physiological maturation has happened. For we have followed the Ugly Duckling through all of his struggles and have watched him bravely triumph over all sorts of adversity.

At the start of the story, he leaves his family and goes out into the wide world to escape ridicule and ostracism. Yet he also commences a difficult journey, an odyssey, that tests his character and makes him every bit as strong, noble, and beautiful inside as he eventually becomes on the outside. Like the Velveteen Rabbit, the Ugly Duckling resists bitterness, jealousy, and resentfulness and instead grows in humility and gratitude for the beautiful world that he has been given. That is why we forget the inevitableness of his physical change and rejoice in the alteration of his appearance as a genuine transformation, a gift from some Higher Power for the duckling's love of beauty, his willingness, even, to abandon himself just to be near to beauty. "He ruffled his feathers and raised his slender neck, while out of the joy in his heart, he thought, 'Such happiness I did not dream of when I was the ugly duckling'" (p. 224).

8

THE GOODNESS OF GOODNESS

The Grimms' "Cinderella" and John Ruskin's The King of the Golden River

Aristotle states in his *Ethics* that the nobility and the happiness of a good individual, of a person whose character is whole and healthy, will be evident, even when that person is living under circumstances that ordinarily inhibit or constrain virtuous behavior. This is because a good individual is in the habit of being virtuous; virtuous behavior is second nature for that individual, more like breathing than choosing. Spinoza sums this up. "Happiness," he explains, "is not the reward of virtue, but virtue itself."[1]

One might reasonably wonder whether we should therefore assume that a bad person can never be happy and a good person never unhappy. This depends on what we mean by happiness. If by happiness we mean the mere felicitous gratification of animal desire and appetite, the sort of emotion that even the most fleeting pleasures bring, then we certainly may say that bad people can be happy. But for Aristotle happiness is something more, something

Tending the Heart of Virtue. Second Edition. Vigen Guroian, Oxford University Press.
© Vigen Guroian 1998, 2023. DOI: 10.1093/oso/9780195384307.003.0009

deeper than that. It is, in fact, altogether different. For Aristotle happiness is part and parcel of living a good and upright life. For that reason, adverse circumstances that would normally make the non-virtuous person unhappy might not have the same effect on someone who is virtuous.

Thomas Aquinas builds on Aristotle. He tells us that there is a transcendental (or supernatural) dimension to happiness. For Aquinas, the realest happiness—"bliss" is the better word—is a taste of beatitude, of divinity itself. Human beings may not be able to be happy all of the time, but happiness that is a taste of the divine or transcendent is possible. Virtue may not guarantee happiness; however, goodness and happiness do go hand in glove. Once again, this is because genuine happiness is not merely a passion, emotion, or mood. It is a state of being.

What does all of this have to do with fairy tales, and especially the two fairy tales discussed in this chapter? I certainly am not suggesting that the inventors of fairy tales owe their knowledge of goodness and happiness to Aristotle and Aquinas. Fairy tales reach back much further in human history than Aquinas or even Aristotle. Yet in the fairy-tale world there are noteworthy characters who exemplify both Aristotle's and Aquinas's understandings of goodness and happiness, characters that endure even the most discomfiting and limiting circumstances and yet do not despair, characters for whom goodness and happiness are, in some real sense, their inheritance. Cinderella, in the Grimms' version of the story, and Gluck, in John Ruskin's Victorian fairy tale *The King of the Golden River*, stand out. And that is the principal reason I have brought these two stories together.

Cinderella and Gluck
Cinderella

The story of Cinderella needs little or no introduction in the English-speaking world, if for no other reason than that Disney has acquainted vast numbers of people with it through both the studio's early animated film and more recent live-action movies. Disney, however, has chosen the seventeenth-century French writer Charles Perrault's version of "Cinderella" for the template of its film productions, not the Grimms'. There are important differences between the two. These differences have to do not only with the course of their respective narratives but with also how Cinderella is depicted.

Perrault's Cinderella is most certainly good, but she also is inherently passive. Things happen *to* or *for* Cinderella. Her triumph is brought about by the unilateral intervention of a fairy godmother who suddenly appears, without explanation, except that she has observed Cinderella in tears. By the mere tap of her magical wand, this fairy godmother provides Cinderella *ex machina* with all that she needs to attend the royal ball and capture the prince's attention. By contrast, the Grimms' Cinderella forges her own destiny, though not without crucial assistance. And she exhibits independence right from the start: "After her mother's death the maiden went every day to visit her grave and weep."[2] Cinderella makes these visits on her own initiative, whereas her father does not once visit his wife's grave. Later she decides on her own, despite the obstacles thrown before her, to go to the royal festival in which a bride will be chosen for the prince.

The assistance that the Grimms' Cinderella does get is the benefaction of a promise. Before her death, Cinderella's mother implores: "Dear child, be good and pious. Then the dear Lord shall always assist you, and I shall look down from heaven and take care of you" (p. 79). The narrator adds that Cinderella "remained good and pious" (p. 79). Furthermore, the strong love that bound mother and child in life continues on after the mother's death. This filial love and piety are at the heart of Cinderella's happiness. These same qualities contrast sharply with the father's shocking forgetfulness of his deceased wife, his callous indifference to the abuse his new wife and her two daughters inflict upon Cinderella, and his own malefic attempts to harm Cinderella.

Gluck

John Ruskin penned *The King of the Golden River* when he was a mere twenty-two years of age, though by this time he already had garnered notice for essays on art and architecture and as a recipient of the Newdigate Prize for poetry. In the summer of 1841, Mr. and Mrs. George Gray visited the Ruskin home with their twelve-year-old daughter, Euphemia (Effie), whom Ruskin later married. In his autobiography, *Praeterita*, Ruskin recalls that during this visit Effie challenged him to compose a fairy tale in the style of the Grimms. He took up the challenge and completed *The King of the Golden River* in just a few weeks. Although he refused to have it printed and never looked with favor upon it, Effie, in collaboration with Ruskin's father, arranged for its publication a decade later. It now stands out as one of the first Victorian fairy tales, and one of the finest.

The protagonist of *The King of the Golden River* is a youth whose name is Gluck (the German word for luck). Gluck has two older brothers, Hans and Schwartz, whom the denizens of the Treasure Valley have nicknamed the Black Brothers on account of their greed and cruelty. Gluck's brothers severely abuse him. They assign him menial and degrading tasks and beat him regularly. "Gluck was not above twelve years old . . . and kind . . . to every living thing. . . . He was usually appointed to the honorable office of turnspit. . . . At other times he used to clean the shoes, floors, and sometimes the plates, occasionally getting what was left on them, by way of encouragement, and a wholesome quantity of dry blows, by way of education" (p. 4). Like Cinderella, Gluck succumbs neither to self-pity nor to bitterness, nor does he turn to revenge. For his goodness and virtue, he, like Cinderella, is raised from poverty to prosperity and from loneliness to happy relations with others.

The resourcefulness with which Cinderella and Gluck hold on to their goodness makes them compelling exemplars for children. Bruno Bettelheim rightly states that "it is not the fact that virtue wins out at the end [in the great fairy tales] which promotes morality," but more precisely "that the hero is . . . attractive" to children, such that children imaginatively identify with the hero, suffer "with the hero through his trials and tribulations," and triumph with the hero "as virtue is victorious."[3] Bettelheim has described in simple terms how the moral imagination is engendered in children and how virtue can be learned through stories.

"Cinderella": A Communion of Love

> Blessed are the poor in spirit, for theirs is the kingdom of heaven. Blessed are those who mourn, for they shall be comforted.
>
> —Matt. 5:3–4

In his unparalleled study of the Grimms' fairy tales, *The Owl, the Raven, and the Dove,* Fr. Ronald Murphy argues that the Grimms' religion—their theology, if you like—adds force and depth of meaning to their story of "Cinderella."[4] The Grimms introduce this religious element at the beginning. Again: "The wife of a rich man fell ill, and as she felt her end approaching, she called her only daughter to her bedside and said, 'Dear child, be good and pious. Then the good Lord shall always assist you, and I shall look down from heaven and take care of you'" (p. 79). Cinderella's affectionate and enduring relationship with her mother may surprise readers who are familiar only with Charles Perrault's story. Perrault neither hints nor suggests that there is a lasting filial devotion of daughter to mother. In the Grimms' fairyland, however, as in the Christian world, birth and death are conjoined, even as they also are in counterpoint to each other. It is not foreordained that after her death Cinderella's mother should drop out of her daughter's life. In other words, in the Grimms' fairyland there exists a communion not only among the living but also between the living and the dead. Death, though it is real and final, is not meaningless, and the dead have a role in the lives of the living. Thus, the dead mother very much belongs to the dramatic action, though the agents of her intent are not angels but creatures of nature—birds that help to secure Cinderella's triumph.

Aschenputtel

The German word that is translated as the name Cinderella is *Aschenputtel*. Its literal meaning, however, is cinder-fool.

Aschenputtel is a double entendre. It may mean fool in the ordinary colloquial sense, but within the Grimms' religious imagination *Aschenputtel* also denotes Cinderella's Christian identity, as when St. Paul declares: "We are fools for Christ" (Cor. 4:10).

Cinderella's family certainly treats her as if she were a fool. They taunt: "Why should the stupid goose be allowed to sit in the parlor with us?" They take away her pretty clothes, dress her in a shabby gray smock, and give her wooden shoes to wear. And they make fun of her appearance: "Just look at the proud princess and how decked out she is!" they exclaim (p. 79). This scene is an allusion to Jesus's scourging before his crucifixion when the soldiers strip him, dress him in a scarlet robe, place a crown of thorns on his head, and mock him, saying, "Hail, King of the Jews."[5]

In biblical faith, ashes (or cinders) are associated with mortality. Yet they also can signify hope for eternal life. "'Ashes to ashes, dust to dust' . . . [A]ll of Christendom covers itself in ashes on Ash Wednesday, at least it did in the Middle Ages, as a reminder of the [mortal] human condition," Fr. Murphy reminds us. Ash Wednesday, however, also heralds the beginning of Great Lent, which leads to the Easter Triduum. This is the final three days of Holy Week, in which occur the Last Supper, Passion, and death of Christ and his triumphant descent into Hades, concluding with the Resurrection on Easter Sunday, the first day of a new week, or the eighth day and first of a new creation. Fr. Murphy adds that "Cinderella is a stand-in for everyman." We may "rejoice with Cinderella over the three days of her predestined rescue by the love of the king's son."[6] For on the day after the festival the prince discovers that Cinderella is the mysterious maiden who has stolen his heart, rescues her from her hostile family, and marries her.

The Grimms' story of *Cinderella* is deeper than Disney's romance or Perrault's moralism. We see that the story they tell draws substantially from the biblical story of salvation. The ashes in which Cinderella sleeps and with which she is covered are an external sign of her inner humility. The servanthood into which she is pressed speaks to the same. This servant status may appear to be entirely coerced. But, I submit, this is not all there is to it. Her humble status is also a marker of her goodness and piety. She accepts her yoke without ire, protestation, or resentment, and she continues to visit her mother's grave and there pray. We may live among "ashes," yet from these ashes there also may arise new life. Bettelheim points out that Perrault's Cinderella chooses "to sleep in the ashes," whereas "there is no such self-debasement in the Brothers Grimm's story; as they tell it, Cinderella *had* to bed down among the ashes."[7] Furthermore, in the Grimms' fairyland it is possible that at the very moment that we are stripped of glory, there may arrive the help of God and his angels—the birds in the Grimms' story—clothing us in rich and golden raiment, as Adam and Eve were "clothed" before the Fall.

A Reproach Unheard and Unheeded

Early in the story, Cinderella's father sets off on horseback to a fair. Before his departure, he asks his stepdaughters and Cinderella what gifts they would like him to bring back for them. The stepsisters request dresses, pearls, and jewels. Cinderella answers: "Just break off the first twig that brushes against your hat on your way home and bring it to me" (p. 80). This is a not-so-guarded reproach. It is as if she pleads, "Father, you so easily forget me. Perhaps this tap on your hat will remind you of me, I who am your only child, flesh of your flesh."

This reproach is as wise as it is brave. It reveals Cinderella's self-possession; in other words, she is not desperate, but has a hold on herself and her situation. The striking contrast between her request and her stepsisters' ought to awaken the father to his shameful neglect of Cinderella. Evidently, it does not. For when, on his journey home, a hazel twig knocks off his hat, the father discovers no special meaning in it other than that he must deliver the branch to Cinderella; he neither comprehends his daughter's distress nor hears her call for help. He hands Cinderella the hazel twig with not a word spoken. Yet Cinderella does not express the disappointment she most certainly must feel. Rather, she courteously thanks her father for his "gift." What Cinderella then does with the hazel twig is a poignant reminder of where her love, her commitment, and her strength lie. Cinderella immediately carries the twig to her mother's gravesite and plants it there. In Celtic and Germanic lore the hazel tree symbolizes wisdom, innocence, and purity, qualities that Cinderella possesses.

A Greening Cross

In his book, Fr. Murphy includes a drawing by Laurence Selim, after an original by Ludwig Emil Grimm, brother of Jacob and Wilhelm. In this image, Cinderella is seated beside a hearth. There is a window above her head and a gothic doorway to her right that opens onto a clear view of her mother's grave. There are three crosses in the drawing: one in the window that the framing forms, a second at the head of the grave, and a cross formed by the hazel tree, with its trunk the upright and its branches the transverse or crosspiece.

However, the wood of the hazel tree is alive, not dead. Life runs through it, life that Cinderella's tears have nourished. Her love may bear a "cross," yet it is a cross of strong love aligned with life. She "wept so hard that the tears fell on the twig and watered it. Soon the twig grew and quickly became a beautiful tree" (p. 80). These are sacred tears. In Christian tradition, tears like these are a gift of the Holy Spirit, beads of prayer offered up to God. Cinderella's tears are the issuances of a blessed sorrow, of a prayerful mourning that reposes in a deep-seated gladness, joy, bliss. "Three times every day Cinderella would go and sit beneath it [the tree] and weep and pray, and each time, a little white bird would also come to the tree." The bird is a dove, *Taube* in German. In all four gospels the Holy Spirit descends upon Christ at his baptism in the form of a dove.[8] Whatever else may be said, the appearances of the small white bird signify the mother's spiritual presence, comfort, and sacred guardianship over Cinderella. "Whenever Cinderella expressed a wish, the bird would throw her whatever she had requested" (p. 80).

The Wedding Feast

> The kingdom of heaven is like a certain king who arranged a marriage for his son; and he sent his servants to call those who were invited to the wedding feast.
>
> —Matt. 22:2–3

> On the third day there was a marriage in Cana of Galilee.
>
> —John 2:1

> Let us rejoice and exult and give him the glory, for
> the marriage of the Lamb has come, and his bride has
> made herself ready; it was granted her to be clothed
> with fine linen, bright and pure.
>
> —Rev. 19:7

Marriage is an important metaphor in the Bible. We glean the depth of its symbolism from these three passages. Matthew associates marriage with the kingdom of heaven. John reports a marriage as the first of seven wonders or miracles that reveal the divine identity of Jesus and herald the advent of the kingdom of God. At the wedding in Cana, Jesus turns the water to wine as he also makes the union of two into one conjugal being. The marriage in Cana foreshadows the eschatological union of the church, as the bride, with Christ, the groom, whose coming the Book of Revelation proclaims.

The Grimms infuse their story with this rich, multivalent symbolism of marriage. They invite us to read the story as a parable, or perhaps even an allegory, of the union of Christ and the church (and on a smaller scale the individual believer's union with Christ). In this respect, the Grimms' decision to introduce the German word *Königssohn* to identify the prince, and not *Prinz*, may be significant. *Königssohn* means literally "son of the king." Jack Zipes, in the translation that I am using, renders *Königssohn* as "prince" in every instance. There isn't a clue of a parabolic or allegorical dimension in this rendering. Most other translators do likewise. Calling him the son of the king, however, points to the prince's relationship with his father, the king, the same who has called the wedding feast in order to find a bride for his son. In other words, *Königssohn* correlates with the symbolism in the biblical passages that I have cited above.

The Grimms make an equally significant word choice to describe the event that the king commands. "In the meantime, the king had decided to sponsor a three-day festival, and all the beautiful young girls in the country were invited so that his son could choose a bride" (p. 80).[9] They use the German word *Fest* here. This is accurately translated as "festival." In every subsequent mention of the event, however, the Grimms employ *Hochzeit*, the German word for marriage or wedding. The word choices of *Königssohn* and *Hochzeit* invite a biblical and theological interpretation of the story. In the Grimms' story, the marital intention is clear from the start. In Perrault's tale, however, the prince announces a ball (the French is *bal*), which is to be a grand social event. Only after the prince has fallen in love with Cinderella is a proclamation issued that the prince intends to marry the young woman to whom the glass slipper belongs.

I have said already that the three-day duration of the wedding carries a religious meaning. But the three-day period also fits with Cinderella's solemn practice of visiting her mother's grave thrice daily. Furthermore, Laurence Selim's inclusion of three crosses in her illustration supports a sacral, indeed Christological significance. The threefold nature of the Godhead—Father, Son, and Holy Spirit—is not far in the background. A trinitarian motif runs deeply within the story: king, the father; prince, the son of the father-king; Holy Spirit, a small white bird or dove.

Danger in the Garden and Revelation in the Home

On each evening of the marriage festival, Cinderella runs home and hides in the garden. Her father suspects that she is the mysterious young woman with whom the prince has danced. On the first night the father takes up an ax and destroys the dovecote wherein he believes Cinderella has hidden herself. On the second night, he fells a pear tree with the same purpose. On all three nights Cinderella stealthily slips back into the house, changes her clothes, and returns safely to her bed of ashes. It is easy to understand why the father, who clearly has favored his stepdaughters, should want to prevent Cinderella from attending the festival. But why such ferocity and homicidal intent? This remains unexplained, though clearly he associates her with the dead, not the living. For as he says to the prince when asked about her, "There's only little Cinderella, my dead wife's daughter" (p. 83).

When the prince arrives at Cinderella's home, the father and stepmother introduce only the two stepdaughters. Each, at her mother's encouragement, cuts off a portion of her foot in order to fit it into the golden slipper. But the prince rejects both when he discovers their deception. Then he asks the father and stepmother if there is another daughter whom they have not shown to him. The father protests that the remaining daughter is his "dead wife's daughter, who's deformed" (the German word is *verbuttes*, which also may be translated "dumb" or "stunted"). The stepmother reinforces this distasteful image of Cinderella. She interjects: "Oh, she's much too dirty and really shouldn't be seen" (p. 83). The prince does not accept any of this. And finally Cinderella is brought forward.

This is a recreation of an important scene in the first book of Samuel. It is when Samuel asks Jesse, the father of David, whether he has another son (1 Sam. 16:1–12), one other than the seven he already has been shown.[10] Samuel is looking for a successor to King

Saul. Jesse demurs. There is his youngest son, the diminutive David. But he is a mere shepherd and could not possibly make an appropriate successor to Saul, the king. Nevertheless, Samuel insists on seeing David, and when David is presented to him, the Lord immediately instructs Samuel to anoint the youth. In the Grimms' story Cinderella's foot fits into the golden slipper: "The prince looked her straight in the face, [and] he recognized the beautiful maiden who had danced with him. 'This is my true bride!' he exclaimed'" (p. 84).

The Bible also reverberates in Cinderella's preparation to meet the prince. "First she [Cinderella] washed her hands and face until they were clean, and then she went and curtsied before the prince" (p. 84). This brings to mind St. Paul's analogy of a wife and the church as bride of Christ. "Husbands, love your wives, as Christ loved the church . . . that he might present the church to himself in splendor, without spot or wrinkle, . . . that she might be holy and without blemish" (Eph. 5:25, 27). Cinderella's bath and curtsey signify her purity and humility, whereas the stepsisters' self-mutilation mocks genuine religious sacrifice.

Conclusion: Why Judgment Belongs to the Story

The first published version of the Grimms' "Cinderella" lacks the ending by which it has since come to be known. This is the scene of Cinderella's entry and departure from the church at her wedding. She enters and exits the church with a dove perched on each of her shoulders. And these doves, though they are not birds of prey, peck out the eyes of the stepsisters, first one eye when they enter the church and then the other eye when they depart.

This scene has been criticized as gratuitously violent and inappropriate for children. Despite this criticism, I believe the scene is valuable and meaningful, though I also am comfortable with the omission of it in the case of the very young. However unsophisticated children may be about justice, they relentlessly look for it in their lives. Indeed, children may well be more able to recognize the poetry in the conclusion of the Grimms' tale than the secular critics who routinely condemn the violence in it. Children exhibit a native moral sense until "sensible" adults quell or inhibit it. But first the ending:

> On the day that the wedding with the prince was to take place, the two false sisters came to ingratiate themselves and to share in Cinderella's good fortune. When the bridal couple set out for the church, the oldest sister was on the right, the younger on the left. Suddenly the pigeons pecked out one eye from each of them. And as they came back from the church later on ... the pigeons pecked out the other eye from each sister. Thus they were punished with blindness for the rest of their lives due to their wickedness and malice. (p. 84)

There are several important questions that this ending raises. The first concerns the violence in it and the second the nature of Cinderella's agency. Maria Tatar objects to the violence as gratuitous and self-indulgent. "The Grimms delight in describing the blood in the shoes of the stepsisters, who try to slice off their heels and toes in order to get a perfect fit," she writes, and points out that "Perrault's Cinderella is, by contrast [to the Grimms'], a model of compassion."[11] While it is true that Perrault's Cinderella forgives her stepsisters, we mustn't overlook the fact that in his story the stepsisters repent of their cruelty: "They threw themselves at her feet, to beg pardon for all the ill treatment they had made her undergo."[12] Whereas in the Grimms' story, the stepsisters remain unrepentant and manipulative to the very end. How, then, is it fair to fault the Grimms' Cinderella for not exhibiting a gesture of forgiveness like that of Perrault's?

Yet Tatar reaches even further. She implies that the Grimms' Cinderella sets up her stepsisters for their punishment. She "invites them to her wedding, where the doves peck out their eyes."[13] But nothing in the text says one way or another that Cinderella has invited the stepsisters to the wedding. It certainly does not indicate that Cinderella wishes them ill; rather, it suggests that the sisters persist in their malicious scheming. Tatar's own translation reads as follows: "On the day of the wedding to the prince, the false sisters came and tried to curry favor with Cinderella and share her good fortune."[14]

Whatever the case may be, it is a stretch to even imply, as Tatar does, that the doves are instruments of Cinderella's will. It is possible, however, that they are supernatural agents. In my college classroom and in teacher and parent seminars I have frequently heard this speculation, prompted by a struggle to make sense of the narrative sequence. How can it be that the stepsisters, who have already had one eye pecked out, do not take precautions to avoid a repetition of the same when they leave the church?

If, however, the doves are supernatural agents, then it is possible to imagine that they are not visible to the stepsisters, who do not belong to the communion of saints of which Cinderella is a member. The Grimms do not offer an explanation, and they needn't do so. Fairy tales are a form of romance fiction in which scenes and actions often cannot be accounted for by ordinary causality, stories where an atmosphere of mystery is deliberately created. "If the writer believes that our life is and will remain essentially mysterious," writes Flannery O'Connor, "if he looks upon us as beings existing in a created order to whose laws we freely respond, then what he sees on the surface will be of interest to him only as he can go through it into an experience of mystery itself . . . because for this kind of writer, the meaning of a story does not begin except at a depth where adequate motivation and adequate psychology and the various determinations have been exhausted."[15]

The goodness of Perrault's Cinderella resides in her compassionate and forgiving nature. The Grimms have something else in mind: judgment. In their story, the stepsisters are not merely jealous or envious. They are genuinely wicked. The same holds for the father and stepmother, who are removed from the story even before it ends. Sometimes, the evil in the hearts of individuals has corrupted nearly the whole of their character. The Grimms' Calvinist faith supports this view.[16] Our modern ears do not welcome this muscular Christianity. Its view of the sinful human condition rubs uncomfortably against an inveterate sentimentality and optimism.

Max Lüthi, in his thoughtful little book *Once Upon a Time: On the Nature of Fairy Tales*, is another critic who has reservations about the ending of the Grimms' "Cinderella." Lüthi, however, is closer to the truth about their purpose and their poetic craft than Tatar, though I question his characterization of the acts of punishment as retribution (or vengeance). "The mutilation of the two stepsisters," he proposes, "is in a way the answer to their self-mutilation: they cut off their toe and heel [in order to fit their feet into the slipper], and then their eyes are taken from them by the forces of retribution; what they themselves began is completed from above."[17]

In other words, the punishment by blinding fits with the stepsisters' self-mutilation. This self-mutilation is sacrilegious and morally repulsive, whereas the physical blindness they must live with for the balance of their lives is religiously and morally meaningful. It is a testimony to the spiritual blindness that prevented them from delighting in the goodness of their stepsister, participating in her happiness, and becoming members of the communion of love to which Cinderella and her mother belong.

Alas, the stepsisters' punishment is a lesson for the reader to ponder. Whose eyes would you choose for yourself? : the stepsisters' of flesh, blind to goodness and beauty, or the prince's spiritual eyes, which from the beginning evidently see the beauty in Cinderella's goodness?

The King of the Golden River: "There Is No Wealth but Life"

Blessed are the meek, for they shall inherit the earth.
—Matt. 5:5

"Inherit the earth," I believe, means the land promised in the psalm: "Thou art my hope, my portion in the land of the living."
—Augustine

I cannot count how many times over the course of my teaching career I admonished my college students that no matter how much they might suspect that an author is influenced by the Bible, it is a hazardous business to try to track down every allusion to it in his or her work. The reason is that in doing so one risks losing a grip on the narrative and missing much of the meaning that is in it. Yet among the writers whose stories I discuss in this book, several knew the Bible extraordinarily well and this knowledge, without question, shaped their literary imagination. John Ruskin is one.

Ruskin's mother, Margaret, was his principal religious influence during his youth. She was an evangelical Christian and taught the Bible to her son daily. Ruskin's biographer Tim Hilton reports: "Every single day of every week, from the time he began to read until he left home to go up to Oxford, Ruskin read two or three chapters [of the Bible] a day with his mother."[18] Consequently, Ruskin committed much of the Bible to memory. And although his religious beliefs underwent several crises and significant changes over his life, Hilton insists that Margaret's early instruction "informs all Ruskin's later writing."[19]

I have said that Ruskin was twenty-two when he composed *The King of the Golden River*. At this time his faith was orthodox and his mother's Bible instruction was fresh in his mind. Thus, it is not surprising that the Bible echoes through its entirety. Occasionally in the classroom I have described *The King of the Golden River* as a mini-Gospel. I have meant that the story is thoroughly imbued with the spirit of the Gospels. Here, however, I do not often pause to identify Ruskin's allusions to the Bible. Instead, I reserve this for the endnotes. My preference is to stick closely to the narrative and let the biblical spirit of *The King of the Golden River* speak for itself.

A Story in Two Parts

Ruskin divides his story into five chapters. Nonetheless, I believe it is helpful to consider it in two parts. The first and by far the shorter introduces all of the principal characters, excepting the King of the Golden River. In this part of the story, we are acquainted with Gluck's humble and generous nature and how he has suffered under his brothers' brutal tyranny. We are introduced to the gnome-like South West Wind, Esquire. And we are given important information about the Treasure Valley: its beauty and fertility, but also the impoverishment of its inhabitants under the greedy domination of the Black Brothers. Last, we hear of a climatic catastrophe that devastates the valley, wreaking even more suffering upon its people. On one level, forces of nature—a wind-driven deluge followed by years of drought—are the causes of this catastrophe. But these events may also be attributed to a supernatural agency, as in Old Testament stories wherein nature delivers and reveals divine judgment and wrath.

The second part of the story tells of the Treasure Valley's restoration and Gluck's role in bringing this about. The King of the Golden River enters early, and quickly we start to suspect that his invisible but evidently providential hand is steering events toward a dénouement in which the Treasure Valley is made fertile again and the people are blessed with a prosperity and happiness they never before have known. Oftentimes my students have speculated whether South West Wind and the King of the Golden River are in some way or another related, or perhaps even the same agent in different manifestations. Children to whom I have read the story have suspected the same. While Ruskin does not overtly connect the two characters and their activities, it is fair to say that their discrete interventions and interactions with Gluck add up to an economy and pedagogy that prepare him to succeed and to become a strong, compassionate, and responsible steward of a renewed Treasure Valley.

Sir Oliver Lodge, in his introduction to an early Everyman's Library edition of Ruskin's writings (1907), describes *The King of the Golden River* as a parable of "Paradise Lost and a Paradise Regained—lost by selfishness, regained by love."[20] Lodge's interpretation is consistent with how Ruskin was taught to read and interpret the Bible: Old and New Testaments in juxtaposition as judgment and selection, prophecy and fulfillment, and, yes, Paradise lost and Paradise regained. Within this framework, Gluck may be seen as a model of the biblical just and righteous man in whom and through whom God labors to redeem the land and its people.

From the start, Ruskin starkly contrasts Gluck's goodness with his brothers' greed, corruption, and cruelty. Hans and Schwartz "lived by farming the Treasure Valley; and very good farmers they were. They killed everything that did not pay for its eating. They shot the blackbirds, ... killed the hedgehogs, ... [and] poisoned the crickets ... They worked their servants without any wages" and kept the corn from market until they could "sell it for twice its value."[21] They were, in sum, wicked men. By contrast, Gluck "was as completely opposed, in both appearance and character, to his seniors as could possibly be imagined." He was "kind in temper to every living thing," and "did not, of course, agree ... with his brothers" (p. 4).

The Mystery and Sublimity of Nature

Recently, Ruskin has gotten attention for his ecological sensibility, notably his conviction that the natural world has an inherent value that transcends any usefulness it might have to human beings and that, therefore, the relationship of human beings to nature ought to be cooperative and not exploitative. The pedagogy of South West Wind and the King of the Golden River ensures that Gluck is prepared to lead in such an ecological project. His stewardship of the Treasure Valley is, in the biblical sense, ordained rather than merely chosen. It is his calling to make the "desert ... blossom abundantly" so that the people may "rejoice with joy and singing" (Is. 35:1–2).

For Ruskin the sempiternal speaks in and through nature. In the fourth volume of his massive work *Modern Painters*, Ruskin explains:

> It seems to me that in the midst of the material nearness of these heavens [the firmament], God means us to acknowledge His own immediate presence as visiting, judging, and blessing us. "The earth shook, the heavens also dropped, at the presence of God" [Ps. 68:8], "He doth set his bow in the cloud" [Gen. 9:13], and thus renews, in the sound of every drooping swathe of rain, His promise of everlasting love. "In them hath He set a tabernacle for the sun" [Ps. 19:4]. ... As the Creator of all the worlds, and Inhabitor of eternity, we cannot behold [Him] ... , but as judge of the earth and the preserver of men, those heavens are indeed His dwelling place. "Swear not at all, neither by heaven; for it is God's throne; nor by the earth, for it is His footstool." [Matt. 5:34–35][22]

Ruskin's portrayals of landscape and skyscape in *The King of the Golden River* are among his earliest expressions of this vision of nature's numinosity. Here is a sample from the description of Hans's climb up the mountain as he encounters an unexpected glacier on the way to the headwaters of the Golden River.

> The ice was excessively slippery, and out of all its chasms came wild sounds of gushing water; not monotonous or low, but changeful and loud, rising occasionally into drifting passages of wild melody, then breaking off into short, melancholy tones, or sudden shrieks, resembling those of human voices in distress. The ice was broken into thousands of confused shapes, but none, Hans thought, like the ordinary forms of splintered ice. There seemed a curious *expression*

about all their outlines—a perpetual resemblance to living features, distorted and scornful. Myriads of deceitful shadows, and lurid lights, played and floated about and through the pale blue pinnacles, dazzling and confusing the sight of the traveller; while his ears grew dull and his head giddy with the constant gush and roar of the concealed waters. . . . [I]t was with a new oppressive feeling of panic terror that he leaped the last chasm, and flung himself, exhausted and shuddering, on the firm turf of the mountain. (p. 17)

Such writing is a far cry from naturalism. It is much more akin to what Russell Kirk describes as storytelling of the "uncanny" and "preternatural" kind, in which the bias is quite the opposite of naturalism.[23] It is a kind of writing that strives to build up the religious and moral imagination. It is related to the romanticism of William Wordsworth, who in "Tintern Abbey" celebrates "a presence that disturbs me with the joy / Of elevated thoughts; a sense sublime / Of something far more deeply interfused, / whose dwelling is the light of setting suns, / And the round ocean, and the living air, / And the blue sky, and in the mind of man." Except in Ruskin's passage the "presence" disturbs not with joy but with fear and dread. Here the elements and forces of nature are not only emblematic of an all-encompassing preternatural reality but also revealing of divine judgment and Hans's haunted and bent soul, tormented by that judgment. Dread and terror overwhelm him, much as water surges and drowns, ice cuts and freezes, and rocks bruise and crush.

A Knock at the Door and the Beginning of a Pedagogy

He [Abraham] looked up and saw three men standing over against him. On seeing them, he hurried from his

THE GOODNESS OF GOODNESS

tent to meet them. Bowing low, he said, "Sirs, if I have deserved your favor, do not go past your servant without
a visit. Let me send for some water so that you may
bathe your feet; and rest under this tree while I fetch a
little food so that you may refresh yourselves...." They
said, "Very well, do as you say."

—Gen. 18:2–5

I was hungry and you gave me food, I was thirsty
and you gave me drink, I was a stranger and you
welcomed me.

—Matt. 25:35

Extend hospitality to strangers.

—Rom. 12:13

In the Christian religious and moral imagination, hospitality
is above all else a fervent reception of God and Christ into one's
life, lived out in deeds of kindness and generosity, especially toward strangers, the most vulnerable, and the least comely. In the
twenty-fifth chapter of the Gospel of Matthew, which I have cited
above, Christ goes on to instruct: "As you did it for least of these
my brethren, you did it for me" (Matt. 25:40).

The story of Abraham's welcome to the three "angelic" strangers
at his encampment by the Oak of Mamre was an important subject
of the earliest Christian art and preaching. We find an expression
of the latter in St. Ambrose of Milan of the fourth century:

Hospitality is a good thing, and it has its recompense: first of all the
recompense of human gratitude and then, more importantly, the
divine reward. In this earthly abode we are all guests ... Let us be
careful not to be discourteous or neglectful in receiving guests, lest
we be denied entrance into the dwelling place of saints at the end
of our life.[24]

Ruskin introduces this theme of hospitality at the start of *The King of the Golden River*. Gluck has been left alone at home to mind a roast that is cooking in the fireplace, when his watch is interrupted by a mysterious knock at the door. It was "a double knock . . . yet heavy and dull, as though the knocker had been tied up—more like a puff than a knock. 'It must be the wind,' said Gluck; 'nobody else would venture to knock double knocks at our door.' No, it wasn't the wind: there it came again very hard" (p. 5). This is not entirely true. In a real, though peculiar, way, it *is* the wind that knocks at Gluck's door, personified, however, as a strange gentleman whose name is South West Wind Esquire.

Gluck's brothers have left him with strict instructions not to let anyone into the home or share the mutton with anyone. Nevertheless, just before South West Wind knocks at the door, Gluck thinks: "What a pity . . . my brothers never ask any body to dinner. I'm sure, when they've got such a nice piece of mutton as this, and nobody else has got so much as a piece of dry bread, it would do their hearts good to have somebody to eat it with" (p. 5). This bids the reader to ask: Have Gluck's thoughts brought South West Wind to the house, or has South West Wind selected Gluck for some special reason? There are no sure answers to these questions. Yet it soon is evident that South West Wind's arrival is *not* accidental.

At first, Gluck is hesitant to let South West Wind in. However, the stranger's unusual appearance intrigues him. It is an appearance that is bound to catch the attention of a child. "He had a very long nose, slightly brass-coloured, and expanding towards its termination into a development not unlike the lower extremity of a key bugle. His cheeks were very round, and very red . . . His eyes twinkled merrily through long silky eyelashes, his mustaches curled twice round like a cork-screw on each side of his mouth...He was about four feet six in height, and wore a conical pointed cap of nearly the same altitude ... His doublet was prolonged" in the shape of a "swallow tail" that was covered almost entirely by "an enormous black, glossy looking cloak" (p. 5). Gluck is fascinated by the stranger and pities him as well. So after some persuasion from the stranger, Gluck invites him in. Once South West Wind has entered the house, he drags Gluck through an ordeal—a test of Gluck's character, perhaps?—which heightens the boy's anxiousness that Hans and Schwartz might arrive at any moment and discover his transgressions.

Meanwhile, unceasing streams of water cascade from the little man's doublet and conical cap onto the hearth and floor, and make puddles that will leave the sure sign that someone other than Gluck has been in the house. Then the stranger makes a request. " 'The mutton looks very nice,' said the old gentleman at length. 'Can't you give me a little bit? . . . I'm very hungry. . . . I've had nothing to eat yesterday, nor to-day " (p. 7). Again, Gluck is moved to remedy his guest's discomfort. In defiance of his brothers' instructions, he graciously prepares to give South West Wind his portion of the roast. Suddenly Hans and Schwartz arrive home, inebriated and hot-tempered.

Gluck has been kind and generous. His good and sympathetic character, no doubt forged and refined, at least in part, by the suffering he has endured at the hands of his brothers, is proved. He has acted hospitably in uncertain and terrifying circumstances. Hans and Schwartz are of a different disposition. They will not listen to or tolerate South West Wind's pleas for food and shelter. After an altercation that magically lands both brothers disarmed on the floor in a corner of the room, South West Wind announces his departure. More important, he hints of his future intentions: "Gentlemen, I wish you a very good morning. At twelve tonight, I'll call again; after such a refusal of *hospitality* as I have just experienced, you will not be surprised if that visit is the last I ever pay" (p. 90, my emphasis).

By morning, a storm has nearly destroyed the brothers' home. Only Gluck's bedroom is left with a roof. Indeed, the storm has reduced the Treasure Valley to "one mass of ruin and desolation" (p. 10). The trees, fruit, and livestock have been washed away and all that is left is a wasteland of sand and mud. The favorable winds that always had dependably brought rain to the Treasure Valley visit no more, and drought carries on from one year to the next.

A Promise of Gold

No longer able to live by farming, the Black Brothers flee the Treasure Valley and move to the city. They have exhausted their wealth, all but for some "old-fashioned pieces of gold plate" (p. 11). Rather than pursue an honest trade of goldsmithing, however, they contrive to mix copper into their gold to swindle their customers. Eventually, just one piece of gold remains, a mug that belongs to Gluck, which he treasures. Hans and Schwartz order Gluck to melt it down, and the boy obeys. As the mug is melting, Gluck peers out the window at the mountain range that towers over the Treasure Valley and from which the Golden River descends. The Golden River had gotten that name because when the sun shone upon it, "it looked like a shower of gold" (p. 3). Gluck muses wistfully how wonderful it would be if the river really were gold.

The boy's thought is interrupted by a "metallic" voice that issues from the molten gold: "No it wouldn't, Gluck." It is the King of the

Golden River. The king asks Gluck to pour him out of the crucible. Instead of molten metal, out cascades "a little golden dwarf, about a foot and a half high" (p. 13) The dwarf again warns Gluck that it would not be at all good if the river really were gold. The dwarf tells Gluck that his actions have released him from the spell of a far stronger, maleficent king. Then, like the genie of Arabian lore, he offers to help Gluck. "What I have seen of you, and your conduct to your wicked brothers, renders me willing to serve you; therefore attend to what I tell you. Whoever shall climb to the top of that mountain from which you see the Golden River issue, and shall cast into the stream at its source, three drops of holy water, for him, and for him only the river shall turn to gold. But no one failing in his first, can succeed in a second attempt; and if any one shall cast unholy water into the river, it will overwhelm him, and he will become a black stone" (p. 15).

At first look, this testimony, this prophecy, would appear to contradict the king's declaration that it would not be a good thing for the river to become real gold. Later, we learn that the gold the king promises is not the element of that name. Rather, gold is a metaphor for the luxuriant and bountiful life that the river will restore to the Treasure Valley when its course is redirected to run through the region. Clive Wilmer explains that in *The King of the Golden River* "the source of value is not gold—that is a token—but light and water, the sources of life."[25] The Golden River will course through Treasure Valley like the river of "the water of life" that runs through the New Jerusalem and makes a garden of it (Rev. 22:1).

The king's admonition carries a moral meaning also. For if the river were to become real gold, it might be a "golden calf," a false god, an idol that corrupts the valley's inhabitants. "Many joys may be given to men which cannot be bought for gold," Ruskin observes in *Unto the Last*, "and many fidelities found in them which cannot be rewarded with it... THERE IS NO WEALTH BUT LIFE... including all the powers of love, of joy, and of admiration.... [T]hat man is richest who, having perfected the functions of his own life ..., has also the widest helpful influence, both personal, and by means of his possessions, over the lives of others."[26] Gluck becomes the bearer of such a private and public virtue, an ensign of this wisdom.

Trial and Pedagogy on the Mountain

A wicked man earns deceptive wages,
but one who sows righteousness
gets a sure reward.
He who is steadfast in righteousness
will live,
but he who pursues evil will die.
—Prov. 11:18–19

The King of the Golden River had intended that Gluck alone hear his promise. Unhappily, Gluck informs his brothers of what the king has told him. We could attribute Gluck's error in judgment to a naive familial love, a love that he bears for his brothers in spite of the cruelty with which they have treated him. Hans and Schwartz have no such love for each other, however, or for Gluck. After hearing Gluck's story, they turn on each other and come to blows. The constable drags Schwartz off to prison. Hans successfully conceals himself and quickly makes off to seek his fortune on the mountain.

When, after a time, Hans does not return, Schwartz, now free and callously indifferent to his brother's fate, sets off to seek his own fortune on the mountain. He, like Hans, encounters obstacles of un-forgiving terrain, a jagged glacier, and spectral occurrences. And he, like Hans, though he makes it to the headwaters of the Golden River and successfully deposits holy water into the river, is not granted the promised reward, but is changed instead into a black stone.

Meanwhile, Gluck patiently awaits the return of his brothers. When it is evident that they will not be returning, he decides to "try his [own] fortune with the Golden River." Though he suspects that the worst has happened and that his brothers have been turned into stones, he reassures himself that the king, after all, had "looked very kind" and "would not turn him into a black stone" (p. 21). Thus it comes to pass that all three brothers journey up the mountain, and all three make it to the headwaters of the Golden River; but only one, Gluck, succeeds in this endeavor and is not turned into a black stone.

There are important reasons Hans and Schwartz are turned into black stones while Gluck not only survives but is granted the reward that the King of the Golden River has promised. On their climbs, both Hans and Schwartz meet three individuals who are dying of thirst and beg for a drink. Each brother denies drink to the supplicants in his path. Hans encounters a dog, a small child, and an old man, in that order: Schwartz a child, an old man, and a spec-tral presence of his own brother Hans. As if these refusals were not proof enough of the brothers' wicked hearts, the environment also testifies to the same. It grows more severe and threatening with each despicable denial. For example, when Schwartz refuses to let the spectral presence of his brother drink from his flask, swordlike flashes of lightning strike everywhere around him, the rays of the setting sun turn blood red, and a darkness descends over him that forebodes his transformation into a black stone.

On his trek up the mountain, Gluck, like his brothers before him, loses all his provisions, except for his flask of holy water. Unlike his brothers, but like the Good Samaritan in the Gospel of Luke (Luke 10: 25–37), however, Gluck stops to help not one but three strangers in distress. He gives a young boy, an old man, and a dying dog a drink from his flask. His brothers' refusals to help the weak and the sick were followed by terrifying occurrences on the mountain. In this case, the stony landscape comes alive with "all kinds of sweet flowers . . . bright green moss, with pale pink flowers, and soft bellied gentians, more blue than the sky at its deepest, and pure white lilies." Butterflies dart about, and the sky sends down "such pure light" that Gluck rejoices (p. 22).

More Mysterious Happenings on the Mountain

All this while, the King of the Golden River has not shown himself, at least not in his familiar shape or form. Like the goddess Athena in *The Iliad* and *The Odyssey*, he has, however, evidently appeared in a variety of guises, as the human beings and animals that all three brothers encounter. He has tested Hans and Schwartz, and they have miserably failed their trials. Mountains in the Bible often bear a sacred meaning. We read in Isaiah: "'They shall not hurt or destroy in all my holy mountain,' says the Lord" (Is. 65: 25). On mountains, theophanies occur and revelations are given. Due to the corruptness of their lives, Hans and Schwartz have no business on this holy mountain. Their actions on it only go to prove their unworthiness and depravity. Their younger brother is a different matter.

After the dying dog consumes the remaining drops of holy water from his flask, Gluck gives up all hope for success. Yet his fear that he has forfeited the promised gold is unfounded, for he has acted com-passionately. The moment the beast finishes drinking, it springs up, stands on its hind legs, and transforms into the King of the Golden River. The king scolds Gluck: "Why didn't you come before ... instead of sending those rascally brothers of yours?" (p. 22); however, the king is not displeased with Gluck. He stoops down and plucks a lily growing at the boy's feet.[27] On its leaves cling "three drops of dew." The king shakes these dewdrops into Gluck's flask and instructs Gluck to cast them "in the river and [then] descend on the other side of the mountain into the Treasure Valley" (p. 23).[28]

Initially, when Gluck pours the dewdrops into the river, he is disappointed because it does not turn to gold. But what he does not know is that the river will take a new path underground down the mountain into the Treasure Valley, where it will replenish the depleted earth and nourish verdant new life.

A Moral Measurement

When I taught *The King of the Golden River* in the college classroom, I often invited the students to stop and consider just what Ruskin is up to by juxtaposing chronologically the three episodes of the brothers on the mountain. This juxtaposition obviously highlights the differences between Hans's and Schwartz's responses and Gluck's to the individuals they meet. More important, however, Ruskin invites a moral measurement of these responses.

Suzanne Rahn cites an unpublished faux epilogue to *The King of the Golden River* attributed to Ruskin. In it he ponders how things might have turned out had Hans, Schwartz, and Gluck responded differently to the entreaties of their beleaguered supplicants. First,

Ruskin points out that the two older brothers were approached by individuals who, in their order of appearance, from first to last, ought to have "excit[ed]" increased "pity." Yet neither brother gives assistance, not even to the third petitioner, for Hans the old man and for Schwartz his own brother. Next Ruskin poses this question: what if, for argument's sake, Hans and Schwartz had rejected the first two appeals but "yielded to the last" and strongest appeal? He proposes that in this instance Hans and Schwartz might not have perished, though they still would have been denied the promised reward"[29]

But how about Gluck? In his case, the three supplicants had, in order, from first to last, "diminishing" moral claims on him; the last of those who approach him is a dog, a mere animal. Nonetheless, Gluck assists all three. For this reason, Gluck received "the full reward." Nevertheless, what if Gluck had not stopped for the dog? In that case, Ruskin concedes that one might reasonably argue that Gluck should still have "received the reward," since a beast has less of a moral claim on us than a human being. But Ruskin rejects this common view. Instead, he interjects a radically different moral calculus. He maintains that had he not stopped for the dog, Gluck "would not have succeeded in his design, although his previous charities might have preserved him from death."[30]

Rahn describes this as a demand for "something like perfection... of him who would save others as well as himself."[31] Another way of stating the matter is that Ruskin prescribes a perfectionist ethic.[32] Biblical pronouncements can certainly be marshaled to support such a perfectionist ethic. "I am the Lord who brought you out of the land of Egypt, to be your God; you shall therefore be holy, for I am holy," says the Old Testament (Lev. 11:45). And in the

New Testament, Jesus commands: "You ... must be perfect, as your heavenly Father is perfect" (Matt. 5:48). Nor should the beatitudes of the Sermon on the Mount be forgotten. These biblical passages and more are most certainly in the background of the ethic Ruskin embraces, an ethic that requires uncompromising benevolence toward the poor and that honors in every case the rule that life must be valued above all other goods. Ruskin proffers this ethic as an alternative to the destructive instrumentalization of life to which he believed the industrialization of society was giving rise. Gluck, who exemplifies this radical ethic, is that "righteous man who walks in his integrity" (Prov. 20:7). Gluck is a worthy heir to the restored Treasure Valley because he is the man who pursues "righteousness and kindness" and, for that, "will find life and honor" (Prov. 21:21).

A Patriarch's Entrance

The Lord said unto Abram ..., Lift up now thine eyes, and look from the place where thou art. ... For all the land which thou seest, to thee I will give it, and to thy seed for ever. And I will make thy seed as the dust of the earth ... Arise, walk through the land in the length of it and in the breadth of it; for I will give it unto thee. Then Abram removed his tent, and came and dwelt in the plain of Mamre, which is in Hebron.

—Gen. 13:14–18

Thou openest thine hand, and satisfiest the desire of every living thing.

—Ps. 145:16

The concluding paragraph of *The King of the Golden River* brings to life the biblical theme of the righteous man and his rewards. The description of Gluck's return to the Treasure Valley carries a cadence that resembles the rhythm of the King James Bible:

> And thus the Treasure Valley was a garden again, and the inheritance, which had been lost by cruelty, was regained by love. And Gluck went in, and dwelt in the valley, and the poor were never driven from his door; so that his barns became full of corn, and his house of treasure. And, for him, the river had, according to the dwarf's promise, become a River of Gold. (p. 23)

Like Abraham, Gluck enters the promised land. His goodness, the fullness of his righteousness, is his special gift to the Treasure Valley and its inhabitants. In Flannery O'Connor's short story "The Lame Shall Enter First," a youth, far removed from the goodness of Cinderella or Gluck, nonetheless speaks a biblical wisdom when he says of the atheist social worker Sheppard: "I don't care if he's good or not. He ain't right."[33] Of Cinderella and Gluck, however, we are able to say that they are not only good but also right, right with God—that is, righteous.

Of Mercy and Wrath

Gluck speaks up when the King of the Golden River appears on the mountain. It is a token of his goodness and an indication of his youthful credulity that Gluck scolds the king for having turned his brothers into black stones: "Oh dear me! . . . have you really been so cruel?" The king responds, "Cruel! . . . [T]hey poured unholy water into my stream: do you suppose I'm going to allow that?" Gluck does not understand. "'Why,' said Gluck, 'I am sure, sir—your majesty, I mean—they got the water out of the church font.'" The king does not bring up the devious and illicit means by which Hans and Schwartz got the holy water. His concern is with how they used the holy water, or, rather, that it was not used when it was needed most. He responds, "The water which has been refused to the cry of the weary and dying, is unholy, though it had been blessed by every saint in heaven; and the water which is found in the vessel of mercy is holy, though it had been defiled with corpses" (p. 22).

In traditional Christian teaching, the most important use of holy water is for the sacrament of baptism. The water of the baptismal font is blessed and holy oil is added to it so that it might become the waters of the Jordan River in which Jesus was baptized, in order that the Holy Spirit, who was there at the Jordan, might bless it and the one who is baptized in the font. Ruskin alludes to baptism throughout his story by his repetition of the water motif. The king's prescription that three drops of holy water must be poured into the headwaters of the Golden River specifically symbolizes baptism in the name of the Trinity.

Ruskin, however, deviates from dogmatic teaching when he suggests that the misuse of holy water or the ill will of its user can affect its spiritual power and render it unholy. Theologically speaking, holy water cannot be made unholy. Ruskin's contradistinction of holy water and unholy water is not theologically correct, but it serves his moralistic purpose. And this is perfectly fine for a fairy tale. Yet there is more to be said about this. Ruskin borrows from St. Paul: "What if God, willing to shew his wrath, and to make his power known, endured with much long-suffering the vessels of wrath fitted to destruction: And that he might make known the riches of his glory on the vessels of mercy, which he had afore prepared unto glory" (Rom. 9: 22–23). However, his invocation of "vessel of mercy" and the meaning he gives to it depart from St. Paul's. Paul contrasts "vessels of mercy" and "vessels of wrath" in order to clarify just how and by what means God accomplishes salvation for those whom he chooses (or elects). Paul's speech is theological and functions within a broader discussion of how God saves both Jews and Gentiles. Only in a secondary sense is Paul concerned with morality.

Ruskin's principal interest is moral. Due to his goodness, Gluck becomes a vessel of mercy, while because of their wickedness, we may say that Hans and Schwartz become vessels of wrath—though Ruskin does not use that phrase. By his goodness, Gluck brings blessings upon himself and the whole of the Treasure Valley, while because of their wickedness, Hans and Schwartz are cursed. Indeed, they are turned into black stones, and to this day, in the evening, as the sun sets, they may be seen enveloped by waters that "howl mournfully" (p. 23). Unlike Cinderella's stepsisters, the brothers do not remain living beings. They become inert objects, like Lot's wife who, when she turned to look back at Sodom and Gomorrah, was changed into a pillar of salt (Gen. 19:26).

An inert object cannot learn from mistakes, repent, or hold out hope for the future. The severity and finality of the brothers' punishment are consistent with how the evangelical Christianity of Ruskin's upbringing stood on salvation and damnation. But *The King of the Golden River* is, after all, a fairy tale. For this reason, I say again, we ought to be careful not to read it through strict dogmatic or biblical lenses. It is unlikely a child will do so, and the child should not be encouraged to. In the mind and moral imagination of a child, Gluck's brothers get what they deserve. They are cruel and wicked men, and they are punished for that. Justice is rightly meted out. Good rightly triumphs over evil, and the inhabitants of the Treasure Valley live happily ever after. The Treasure Valley became a garden again, and what was lost by cruelty was regained by love. And that is as it should be in a fairy tale.[34]

9

OBEDIENCE AND THE PATH TO PERFECTION IN GEORGE MACDONALD'S *THE WISE WOMAN*

A Double Story

> When I say the book is full of truth, I do not mean either truth of theory or truth in art, but something deeper and higher—the realities of our relations to God and man and duty . . . If a man will not have God, he never can be rid of his weary and hateful self.
>
> —*George MacDonald, Preface to Letters from Hell,*
> *by V. A. Thisted*

In Chapter 2 I brought up Maurice Sendak's strong dislike for Carlo Collodi's *Pinocchio*. Sendak has similar things to say about the subject of this chapter, George MacDonald's *The Wise Woman*. *Pinocchio* and *The Wise Woman* depict ill-behaved children who resist discipline and struggle to be responsible moral persons. Sendak is troubled by Collodi's and MacDonald's tough-minded

Tending the Heart of Virtue. Second Edition. Vigen Guroian, Oxford University Press.
© Vigen Guroian 1998, 2023. DOI: 10.1093/oso/9780195384307.003.0010

views on human nature, though this always has struck me as a little odd coming from the author of *Where the Wild Things Are*.

Whatever the case may be, Sendak describes *The Wise* Woman as "a harsh, angry tale whose magic, unlike the crystal-clear fantasy of MacDonald's earlier stories, is black, erratic, and appears finally to be nearly impotent against the forces of evil." "There is a falling off," he adds, "not of creative power, but rather of . . . faith in moral power."[1] And he warns that those who have admired the character Irene in *The Princess and the Goblin* "might very well be put off by the harshness" of *The Wise Woman*.[2]

Although this is not my opinion, one might just as well argue that Irene is too sugar-sweet to be an attractive or believable character. I cannot imagine how Sendak would disagree that most if not all children manifest the kinds of poor behavior that the two young female protagonists in *The Wise Woman*, the princess Rosamond and the shepherd girl Agnes, exhibit. Moreover, MacDonald does not pretend that his story is "realistic." He has written *The Wise Woman* as a parable, and in a parable an author is at liberty to overstate traits of character, exaggerate the dramatic action, and ignore common rules of narration in order to teach important lessons about human behavior.

C. S. Lewis disagrees with Sendak. He ranks *The Wise Woman* among MacDonald's greatest fantasies, along with "*Phantastes*, the *Curdie* books, *The Golden Key*, and *Lilith*."[3] I side with Lewis. In *The Wise Woman* MacDonald does not lose "faith in moral power." Quite the contrary: his story probes, as few children's stories do, the deeply rooted sources of morality. It casts a penetrating light on the psychological and spiritual complexity of personal morality and the difficult struggle to be virtuous. Far from proving our impotence against evil, *The Wise Woman* affirms our shared human capacity to be good. Yet MacDonald is not sanguine about this. He demonstrates that within all of us there are also deep-seated forces that fight against our better selves.

Early in the story, both Rosamond and Agnes come under the discipline of the mysterious Wise Woman. The two girls have vastly different upbringings, but both exhibit the same destructive propensities of egocentricity, self-satisfaction, and pride. As MacDonald puts it, both think of themselves as a very special "Somebody." Both resist correction and reform. The girls' parents are, in their own fashion, enablers of their daughters' selfishness and self-centeredness. The Wise Woman intervenes in the girls' lives with the intent to correct their bad habits and draw out from them what is best in them. Her uncanny interventions intertwine the lives of these two young girls, though throughout most of the story the girls are unaware that their destinies are interlaced.

The Wise Woman *as Parable*

Before I enter fully into the stream of the narrative, it helps to discuss four keys to the story's meaning. The first, as I have mentioned already, is that *The Wise Woman* is a parable. Like Jesus's parables, it is a story about the path to blessedness and inheritance of the kingdom of heaven. Most commentators have either ignored or not looked seriously enough at the parabolic character of *The Wise Woman*. Thus, for example, these commentators sometimes leave their readers with the mistaken impression that MacDonald commends to parents even the severest of the Wise Woman's tough disciplinary measures.

The Wise Woman certainly is a stern taskmistress. She kidnaps Rosamond and Agnes, then subjects both of them to life-threatening encounters with wild beasts, after which she shuts them up alone in her cottage for days without evident rationale, and submits them to trials that in the real world would unquestionably be extreme. If, however, we view *The Wise Woman* as a religious parable, nothing in it need be taken as a literal prescription for childrearing. Indeed, when it was first published in 1875, the story was subtitled *A Parable*.[4] The *Oxford English Dictionary* has defined a parable as a "fictitious narrative (usually something that might naturally occur) by which moral or spiritual relations are figured [metaphorically represented] or set forth."[5] MacDonald believed that parables are especially suited to explore not just the psychological but, more important, the moral and spiritual aspects of human existence. "Parables are stories, tales, incidents . . . by which we are to measure the action of our lives," he writes.[6] "There is a thing wonderful and admirable in the parables [of Jesus], not readily grasped, but specially indicated by the Lord himself." Parables are not intelligible to the mere intellect. They are "addressed to the conscience and . . . to the will . . . They are strong and direct but not definite. They are not meant to explain anything, but to rouse a man to the feeling, 'I am not what I ought to be, I do not the thing I ought to do!'"[7]

Gisela Kreglinger correctly points out that MacDonald understood how parables "invite the hearer to participate" in their stories and in that way figure out the meaning in them.[8] At the beginning of *The Wise Woman*, MacDonald invites the reader to do just that. "There was a certain country where things used to go rather oddly," the narrator reports. And in this country you could never tell whether it was going to rain or hail, or whether or not the milk was going to turn sour. It was impossible to say whether the next baby would be a boy or girl, or even, after he was a week old, whether he would wake sweet-tempered or cross.[9]

Indeed, this country was so peculiar, the narrator continues,

> that my reader must not be too much surprised when I add the amazing fact, that most of its inhabitants, instead of enjoying the things they had, were always wanting the things they had not. (p. 4)

This is a literary exaggeration, and a humorous one at that, which indicates the precise opposite of what is premised. In other words, the world of *The Wise Woman* is not different from but rather very much like our own. For in our world, also, one cannot foretell with certainty whether it will rain or hail tomorrow or the next day, or whether a newly born infant will grow up to have a mild or tempestuous temperament. And we would be foolish if we failed to recognize that in our world, much as in the world of *The Wise Woman*, discontentedness, envy, and greed are found most everywhere. In other words, the ordinary course of events in MacDonald's imaginary country and in our world are very much alike.

Wisdom

> Howbeit we speak wisdom among them that are perfect; yet not the wisdom of this world ... But we speak the wisdom of God in a mystery.
>
> —1 Cor. 2:6–7

Wisdom is the second key to the meaning of *The Wise Woman*. The Wise Woman is one of MacDonald's special female characters who possess preternatural powers, like the great-great-grandmother in *The Princess and the Goblin*. The reputation of the Wise Woman's wisdom has reached even the ears of the king and queen, who are desperate to rein in their daughter Rosamond's wild mood swings and the fits of uncontrollable rage that inflict havoc upon the entire royal household. So the king summons the Wise Woman to the palace.

"In some countries . . . [the Wise Woman] would have been called a witch, but that would have been a mistake, for she never did anything wicked, and had more power than any witch could have" (p. 7). Indeed, the power, the wisdom, of the Wise Woman is not the wisdom of this world. Her wisdom is of a biblical pedigree: it is creative and redemptive. The Christian faith associates this sort of wisdom with holiness and in particular with Christ himself (1 Cor. 1:23–24). But wisdom often assumes a feminine form (the Greek word for wisdom is *sophia*), and in the Bible as well as in Jewish and Christian literature it is sometimes personified that way. "Blessed is a man who finds wisdom," the Book of Proverbs proclaims. "Nothing evil will withstand her . . . length of days and years of life are in her right hand . . . Righteousness proceeds from her mouth. And she carries law and mercy upon her tongue. Her ways are good ways. And all her paths are in peace. She is a tree of life to all who cleave to her" (Prov. 3:13, 15, 17–20).[10] The Wise Woman is not Christ, nor is she a goddess. She is, however, a holy figure not unlike the personification of wisdom in the Book of Proverbs.

Royal Sons and Daughters: The Meaning of Being a Real Princess

The third key to the meaning of *The Wise Woman* also has biblical connotations. It is a theme we have come across in *The Princess and the Goblin* as well: membership in the royal household of God. Near the end of the story, just before the Wise Woman submits Rosamond to the three tests that will determine whether she has genuinely changed for the better, she instructs Rosamond about what a "real princess" is.

> Nobody can be a real princess—do not imagine you have yet been anything more than a mock one—until she is a princess over herself, that is, until, when she finds herself unwilling to do the thing that is right, she makes herself do it. . . . Whoever does what she is bound to do, be she the dirtiest little girl in the street, is a princess. (pp. 82–83)[11]

Here, as in *The Princes and the Goblin*, MacDonald invests this idea of a princess with a moral and spiritual meaning that applies to our common humanity. A true princess has mastery over herself and the discipline to do what is right, especially when she is pulled by her passions or desires to behave differently. To be a true princess transcends all of the inherited worldly stations that carry this title, and so it is possible for even the lowliest and most impoverished individual to be a real princess. To be a real princess is to humbly accept, embrace, and try to live up to the spiritual vocation of a child of God—or, as the New Testament states, to be a member of God's royal household, "a royal priesthood, an holy nation, a peculiar people" (1 Peter 2:9). "Until our outward condition is that of sons royal, sons divine," McDonald argues, "so long as the garments of our souls ... are mean—torn and dragged and stained; ... we are but getting ready one day to creep from our chrysalises, and spread the great heaven-storming wings of the psyches of God."[12]

Divine Grace and the Mysteriousness of Human Freedom

What parent, teacher, or friend of a family has not wondered why one sibling turns out so well and the other seems destined for misadventure, why the character and behavior of one are pleasing and those of the other utterly vexing, and why one excels in life and the other falls short? Rosamond and Agnes are not siblings, and they have grown up in vastly different environments. Yet it is significant that they are born at approximately the same time and under the same symbolic storm cloud. This storm cloud showers "golden rain" (p. 3) over the palace of the newborn princess and dashes "huge fierce handfuls of hail" (p. 4) over the wild countryside where the shepherd girl is born. What possible meaning can this have? Do the rain and hail symbolize the grace that, in the language of the King James Bible, God "sendeth ... on the just and on the unjust," as also "he maketh his sun to rise on the evil and on the good" (Matt. 5:45)? Or is it the contrast between golden rain and driving hail that should catch our attention, perhaps portending that, while the destinies of the two girls intertwine, their lives will take very different courses, like Cain and Abel, or Jacob and Esau? Or are both meanings plausible?

As I already have suggested, the world of *The Wise Woman* is a fairy-tale version of a grace-filled world. And if this is so, the two girls' destinies are not solely of their own doing. Mystery enters into their lives, mystery that is the fullness of wisdom and grace. The destinies of both are contingent upon the nature and quality of their relationship to the wisdom and mystery that the Wise Woman embodies. Yet each girl also is responsible for her own character, for being and becoming who she is.

How freedom and grace are related is the fourth and final key to a comprehension of the story's deeper meaning. MacDonald believed that grace is at work in all of our doings. But he also argued that God does not unilaterally predetermine a person's character and destiny. "God [also] gives us the will wherewith to will, and power to use it, the help needed to supplement the power, whatever the need ... may be." This "power of willing," MacDonald explains, is "created," it is creaturely, it is our own, and yet, he maintains, "the willing [itself] is begotten," that is, it is a work of God within us.[13]

This affirmation of both human freedom and the efficacy of grace is at the heart of MacDonald's moral and religious vision. MacDonald embraces the distinction that the Nicene Creed of the Christian church makes between that which is *created* and that which is *begotten*. The creed states that Jesus Christ, the Son of God, is eternally begotten of the Father, and not made (i.e., not created); Christ is from the Father, eternally with the Father, and of the same Being as the Father. It is relatively easy to comprehend that the will, our "power of willing," is created. We are, after all, creatures, and our wills, however free they may be, are finite and limited, thus vulnerable to sin and error. Yet MacDonald also maintains that our willing of that which is good, that which is righteous (in the Bible's speech), is God acting within us. In other words, when a person wills that which is good or righteous, this is by and through

God's grace.[14] Therefore, we are bound to say that God *begets* this willing in us.

MacDonald is not finished. Behind this truth about our "ingraced" willing of the good is a deep paradoxical truth: "*Because God wills first, man wills also*" (my emphasis).[15] That is to say, God's grace, his willing, is antecedent to all of our willings. What is more, no matter whether we ourselves will for good or for ill, it is the will of God that will ultimately prevail in his Creation.

By defining the relationship of freedom and grace in this way, MacDonald sought to avoid or overcome the strict Calvinist predestinarianism of the Scottish Congregationalism in which he was raised. It bears repeating that he strongly insists that the kind of moral and spiritual person we become is not fated. Rather, *character must be understood as a destiny enacted freely under a sign of divine wisdom and mystery*. In the best of his fiction, MacDonald does not argue this truth so much as enable his reader to vicariously and imaginatively experience it through the characters he presents. A mind that is able to understand good fiction, Flannery O'Connor writes, is one that is "willing to have its sense of mystery deepened by contact with reality, and its sense of reality deepened by contact with mystery."[16] MacDonald follows out this truth in *The Wise Woman*.

How Character Is Forged

We need now to enter more fully into the story, first by looking at Rosamond's and Agnes's respective stays in the Wise Woman's cottage. These visits occur early in the story, in each case immediately after the Wise Woman has stolen the girl from her parents.

In these episodes, we learn much about the girls' personalities. We also begin to suspect how difficult it will be for even the Wise Woman to reform the girls and put them on the path to living virtuous lives.

During their visits in her cottage, the Wise Woman assigns to Rosamond and Agnes ordinary household tasks, such as stoking the fire, cleaning the dishes, sweeping the floor, and washing their own faces. Rosamond fails dismally to perform her duties, but Agnes succeeds. The princess's failure may in part be accounted for by the fact that she has grown up in a palace where attendants have seen to her every need, whereas Agnes's success may be attributed to the fact that she has been brought up on a farm where each family member must perform essential household activities.

Nonetheless, these differences in their upbringings do not completely explain their responses to the Wise Woman's instructions. The girls' temperaments and character traits are different. Rosamond is not lazy. She is, however, proud, obstinate, and contrary. "In truth she would have been glad of the employment, only just because she had been told to do it, she was unwilling; for there *are* people—however unlikely it may seem—who object to doing a thing for no other reason than that it is required of them" (p. 28).

Agnes may do much better at performing the jobs that the Wise Woman assigns, yet her motives and reasons for doing so are no more laudable than Rosamond's refusals. Agnes does not conceive of duty as the performance of responsibility toward others. Neither is the virtue of diligence in doing one's duty fixed in her character. Rather, Agnes prides herself on being superior to others for performing her tasks. "What honest boy would pride himself on not picking pockets? A thief who was trying to reform would. To be conceited of doing one's duty is then a sign of how little one does it, and how little one sees what a contemptible thing it is not to do it. Could any but a low creature be conceited of not being contemptible? Until our duty becomes to us common as breathing, we are poor creatures" (p. 53). In other words, Agnes's egocentricity, smugness, and conceit hamper her from becoming a genuinely responsible person.

Are there, however, grounds on which to judge which girl is initially the better, and in this way reach a reliable conclusion about which girl might turn out better? Midway in the story, MacDonald pauses to reflect on this conundrum. He cautions his readers to hold off from premature conclusions about the girls' destinies. "What is there to choose between a face distorted to hideousness by anger, and one distorted to silliness by self-complacency?" he asks. "True, there is more hope of helping the angry child out of her form of selfishness than the conceited child out of hers; but, on the other hand, the conceited child was not so terrible or dangerous as the wrathful one. . . . I would say that the king's daughter would have been the worse, had not the shepherd's been quite as bad" (pp. 42–43). Is it luck, something inside herself, an imponderable providence, or a combination of all three that makes the difference and leads one girl onto a path toward membership in the royal household of God and leaves the other far behind in her moral and spiritual journey? These are the questions that MacDonald invites us to ponder.

Obedience

O obedience, salvation of the faithful! O obedience, mother of all the virtues! O obedience, discloser of the

kingdom! O obedience, opening of the heavens . . . ! O
obedience, food of all the saints, whose milk they have
sucked, through you they have become perfect! O obedience, companion of the angels!

—Father Rufus

From these descriptions of the two girls and their behavior in the
Wise Woman's cottage, we might well, setting aside MacDonald's
admonitions for the moment, judge Rosamond the worse of the
two. The shortcomings of her temperament impede the very
doing of duties, whereas Agnes at least perfunctorily performs
the tasks the Wise Woman assigns to her. Nonetheless, the
differences between the two girls are not nearly as significant as
the resemblances. Both lack what might be called a habit of naive
or artless obedience, an obedience that, although lacking fore-
thought or conscientious effort, is consistent and habitual.

In children, naive or artless obedience normally centers on
parents or guardians, individuals whom, from their earliest experience, children recognize as authorities over their behavior.
Lack of this obedience can retard the emergence of a strong sense
of moral responsibility. In Rosamond it seems all but absent. And
while such an obedience may appear to be present in Agnes, the
performance of her duties is inherently self-centered. Thus, in neither girl do we find much reason to expect that she will mature
into a conscientious individual, a good and morally responsible
person, with a moral imagination.

A person who possesses a good and righteous character is
someone in whom duty is ingrained as virtue itself—as a power,
in other words, to choose to do what is right in all circumstances,
a habitual intentionality that is much more than thoughtless habit

or even a wishing or desiring to do what is right. *A good or righteous person is someone in whom there is a complete identification of who one is with what one is supposed to do and to become.* MacDonald, however, counsels that even the thought of righteousness or of striving to be righteous vanishes "in the fact of righteousness. When a creature is just what he is supposed to be . . . he is truly himself" and "never thinks what he is. *He is that thing*" (my emphasis).[17]

"That thing," which is righteousness itself, has, according to MacDonald, not merely human but also divine qualities: "It is simply the thing that God wants every man to be, wrought out in him by constant obedient contact with God himself. It is not an attribute either of God or man, but a fact of character in God and in man. It is God's righteousness wrought out in us, so that as he is righteous we too are righteous."[18]

For most of Christian history, obedience, aligned with faith, hope, charity, and all of the other cardinal virtues, ranked high in the religious imagination. This strong regard for obedience belonged even to the secular imagination. But obedience has fallen upon hard times. Peter Baelz comments that obedience is considered by many "the mark of a slave mentality, a craven spirit." For example, "the obedient child is the convenient child," broken in like a horse or mule, wrongfully manipulated by exploitative adults.[19] Some feminists insist that an ideology of obedience historically has held down women and calls for obedience must be viewed with suspicion. Finally, in our day, the objective language of obedience and duty before God is supplanted by the subjectivistic language of self-fulfillment and being true to oneself.

Yet obedience is one of the most important themes in MacDonald's thought. We cannot ignore it. It is in *The Princess and the Goblin*, and we find it even more thoroughly emphasized and explored in *The Wise Woman* "Obedience is the road to all things. It is the only way to grow able to trust him [God]. Love and faith and obedience are sides of the same prism," MacDonald declares.[20] "Will is God's will, obedience is man's will: the two make one."[21]

Paradoxically—perhaps even counterintuitively— belief in the Wise Woman's goodness is consequent upon an act of obedience to her, not vice versa. "Obedience is the opener of eyes," MacDonald writes.[22] Genuine obedience is not just an intention but must be enacted. This enacted obedience is "the very thing to make you able to trust in him [God], and so receive all things from him."[23] "Obedience is not perfection, but trying." Jesus "knows that you can try, and that in your trying and failing he will be able to help you, until at length you shall do the will of God even as he does it himself."[24] In MacDonald's parable, the Wise Woman stands in for Jesus and not for a parent, as some commentators have thought.

Rosamond's Escape from the Wise Woman's Cottage

Throughout most of the story, Rosamond resists the Wise Woman's discipline and guidance and stubbornly persists in her selfish behavior. This, as I already have shown, is displayed especially during her stay in the Wise Woman's cottage. When Rosamond realizes that she can escape from the cottage by stepping into a painting that hangs in a mysterious picture gallery, she seizes the opportunity to avoid her duties and the Wise Woman's oversight.[25] Regrettably, she flees from the path on which the Wise Woman has put her.

In spite of this, Rosamond does not slip free of the Wise Woman's provident care. For not through happenstance, but evidently by the Wise Woman's design, the picture into which she steps is of the countryside close to Agnes's home, where Agnes's parents, whose daughter the Wise Woman has stealthily stolen, find Rosamond and take her in to live with them. The shepherd and shepherdess have far too readily heaped praise on Agnes, who is already disposed to smugness and self-conceit. Their simple, frugal way of life, however, benefits Rosamond, who has been spoiled near to death with material possessions.

Furthermore, the Wise Woman, in the disguise of an old beggar woman, has left in the care of Agnes's father a sheepdog with the propitious name Prince.[26] Prince watches over Rosamond in a doggishly angelic way, showing her love and affection, while he also checks her passions with a fierce animal force. As no human would be able to do, he teaches Rosamond obedience. This stay with Agnes's parents under Prince's supervision prepares Rosamond for her final ordeals and trials and the responsibility she will have to assume for the care of her parents at the end of the story.

The Hollow Sphere

The episode of the hollow sphere is one of MacDonald's most imaginative literary inventions.[27] After she has stolen Rosamond from her father and mother, the Wise Woman does the same with Agnes. Agnes proves at least as intransigent as Rosamond. "Agnes was guilty of such a meanness as many who are themselves capable of something just as bad will consider incredible" (p. 44).

And she was fearless, so she would not follow the Wise Woman if released from the Wise Woman's black cloak, which magically hides and confines whoever is beneath it.

The Wise Woman decides that before Agnes can be introduced successfully to her cottage, she needs to be taken to another place, "such a one as is to be found nowhere else in the wide world. It was a great hollow sphere," made of a mirrorlike substance, which had "neither door, nor window, nor any opening to break its perfect roundness" (p. 48). In it the Wise Woman puts Agnes through an ordeal designed to make the girl aware of the loathsomeness of her conceit and the ugliness of her attitude toward others.

Agnes, when first sealed inside the sphere, is fearless and content with where she is.[28] With the passage of time, however, she grows weary and tired of being with herself, that very Somebody that has been so important to her. MacDonald's description of this experience is gripping:

> Nothing was overhead, nothing under foot, nothing on either hand, but the same pale, faint, bluish glimmer. She wept at last, then grew very angry, and then sullen; but nobody heeded whether she cried or laughed. It was all the same to the cold unmoving twilight that rounded her. On and on went the dreary hours—or did they go at all?—"no change, no pause, no hope";—on and on till she felt she was forgotten. (p. 49)

On the third day of Agnes's imprisonment in the sphere, something changes. There appears to be someone else inside the sphere. In fact, this other is merely Agnes's own reflection, yet in her eyes there is another person, a young girl like herself. Agnes asks, "Who are you?" and the girl answers, "Who are you?" (p. 51). The girl responds to all Agnes's questions in this fashion and likewise imitates her every movement. Agnes loses her temper and attempts to seize the girl, but the girl disappears and Agnes finds herself "tugging her own hair." When she lets go, the girl reappears. When she flies at the girl "to bite her," Agnes discovers that she has only bitten herself in the arm, and again the girl disappears. Each time the girl reappears, she is "tenfold uglier than before." But now the Wise Woman's plan begins to work. Agnes begins to hate herself "with her whole heart" (p. 51). "There is no spectre so terrible as the unsuspected spectre of a man's own self," MacDonald comments in another of his stories.[29]

Then Agnes is struck with a shattering realization. "It flashed upon her with a sickening disgust that the child was not another, but her Self, her Somebody, and that she was now shut up with her for ever and ever—no more for one moment ever to be alone" (p. 51). For three more trying days, Agnes painfully lives with this terrible knowledge that the" hateful, ape-like creature" she is with is herself (p. 51). On the third day she is exhausted and falls asleep. The next morning—the symbolic seventh day since her ordeal in the hollow sphere began—the Wise Woman carries Agnes to her cottage.

When Agnes awakens she is "in the arms of the wise woman" and "two heavenly eyes [are] gazing upon her" (p. 52) "Heavenly" is not a casual description. It reveals *who* the Wise Woman really is, what kind of being she is. Her identity is paradisical, reflected in her eyes and in her entire countenance, also her kiss. Earlier, MacDonald has compared this kiss to "the rose-gardens of Damascus" (p. 25). The Damascene rose is a hybrid of the *Rosa gallica* that was grown in monastic gardens for its exceptional fragrance and medicinal powers. In the Christian imagination it is associated with the garden of Eden.

Agnes weeps in the Wise Woman's arms, and the more she clings to the Wise Woman, "the more tenderly . . . the great strong arms close around her" (p. 52). Then the Wise Woman washes her in the little well inside the cottage, dresses her, and feeds her with "bread and milk" (52). These are distinctly baptismal and Eucharistic actions. But Agnes subsequently resists this grace and reverts to her old ways.

Agnes's Escape

In the cottage, Agnes initially responds positively to the Wise Woman and follows her instructions. Soon, however, Agnes's old disposition reemerges. She, like Rosamond, who precedes her, finds the way to the mysterious picture gallery. She initially comes across a picture of her own home with an unfamiliar young girl in it; next to it is a painting of a royal city with a magnificent palace. Agnes has not met Rosamond and has no way of knowing that the royal city is Rosamond's home. But her eyes are drawn to a proclamation posted on the palace gates which states: "By the will of the king . . . every stray child found in the realm shall be brought without a moment's delay to the palace. Whoever shall be found having done otherwise shall straightway lose his head by the hand of the public executioner" (pp. 53–54). Agnes turns her back on the picture of her home and fixes on the painting of the palace. She imagines that she might find favor with such a king and become a great lady of the court.

Like Rosamond, Agnes finally surmises that the scene in the picture is real, that the palace is a real palace and not just a painting. She decides that this is her chance to, "make my fortune" (p. 55). So she steps over the frame into the picture and eventually arrives at the city, wearied and bedraggled, having gone through a drenching thunderstorm. A soldier offers to take her to the king and queen. However, her disheveled appearance and ugly countenance thoroughly repulse the royal couple; and they immediately dispatch her to the kitchen as a scullery maid.

The palace servants dislike Agnes from the start and treat her badly. But nothing that she endures moves her to question her own vexatious nature; in fact, she only grows worse, as she schemes to advance herself. In time, Agnes learns of the lost princess, and from a portrait she is shown recognizes Rosamond as the child she had seen in the picture of her own home in the Wise Woman's cottage. Without a thought given to the danger into which she might be placing her parents—for according to the proclamation they would be in jeopardy of losing their heads—she tells the lord chancellor that she knows where Rosamond is. This self-serving act precipitates a series of events that culminate in a complex judgment scene at the royal court where all of the major characters of the story are brought together.

Rosamond's Conversion: The Three Tests

Just as MacDonald does not place God or Christ in his story, neither does he even once introduce the word "conversion." Nonetheless, the Wise Woman endeavors to engender a conversion in both girls—in other words, a turning around to be their "right selves."

The episode of the hollow sphere suggests that a conversion is not likely to happen for Agnes, at least not in the short term. The outcome for Rosamond is different. Over the course of three tests, which she willingly undergoes, Rosamond repents and commits herself entirely into the care of the Wise Woman. She emerges from these trials a real princess: someone who is in possession of herself precisely because she is obedient to an authority higher than herself.

We left Rosamond living with Agnes's parents under the tutelage of the shepherd dog Prince. At the appointed time, the Wise Woman removes Prince from the shepherd's home, and sadly, by degrees, the princess lapses "back into some of her bad old ways" (p. 74). She eventually becomes so unruly that the shepherd couple regretfully expel her from their home. She is hampered by an injured foot as she traverses the countryside on her way to the palace and her parents. The Wise Woman, disguised as an old peasant, once more intervenes. She heals Rosamond's foot, but the girl ignores the old woman's warning that she is about to take a wrong turn in the road. After misadventures that test her courage and try her conscience, Rosamond arrives once again at the Wise Woman's cottage. This is when the Wise Woman tells her that the only way past her miserable condition is to submit to being tested.

For the first of three tests, the Wise Woman magically returns Rosamond to her old nursery, where she finds her nurse and her pet white rabbit.[30] Rosamond orders the nurse to fetch the Queen. After the nurse refuses to do as she is told, Rosamond trips over the white rabbit and furiously throws it at the nurse. She has slipped back into her old behaviors of rage and retaliation, and fails this first trial.

The second test is more complicated. And although she fails it, MacDonald has already begun to reveal that the path to Rosamond's recovery and redemption is sited in her attraction to beauty. She must practice self-restraint, however, when beauty is present, and must not be possessive of it, lest she make beauty serve her acquisitive self. For this test, the Wise Woman places Rosamond "in a beautiful garden, full of blossoming trees and the loveliest roses and lilies." There also is a lake in the midst of the garden, and Rosamond loses herself "in the joy of the flowers and the trees and the water" (p. 85).

This panorama is evocative of Eden and also the garden of the New Jerusalem in the Book of Revelation. Within the garden of the New Jerusalem, fruit-bearing trees line a river that runs through the eternal city. It is "a pure river of the water of life." The leaves of the Tree of Life are "for the healing of the nations" (Rev. 22:1–2).[31] Likewise, all of the plants of the garden in which Rosamond finds herself—the flowering trees, the lilies, and the roses—possess medicinal powers.[32] The Tree of Life is emblematic of both wisdom and beauty. Like wisdom, with which it is closely associated, beauty possesses healing power. The Wise Woman is a healer and, we learn soon that in her "truest" manifestation she is extraordinarily beautiful.

Rosamond espies a "lovely little boy" at play in the garden (p. 86) and she races to embrace him. The boy, however, runs off to the lake, where a small boat is docked. Rosamond follows after him, and together they get into the boat. Their attention quickly turns to a "great white flower" that floats on the water, "huge and glowing as a harvest moon" (p. 86).[33] The boy pulls at the flower, and it eventually comes free in his hands. However, this motion launches the boy backward into the bottom of the boat. Rosamond is overtaken by "a great desire to have it [the flower] herself." In a frantic tussle over it, Rosamond flings the boy out of the boat into the lake, where he drowns. The Wise Woman, in the guise of the boy's mother, now makes her entrance. She holds the limp body out to Rosamond and announces: "This is your second trial, and also a failure'" (p. 87).

In the first trial, Rosamond's intemperance undid her. In this instance, greed and rapacity ensure her failure. Rosamond is mortified, yet her devotion to the Wise Woman has become only stronger. "Couldn't you help me?" she pleads. "I will help you all I can," the Wise Woman responds, "perhaps I could, now you ask me" (p. 87).

For her third test, the Wise Woman transports Rosamond to a forest that is exquisitely beautiful, "half wild, half tended. The trees were grand and full of the loveliest birds, of all glowing, gleaming, and radiant colours. . . All the gentle creatures of a forest were there, but no creatures that killed" (p. 88).[34] MacDonald draws our attention to the butterflies in this garden. "Words would but wrong them if they tried to tell how gorgeous they were" (p. 88). The butterfly is a symbol for the soul and its progress through stages of transformation, rebirth, or resurrection. In this instance, the butterflies are also physical signs of the spiritual changes happening inside of Rosamond.

Immediately, Rosamond notices that there are no flowers in the garden. She "could not help feeling that flowers were wanted to make the *beauty* of the forest complete" (p. 88, my emphasis). Then, in a nearby glade, as if to make a wish come true, Rosamond catches sight of "the loveliest little girl, with her lap full of flowers of all colors, but of such kinds as Rosamond had never before seen" (pp. 88–89). When this young child tosses the flowers, one by one, out onto the forest floor, they instantly take root. Rosamond rushes to pick up one of these flowers, but it withers and dies in her hands. This disturbs her profoundly. She can no more make these flowers her own than possess the moon that she demanded her parents give to her.

Rosamond asks the girl why the flowers do not wither and die in her hands. The child answers: "I don't pull them; I throw them away. I live them" (p. 90). Beauty exists not for just one but all to behold. Yet if we respect the integrity of beauty, we may experience it alive and living in ourselves, and we may even give birth to beauty in what we ourselves do. "Where do you get them?" Rosamond inquires further. "In my lap," the girl answers (p. 90). Rosamond initially feels that the girl is making fun of her. However, when the child looks "her full in the face, with reproach in her large blue eyes," Rosamond senses that the truth about the origin of the flowers and their beauty resides entirely within this child. "'Oh, that's where the flowers come from!' said the princess to herself . . . , hardly knowing what she meant" (p. 90). Beauty is not merely an object of sight: beauty is mysteriously related to purity, to a seeing and a doing that are not greedy, grasping, or self-referential.

Suddenly, a lovely snow-white, blue-winged pony alights in the glade. His name is Peggy (short for Pegasus). This arouses Rosamond's love of animals and her attraction to beauty. Her encounter with the pony is strained from the start, however. She does not know how to treat animals gently or respectfully, not as possessions that are there for her pleasure. Rosamond's rough advances fluster and aggravate the pony. With swift blows of his tail, Peggy throws her twice to the ground. The second blow prevents Rosamond from calamitously acting out her rage.

Rosamond is stunned. A tremor runs through her heart as she discerns how uncouth and selfish she has been for as long as she can remember. In a spirit of genuine penance, Rosamond thinks: "What a wretched, coarse, ill-bred creature I must be! There is that lovely child giving life instead of death to the flowers, and a moment ago I was hating her!" (p. 92). On the heels of this confession, Rosamond spots "a silvery flower, something like a snowdrop" (p. 95). The flower increases in size and loveliness, and then is transformed into "a woman perfectly beautiful, neither old nor young, for hers was the old age of everlasting youth" (p. 95). It is the Wise Woman in her truest, most beautiful presence.

Were it not for her confession, Rosamond could not have seen the Wise Woman in this form. Something had to change within her to see the Wise Woman in her full beauty, a beauty that evidently transcends time and age. Nor should we ignore the priestly absolution the Wise Woman performs. "If I had not forgiven you, I would never have taken the trouble to punish you," she says. "If I had not loved you, do you think I would have carried you away in my cloak? . . . I saw, through it all, what you were going to be. . . . But remember you have yet only begun to be what I saw" (p. 97).

Just before the Wise Woman reveals herself, one final important thing happens. In a great bound the pony, with the lovely little girl astride, leaps over Rosamond in a high arc. The Greek root of Pegasus is *pege*. The word means spring or fountain. In the cottage, Rosamond several times washed herself or was bathed by the Wise Woman. None of these, however, was the spiritual bath of baptism that Rosamond now receives beneath Peggy. This is just the beginning, however, of the changes in Rosamond that will follow "There are many rooms in my house you may have to go through," says the Wise Woman to Rosamond, "but when you need no more of them, then you will be able to throw flowers like the little girl you saw in the forest" (p. 96).[35] Conversion may yet be a long way from perfection, but conversion does clear a path to it. For MacDonald, sanctification is not a station achieved. Rather, it is dynamic and ongoing, and extends into the life everlasting.

Judgment and Forgiveness

> For He regards men not as they are merely, but as they shall be; not as they shall be merely, but as they are now growing, or capable of growing, towards that image after which he made them that they might grow to it. Therefore a thousand stages, each in itself all but valueless, are of inestimable worth as the necessary and connected gradations of an infinite progress. A condition which of declension would indicate a devil, may of growth indicate a saint.
> —George MacDonald, "The Consuming Fire"

With her third trial, Rosamond has proven herself a real princess and a true child of God and now is ready to return to her parents' home. For she now is equipped to assume a redemptive role in their lives. She reaches the palace and from a hiding place behind a curtain, witnesses a tragicomic drama that is unfolding in the throne room. Her father is meting out punishments for Agnes and her parents, whom he accuses of mistreating his daughter.

As he orders the palace guards to take Agnes and her parents to the rack, Rosamond bursts into the hall. She rushes not, as one might expect, to her parents' side, but rather to the shepherd and shepherdess and declares that they have been good and kind to her. Initially, the king and queen do not recognize Rosamond. When at last they do, the Wise Woman steps forward and addresses the king and queen in words that are audible only to them:

> I took your daughter away when she was worthy of such parents. I bring her back, and they are unworthy of her. That you did not know her when she came to you is a small wonder, for you have been blind in soul all your lives: now be blind in body until your better eyes are unsealed. (p. 106)[36]

The Wise Woman throws open her black cloak and lets it fall to the floor. From her inner snowy white garment flashes a luminescence that surrounds her in an aureole of light. Light radiates from "her face of awful beauty and from her eyes," which shine "like pools of sunlight" (p. 106). The light blinds the king and queen and renders the Wise Woman invisible to all but a few in the room. Rosamond and "the woman who swept and dusted the hall and brushed the thrones" see her, and the shepherd has "a glimmering vision of her." And Agnes feels the Wise Woman's presence "like the heat of a furnace seven times heated" (pp. 106–7).

This closing scene is a little parable inside the larger story. It is about justice cast in ironic terms. It defines the difference between God's justice and worldly justice. MacDonald maintained that in God justice and mercy are one, because the aim of divine justice is not punishment but rather the destruction of sin and refinement of the image of God in his creature. The justice the king is prepared to mete out lacks mercy and has no redemptive purpose.

Such a justice is not easily distinguished from vengeance, whereas the Wise Woman's punishment of the king and queen is a call for them to repent of their selfishness, spiritual blindness, and damaging neglect of their daughter. The physical blindness that the Wise Woman inflicts upon the king and queen may be proportional to their spiritual blindness; nevertheless, is not an end in itself. It is, rather, a means to their rehabilitation. "Now be blind until your better eyes are unsealed."

Divine justice is not an eye for an eye. Were that so, the Wise Woman would leave Rosamond's parents desolate, alone in their misery for perpetuity, without hope.[37] Instead, she returns their daughter, who forgives them, much in the way that the Wise Woman has forgiven her. MacDonald argues that "punishment is for the sake of amendment and atonement."[38] Rosamond is made the agent of the Wise Woman's atoning justice, which is itself a mercy. "God is merciful: we must be merciful. There is no blessedness except in being such as God; it would be altogether unmerciful to leave us unmerciful," MacDonald writes.[39] This is the Wise Woman's meaning when she speaks of the "better eyes" that the king and queen must one day possess before they may be cured of their physical blindness. These "better eyes" will be eyes spiritually capable of perceiving in others "that image after which he [God] made them."[40] The most damaging and punishable offense of the king and queen has been their failure to perceive the spiritual needs of their daughter.[41]

In the meantime, Rosamond must serve her parents as they have failed to do for her. "Do let them see. Do open their eyes, dear good, wise woman," Rosamond pleads. The Wise Woman answers: "I will one day. Meanwhile you must be their *servant*, as I have been yours. Bring them to me, and I will make them welcome" (p. 106, my emphasis). "For . . . the Son of Man did not come to be served, but to serve," Jesus says to his disciples (Mark 10:45). Rosamond will become a participant in the goodness and wisdom of the Wise Woman. This much is clear.

While much is exposed and resolved in this final scene of *The Wise Woman*, mystery remains. We have no definitive answer as to why Rosamond ultimately responds favorably to the Wise Woman, while Agnes does not. Is there something within Rosamond, perhaps a seed of undefined, unseen potency that germinates, grows, and blossoms into personal integrity, incorruptibility, and consistency of intention, all three of which together make good character?[42]

The fact that just a few in the throne room are able to see the Wise Woman in her beauty and glory suggests a spiritual hierarchy. Few in this world experience such a pronounced taste of the kingdom of heaven as Rosamond. Others are on various stages of their spiritual journey and in need of attendance by visiting angels. The Wise Woman returns Agnes and her mother to the farm to suffer each other's presence. The shepherd begs to accompany the Wise Woman, and she agrees to take him with her. Perhaps she assesses him as ready for a pedagogy that will increase his spiritual stature sufficient to do for his wife and Agnes what Rosamond will do for her parents.

How Double Is the Story?

The concluding paragraph of *The Wise Woman* begins with this statement: "And that is all my double story. How double is it, if you care to know, you must find out. If you think it is not finished—I never knew a story that was." The narrator concedes that he could say a great deal more about his characters and their destinies but reckons that in his story he already has "told more than is good for those who read but with their foreheads, and enough for those whom it has made look a little solemn, and sigh as they close the book." (108).

The first kind of readers to which the narrator refers are like the critics who do not think very much of MacDonald's "double story" because it seems to them unreasonable or irrational. They read "with their foreheads," not with their hearts or a moral imagination. The second kind are the proudly pious who take delight in and are quite content with the here and now of the Wise Woman's judgments and punishments. They look for nothing else and assume that the "duality" of the story is absolute, that it is about those who are "saved" and those who are not.

But MacDonald allows for a different view on the matter. He says: "How double it is, if you care to know, you must find out." This is a summons to use our imaginations, and not to be content with what we know from what is written. The clear implication is that neither the story nor its characters' spiritual journeys terminate in the present. The duality extends into an unknown, untold future, and belongs not just to the story, but also to the world in which we live. Whether or not the duality in the story can or will be resolved is covered in mystery. But we have been given good reason to believe that there is hope for Agnes and her mother and for the king and queen.

The best way to proceed is neither to be content with what we know nor to put the story behind us as an unsolvable riddle.

Rather, we should turn back to the beginning of the story and read it again, and yet again, until, as every parable challenges its readers and listeners to do, we take the fullest possible measure of our own lives, all the while reminding ourselves: "I am not what I ought to be, I do not the thing I ought to do!"[43]

CONCLUSION

A Bibliographical Essay

In the poem *East Coker*, T. S. Eliot opines that "old men ought to be explorers." I was nearing fifty when I cited this verse in the first edition of this book; now, at seventy-four years of age, I value this kernel of wisdom that much more. Eliot speaks metaphorically, of course. He is not recommending that octogenarians literally go on long voyages across the vast seas like Magellan or Columbus, or traverse the great continents, like Marco Polo. He does mean, however, that the moral and spiritual truths that make us complete human beings are not so much objectives that we grasp with our minds as they are visions we hold up in our hearts and imaginations and which we constantly strive for. We envision truth and it captures our whole being, drawing us continually forward "into another intensity / For a further union, a deeper communion."

When Eliot implores that "old men ought to be explorers" he also is hinting at a mystery, that "in my beginning is my end" and "in my end is my beginning." That is, if we wish to be genuine seafarers and explorers in old age, we must begin to learn and practice the skills of virtuous living when young. Our children

Tending the Heart of Virtue. Second Edition. Vigen Guroian, Oxford University Press.
© Vigen Guroian 1998, 2023. DOI: 10.1093/oso/9780195384307.003.0011

cannot learn these skills on their own. They need guidance. The moral imagination must be cultivated like the tea rose in a garden. Left unattended and unfed, the rose will languish and thistle will grow in its place. But if fed, watered, and pruned properly, the rose will prosper and be beautiful.

Throughout this book I have endeavored to demonstrate how fairy tales nourish the moral imagination with the best food. There is no single solution to the moral crisis of childhood in our culture. But I do not doubt that something is seriously awry. My good friend Gilbert C. Meilaender has written that "if Plato is correct, if we cannot insert vision into the blind and our environment shapes our perceptions and judgments of goodness, one whose vision of the good is not properly shaped in childhood may never come to see—except perhaps by 'divine intervention.'"[1] We are at a point in many Western societies, including our own, where Plato's admonition points straight at us. Our children are in jeopardy, and so is the future of virtue and human goodness. The sort of ship in which we send our children out onto the sea of life makes a profound difference as to whether they drown in the abyss or reach the shores of Paradise.

As Steve Harvey quipped one evening on *Showtime at the Apollo* (my daughter Victoria's favorite television show in the early 1990s): "Now there isn't anything wrong with our children. But there is something the matter with the way we are raising them." Our concern for our children can bring us together. The parents, teachers, pastors, and rabbis whom I have taught or spoken to over many decades all have wanted something better for our children. A message of this book has been that reading good stories to children is one small but very important way to begin to do that something.

My greatest frustration when writing this book has been that for the sake of economy I have had to select but a few of the stories that my children, grandchildren, and I have read together and that for over twenty-five years were the staple of my classroom instruction. In the few pages I have allotted myself here, I have taken the opportunity to pass on the titles of some of the other stories that children can enjoy and from which they might benefit. My comments are ordered along the lines of the topics I have brought to our attention through the stories I have discussed. I have not set out to present a comprehensive list. Rather, I have settled on just one or a few stories under each topic, whether it be self-sacrificial love, friendship, faith, courage, or beauty.

Becoming Real

Stories about becoming real (or transformation) abound in the fairy-tale and fantasy genres. I have said at the end of Chapter 7 that "The Ugly Duckling" is just such a story. Let me, however, turn to Maurice Sendak's *Where the Wild Things Are* as yet another. *Where the Wild Things Are* is a modern classic. I have read it over and over again, on demand, to my grandchildren with all the appropriate intonations to emphasize the humor it contains and the terror it evokes. With its wonderful illustrations and crisp text, *Where the Wild Things Are* achieves brilliance in its simplicity and direct speech. It is a story about learning to discipline one's passions and one's appetites, lest one become a "beast," one of the "wild things." It is about the difficulty of training one's imagination and keeping focused on what is right. And it teaches the important lesson that every child needs both the discipline and the love of his or her parents in order to become a true son or daughter and to become wholly human.

Laurence Houseman's "Rocking Horse Land" has much in common with *The Velveteen Rabbit* in that it is built around the relationship of a child with his toy. Prince Fredolin's love of his rocking horse makes the wooden horse come alive. The young prince releases his friend from the nursery to join forever the real and alive horses in Rocking Horse Land. The story also teaches a lesson about friendship: we must always respect the freedom of a friend, because in the absence of that respect, genuine friendship cannot survive, nor do the friends grow to be mature and responsible persons.

Love and Immortality

The Grimms' "Snow White" (or "Snow-drop") is among the most beloved of fairy tales. But first we must set aside the Disney version. While I favor it as one of the best of the Disney fairy-tale animations, with a healthy share of faithfulness to the Grimms' story, nonetheless it is a romanticized retelling of a story that in its original nears being tragic were it not for the Prince's Christlike rescue of Cinderella from cold death and invitation to come with him "to my father's castle" to be wed. In fairness to Disney, the last scenes of the animated film do capture the spirit of the Grimms' ending.

It is said that our going to sleep at night and arising in the morning is a rehearsal of our death and awakening to eternal life. It seems to me also that this is the deep intuition on which this story is built. Because they love her so much, the Seven Dwarfs do everything within their power to prevent the worst from happening to Snow White at the hands of her wicked stepmother, the queen. Nor do they cease to love her even in her "death." For three symbolical days, all seven "watched and bewailed" Snow White's fall into the deep sleep that they feared was death. But "because her cheeks remained rosy, and her face looked just as it did when she was alive," they did not bury her in the "cold earth" but placed her in a "coffin of glass." The dwarfs continue to hope for Snow White's awakening, until the day a prince comes who falls in love with her at first sight and carries her off to his father's kingdom.

George MacDonald wrote a precious, beautiful little story that has been published in lovely picture book versions. "Little Daylight" is based on the story of "Sleeping Beauty" and also contains important elements of "Snow White" and "Beauty and the Beast." It concerns a young princess who at her christening has a curse placed upon her by an evil fairy. The princess is condemned to sleep during the day and to awaken at night. Her vitality when awake is determined by the waxing and waning of the moon. Eventually, a young prince discovers her and breaks the spell. One night when the moon has waned, he finds the princess in the appearance of an ugly old woman, and does not recognize her as the young maiden he loves. He thinks the old woman is dying and out of pity kisses her on the lips. Then she stands up transformed back into Little Daylight and says to him, "You kissed me when I was an old woman: there! I kiss you when I am a young princess . . . Is that the sun coming?" I regard this as one of the most beautiful and moving of all fairy-tale stories.

A third story that merits mention is Oscar Wilde's masterly telling of "The Selfish Giant." It can be read at many levels. It is appealing to the young because it is about the role that children play in helping a great Giant to repent of his selfishness and give his beloved garden over to them to play in. I leave the allegory and biblical allusions for you to discover.

George MacDonald's *The Golden Key*, which I have mentioned several times in this book. is a far more difficult and complex story than the three I have already discussed. It is symbolical and allegorical. It tells a tale of the mysterious journeys of a young girl and boy named Tangle and Mossy. They are joined, then separated, and finally reunited in a place where the rainbow ends, beyond the earth in "the country whence the shadows fall." I read *The Golden Key* to my son, now a grown man with three children of his own, one evening when he was eight or nine. Rafi fell asleep. I, however, did not notice this, and must have gone on for some time as he slept. I lost track of time, completely enthralled by the pictures that MacDonald was painting and the mood and atmosphere of the story. Rafi probably was too young for it. I don't know whether one is ever ready for it.

Friends and Mentors

In his enchanting and also humorous tale *The Reluctant Dragon*, Kenneth Grahame gives to us the most endearing dragon in all of children's literature. This dragon prefers poetry and good conversation to pillaging and destruction. He befriends a boy and teaches him about loyalty, trust, and the responsibilities of friendship. A dragon may seem to be the most unlikely of mentors. Yet here is one such dragon.

As much as I like E. B. White's story *Charlotte's Web*, I sometimes think I have enjoyed *The Trumpet of the Swan* even more. I admit that this may have to do with the fact that I was a boy once who also spent much time out of doors looking for wild creatures. *The Trumpet of the Swan* is the story of the adventures of a boy named Sam Beaver who finds and befriends a trumpeter swan who is without a voice. Much humor and good fun is built on this premise. But most of all, this is a story about friendships and how they can help us to succeed in life and become better persons in the process. The character of Louis the trumpeter swan is unforgettable for his sincerity, integrity, and sheer joy in living.

Evil and Redemption

Fairy tales and children's fantasy stories almost inevitably present us with good characters who struggle against evil, find evil in their path, or have to learn how to know when evil is present, when to avoid it, and when to meet it head-on. But here I restrict myself to just one such story. I am speaking of C. S. Lewis's final book of the Narnia series, *The Last Battle*. While *The Lion, the Witch and the Wardrobe* may be the best-known of the series, *The Last Battle* is the only one to have won a literary award. It received the Carnegie Medal for the best children's book in 1956.

My oldest grandchild, Virginia, finished fourth grade a year ago. At the end of the school year she read all seven Narnia books in the original order of publication. One day she spoke to me about her reaction to *The Last Battle*. Virginia was deeply moved by it, more so than by any of the other books. The reality of evil and death, and that all things come to an end, made an impression upon her, as did Lewis's beautiful portrayal of redemption on the other side of the stable door. Ultimately, *The Last Battle* is not a dark tale. Even though evil appears to triumph, heroism, goodness, and truth do find their reward in an eternal Narnia that is more real, more alive, more vivid, and more beautiful than anything in the old Narnia. In this book Lewis manages to teach a strong lesson about how wretched and destructive selfishness and falsehood really are and presents a compelling vision of death that transcends tragedy.

Heroines and Heroes of Faith and Courage

In Chapter 6 I discussed the first of George MacDonald's Curdie and Irene stories, *The Princess and the Goblin*. In the sequel, *Curdie and the Princess,* the mysterious grandmother sends Curdie on a mission to save Irene and her father from a vicious plot that threatens them and the kingdom. Not only is Curdie's faith tested but so are his native courage and wit, and in such a way that he truly grows up and matures as a leader. In the first half of the story, MacDonald teaches some wonderful lessons about character and the vision to succeed in the good. If we are ugly inside, then we may see or experience virtue and goodness themselves as ugly or unpleasant, even threatening. If, however, we are obedient and trusting, we stand to gain a special capacity to distinguish good from evil, even when evil hides beneath deceptive cover.

L. Frank Baum's *The Wonderful Wizard of* Oz (and its sequels) and Madeleine L'Engle's *A Wrinkle in Time* (and its sequels) are far better known to contemporary parents and children that the Irene and Curdie books. Little need be said about these stories. *The Wonderful Wizard of Oz* deserves to be read, in spite of the great attraction, excellence, and success of the movie with Judy Garland. There is much more in the book, though one can argue about which is better, the book or the movie. Courage stands out in both as a strong leitmotif. The illusion and trickery of the Wizard present an opportunity to consider the roles that trust and belief play in our lives.

The two books that many of my college students had read are *Charlotte's Web* and *A Wrinkle in Time*. Meg, Irene, and Lucy are heroines every young girl should meet. *A Wrinkle in Time*'s Meg, of course, is called upon to outgrow her adolescent insecurities and trust in herself and interplanetary mentors in order that she may succeed in rescuing her brother and father from captivity under a cosmic power of darkness personified as the It. *A Wrinkle in Time* could also be interpreted profitably under the topic of evil and redemption.

Beauty

I have discussed "Snow White" under love and immortality. Still, it seems to me beauty is as important a theme of the story, though in a different way than in "The Nightingale" or "The Ugly Duckling." In "The Nightingale" there is a strong aesthetic component—in other words, reflection on *what* beauty is. In "The Ugly Duckling," Andersen explores how a love of beauty can be transformative.

In "Snow White," the Grimms' interest in beauty is in its relation to morality and the distinction we draw between good and evil. Disney had it right in depicting the beauty of the stepmother queen as dark, macabre, and menacing. The Grimms describe her as "beautiful" with the qualifier that she also is "proud and haughty." Her arrogance, cruelty, and wickedness contrast with Snow White's innocence, humility, and goodness. The stepmother's competition with Snow White over who is the more beautiful is hard to forget. The repetition of the stepmother's question "Who is the fairest of all?" (*pace* Disney) has become a kind of signature of the story.

Yet the envy and rage of the stepmother when at last the mirror declares Snow White to be "a thousand times more fair" than her is not the end of it. We must ask ourselves the question: how is Snow White a thousand times more fair than the stepmother? The answer is that her beauty is pure, without pride or envy of anyone else. The evil queen will not rest until she has done away with Snow White. She will not allow Snow White to thrive no matter how far removed the younger woman is from her presence. And thus we come to the symbolical three temptations that the stepmother queen contrives in order to snuff out Snow White's life. Famously, the queen succeeds in her third try with the offer of an apple, reminiscent of the biblical story of the temptation to which Adam and Eve succumbed.

The temptations that the queen stepmother contrives are conceived to make Snow White more like herself. This is ironical and makes her attempts to destroy Snow White's innocence and unaffected beauty more complex than they may seem at first. The first of the wares that the disguised queen offers to Snow White are colorful stay laces. When these laces fail to press the breath out of Snow White, the queen returns with a poisoned comb. Both of these items, the stay laces and the comb, are women's accessories for beautification. The queen counts on the lure of a superficial, false beauty to corrupt and kill Snow White. The queen initially had ordered the huntsman to kill Snow White and bring the young girl's innocent heart to her in order that she might consume it. Now she seeks to corrupt that heart. Snow White falls for the queen's first two tricks, accepting the gift of the stay laces and then the comb. It is only by chance that the dwarfs twice find Snow White early enough to save her.

The third gift, an apple, is a subtler subterfuge, though it too is centered in beauty. It is made in the image of Snow White herself, whose skin is white as snow and whose cheeks are red as blood. The poison apple the queen concocts is "beautiful—white with red cheeks." She intends that it draw out of Snow White a latent narcissism. And indeed, the apple catches Snow White's eye: "Snow White was eager to eat the beautiful apple." The queen gives the red poisonous portion of the apple to Snow White and consumes the harmless white half herself. This ruse also works.

Perhaps there is a lesson in this story for our day when the cosmetic and fashion industries craftily appeal to both the insecurity of young girls and their desire to be beautiful. Even the apple may be interpreted in this way, albeit on a symbolical level. The color red is evocative of passion and desire. Snow White feels "a craving for the beautiful apple." This is not just a hunger of the stomach. It reaches to the heart and can corrupt it. As we know, all ends well: Snow White is protected not just by the dwarfs but by forces of goodness stronger than the evil of the queen.

I want also to mention a lovely story in Hans Christian Andersen's corpus, titled simply "The Bell." In it Andersen approaches beauty from yet another perspective, different from that in the two stories I have discussed in Chapter 7. This story concerns a bell that is very far away yet whose sound reaches even the ears of the busy denizens of the city. The bell itself and where it might be, however, remain a mystery. Curiously, the farther one gets from the city the more distinct the beautiful sound of the bell is. The question is whether physical distance alone explains the phenomenon

TENDING THE HEART OF VIRTUE

or whether the bell's increased audibility should be credited to the reduction in distractions that removal from urban life allows.

"On the outskirts of the city, where the houses were farther away from each other and had gardens around them . . . the sunset was much more beautiful and the sound of the bell much louder." The romantic aversion to cluttered and hurried urban life is clear. So too is the romantic belief that the urban shuts out natural beauty. But the lesson of the story is deeper, more profound, and more spiritual than that. When the city dwellers are drawn out of their surroundings to search for the bell, though most do not get very far, they become either discouraged or seize the opportunity for commercial profit. Rich and poor come upon some weeping willows at the edge of the woods and mistake them for the woods itself. Two bakers set up shop and the business is good. One baker even hangs a bell in his tent, but it is "tarred on the outside to protect it from the rain" and has "no tongue." This bell is an emblem of how commercialism and consumerism can quell the love of true beauty.

On a beautiful Sunday a group of children, who have just been confirmed, set out from church to find the bell. Only two, however, go so far as the point at which the forest becomes a garden where beautiful things grow: "lilies shaped like stars," "tulips as blue as the sky," and "apple trees" with fruit that "looked like soap bubbles." There also are "lakes in which swans swam." We follow the course of just one of these boys, however. He is the son of a king. He reaches the sea when the sun is setting, like a shining red altar standing "where sea and sky meet." The other boy is a poor youth. He takes a different, more difficult path than the son of a king, going through "the densest part of the forest, where brambles and thorns" grow that tear and scratch. Yet he too reaches the same clifftop overlooking the ocean and the setting sun. On this spot the "great invisible holy bell" sounds "in loud hosanna"; all of nature is "a great cathedral." The flowers form its "mosaic floors, the tall trees and the swaying clouds . . its pillars and heaven itself . . . the dome." Though nature exhibits a native beauty, even this beauty points to, participates in, a transcendent beauty. One important lesson of the story is that beauty avails itself to rich and poor alike. Though for the poor the way may be more difficult, the reward is no less great.

Goodness

The Little Lame Prince and His Travelling-Cloak (1875) by Dinah Maria Mulock Craik is the story of the son of a king who in infancy is dropped by his nurse and injured so severely that his legs grow malformed and he cannot stand or walk. His mother dies soon after his birth, and when his father not long afterward also passes away, Prince Dolor's uncle, the Prince Regent, declares that the child has died and makes himself king. But this is a lie. Prince Dolor is sent secretly into a lonely exile far away in a desolate region named Nomansland. There he lives, captive in a high tower with just a nurse to care for him.

Prince Dolor has a magical godmother, however, who gives him the gift of a magic cloak that will fly him wherever he wishes to go. The boy does not know he is a captive or that he is the rightful heir to the throne, and learns to live a solitary existence without complaint, books his only companions. "When we see people suffering or unfortunate," the narrator interjects, "we feel very sorry for them. But when we see them bravely bearing their suffering and making the best of their misfortunes, it is quite a different thing. We respect, we admire them."

For a long time, Prince Dolor does not make use of his fairy godmother's magic cloak. When, however, he reads about places beyond his tower-top prison, he begins to wonder how it would be to live in those places, and he sets off to see them. He discovers a wide, wondrous world beyond his imaginings. Aware that he is a prince, he begins to wonder whether he mightn't also be a king one day. Eventually he asks his nurse about this, and she informs him of his rightful claim to the royal throne.

When his uncle dies the realm descends into revolution and tumult. Prince Dolor's nurse boldly takes the initiative and with the help of others spreads the word that the prince is alive. "The country, weary perhaps of the late King's harsh rule, and yet glad to save itself from the horrors" that have come upon it, embraces Prince Dolor. And so he rules for many years, both temperately and justly, and is loved by all of his subjects. "Whether he was happy," the narrator conjectures, "is a question no human can decide. But I think he was, because he had the power of making everybody about him happy."

Prince Dolor was loved, "first because, accepting his affliction as inevitable, he took it patiently; secondly because, being a brave man, he bore it bravely, trying to forget himself, and live out of himself, and in and for the other people." This is a description of a saint. And that is why I believe the story is so powerful. Today our children need exemplars such as this, heroes of humility forged in the furnace of personal affliction and suffering.

Obedience and Perfection

I venture to say that George MacDonald had more to say about obedience as the cardinal condition for the perfection of our humanity than any writer of his time, or of ours. He discussed this connection between obedience and perfection not just in his sermons and essays but also, as we have seen, in his fiction. Obedience is not, as some imagine, a choice to accept things blindly, but rather a path of knowing that enables us to act in a way consistent with our very nature and its perfection. "Until a man begins to obey," MacDonald writes in his tract *The Hope of the Gospel,* "the light that is in him is darkness." We come to our true selves in relation to God by obedience, even before faith matures.

In his fantasy stories, MacDonald explored how obedience is needed for perfection. He wrote parables that do not necessarily make mention of God or Jesus, but the premise of which is that our perfection is possible only when we believe in and trust in God. We have seen how he works this out in *The Wise Woman.* I said in Chapter 9 that in a literary sense the Wise Woman stands in for Jesus. Obedience to her is the precondition for the needed correction in the lives of the two girls so that they turn from being selfish miscreants to being good servants.

This theme of obedience and spiritual or moral improvement is also at the heart of MacDonald's endearing fantasy novel *At the Back of the North Wind.* In it MacDonald blends fantasy with a social realism like that of Charles Dickens. Like Dickens, MacDonald poignantly portrays the urban poverty of the early industrial revolution. The chief protagonist of *At the Back of the North Wind* is a young child named Diamond, the son of a cabby. Diamond comes under the compelling influence of a mysterious feminine persona. Like the Wise Woman, North Wind, for that is what she is and is called, possesses and exercises transformative powers. She can change appearance and size, though for Diamond she is a lovely woman. She carries Diamond to different places on earth and in heaven. Indeed, North Wind carries Diamond to her "back," which is somewhere beyond the North Pole. Interpreters have identified this place as Purgatory, and there are reasons to reach this conclusion. For instance, MacDonald mentions Dante, whom he calls Durante, in the chapter about Diamond's visit to the back of the North Wind. I see no pressing reason, however, to speculate about this. The importance of Diamond's peregrinations with the North Wind and the places she takes him (including to her back) is that by these means Diamond learns an almost divine wisdom.

North Wind hasn't the kind of deep knowledge of things that the Wise Woman has. She is not a wisdom figure like the Wise Woman or Irene's great-great-grandmother. She causes both beneficial and harmful things to happen in her wake. Yet North Wind admits that she doesn't know why what she causes to happen should or must be, whether sinking a ship or taking Diamond to places where he can be of help to others. She and her doings are surrounded in mystery. From a transcendent perspective, however, it is possible to say that all that North Wind does is necessary—that what she does is God's will, that she is a messenger or an angelic agent of a Higher Power that transcends her own knowing (although she is vaguely aware that there is a design in all that she does).

Unlike the two girls in *The Wise Woman*, Diamond is an innocent. He is in need not of correction but rather of a pedagogy that will lead him on a path to perfection. He must obey and trust North Wind in order that she can reveal to him a world and people who do need help and reform, places where he, in spite of his tender age, can be an agent of the good. Some characters in the story mistake Diamond's innocence and wisdom as foolishness, even accuse him of a mental disorder. They call him "God's baby" and say that he is "not right in the head." But the reader knows better.

In an Afterword to the Signet Classic edition, Michael Patrick Hearn describes *At the Back of the North Wind* as "a story of Diamond's spiritual evolution." So far as this goes, I do not disagree. But I do not agree with Hearn's conclusion that the story "is not about growth but awakening." It is hard sometimes to distinguish awakening and growth from each other. However, North Wind's pedagogy more than awakens Diamond to spiritual realities. It engenders in him a spiritual growth. Spiritual growth needn't be measured from a start that is sinful or corrupted. Diamond is an innocent throughout, yet even as an innocent he matures spiritually as he precociously commences his unconditional service to others, such as a drunken cabby and his family and the street urchin Nanny. In this sense, he matures, as St. Paul puts it, into the fullness that is the perfection of our humanity in Christ (Eph. 4:13).

The narrator enters the story in the final chapters of *At the Back of North Wind.* In these chapters, he reports on the last days of Diamond's life. Diamond dies when by temporal measure he is still a young child. Nonetheless, we readers oughtn't to be saddened by his death. He, unlike most of us—excepting perhaps the saints, of which he may be one—completes the course and grows into perfection. His death is perfectly a passage into new life. With just this meaning, the narrator confidently concludes: "They thought he was dead. I knew that he had gone to the back of the north wind."

In closing, I leave a short list of anthologies in which many of the stories I have discussed in this Conclusion appear, excepting the novels and *Where the Wild Things Are*. I do not include in this list picture books of the classic fairy tales because so many, indeed most, are abridged, bowdlerized, recast, or paraphrased versions of the originals. There may be occasions when the best of these warrant attention and use, especially when parents or teachers have legitimate concerns about difficulty and length for the young, and the illustrations add a special value.

A Short List of Anthologies

Hans Christian Andersen: The Complete Fairy Tales and Stories, translated by Erik Christian Haugaard (Anchor Books, 1983)

The Complete Fairy Tales of the Brothers Grimm, translated by Jack Zipes (Bantam Books, 1987)

The Classic Fairy Tales, edited by Iona and Peter Opie (Oxford University Press, 1980)

The Oxford Book of Modern Fairy Tales, edited by Alison Lurie (Oxford University Press, 1993)

The Victorian Fairy Tale Book, edited by Michael Patrick Hearn (Pantheon Books, 1988). Several of the stories I discuss in this Conclusion that are not usually found in book form or collections of the Grimms' or Andersen's work may be found in Hearn's splendid anthology, notably "Rocking Horse Land, "The Selfish Giant," *The Golden Key, The Reluctant Dragon*, and *The Little Lame Prince*.

NOTES

Preface to Second Expanded Edition

1. On these matters, see my article "The Fairy Tale Wars: Lewis, Chesterton, et al. Against the Frauds, Experts, and Revisionists," *Touchstone*, March–April 2020, https://www.touchstonemag.com/archives/article.php?id=33-02-045-f.

Introduction

1. C. S. Lewis, *The Abolition of Man* (New York: Collier Books, 1947), p. 35.
2. Bruno Bettelheim, *The Uses of Enchantment* (New York: Alfred A. Knopf, 1975), p. 5.
3. See Vigen Guroian, "The Fairy Tale Wars," *Touchstone Magazine*, March/April 2020, pp. 45–49.
4. See chapter 11, "Childhood," in my book *The Orthodox Reality* (Grand Rapids, MI: Baker Academic Books, 2018), pp. 159–77.
5. C. S. Lewis, *Of Other Worlds*, edited by Walter Hooper (New York: Harcourt Brace Jovanovich, 1975), p. 24.
6. Robert Coles, "Children and Literature," in *A Robert Coles Omnibus* (Iowa City: University of Iowa Press, 1993), p. 206.
7. Gilbert K. Chesterton, *Lunacy and Letters*, edited by Dorothy Collins (New York: Sheed and Ward, 1958), p. 107.
8. Gilbert K. Chesterton, *Orthodoxy* (Garden City, NY: Image Books, 1959), p. 60.
9. George MacDonald, *The Golden Key* (New York: Farrar, Straus and Giroux, 1967), p. 57.

Chapter 1

1. Flannery O'Connor, *Mystery and Manners* (New York: Farrar, Straus and Giroux, 1990), p. 96.

2. Alasdair MacIntyre, *After Virtue: A Study in Moral Theory*, 2nd ed. (Notre Dame, IN: University of Notre Dame Press, 1984), p. 216.
3. Gilbert K. Chesterton, *Orthodoxy* (Garden City, NY: Image Books, 1959), p. 50.
4. Chesterton, *Orthodoxy*, p. 52.
5. Martin Buber, *Between Man and Man* (New York: Macmillan, 1978), p. 105.
6. Ionia Opie and Peter Opie, eds., *The Classic Fairy Tales* (New York: Oxford University Press, 1980), pp. 182–83. This is the 1761 English translation of Madame de Beaumont's version of the fairy tale, published originally in French in 1756. All subsequent page references to this edition will be made parenthetically in the text.
7. George Santayana, *Interpretations of Poetry and Religion* (New York: Charles Scribner's Sons, 1924), p. 2.
8. See chapter 4 in my book *Rallying the Really Human Things* (Wilmington, DE: ISI Books, 2005), esp. pp. 56–60.
9. George MacDonald, *A Dish of Orts* (San Bernardino, CA: Bibliobazaar, 2014), pp. 16, 17.
10. Gertrude Himmelfarb, *The Demoralization of Society: From Victorian Virtues to Modern Values* (New York: Alfred A. Knopf, 1995), p. 10.
11. Himmelfarb, *The Demoralization of Society*, p. 11.
12. These are collected in Gilbert K. Chesterton, *What's Wrong with the World* (New York: Dodd, Mead, 1910).
13. Chesterton, *What's Wrong with the World*, pp. 252–53.
14. Chesterton, *What's Wrong with the World*, p. 254.
15. Chesterton, *What's Wrong with the World*, p. 253.
16. Chesterton, *Orthodoxy*, p. 59.

Chapter 2

1. Maurice Sendak, *Caldecott & Co.: Notes on Books and Culture* (New York: Noonday Press, 1990), p. 114.
2. Sendak, *Caldecott & Co.*, p. 113.
3. Sendak, *Caldecott & Co.*, p. 115.
4. Carlo Collodi, *Pinocchio*, translated by E. Harden (New York: Puffin Books, 1974), p. 132. All subsequent page references to this edition will be made parenthetically in the text.
5. C. S. Lewis, *Mere Christianity* (New York: Macmillan, 1960), p. 154.
6. Lewis, *Mere Christianity*, p. 154.
7. Sendak, *Caldecott & Co.*, p. 113.

8. Josef Pieper, *A Brief Reader of the Virtues of the Human Heart*, translated by Paul C. Duggan (San Francisco: Ignatius Press, 1991), p. 21.

9. Josef Pieper, *Josef Pieper: An Anthology* (San Francisco: Ignatius Press, 1989), p. 53.

10. I am citing here the less readily available critical English-language edition: Nicholas J. Perella, trans., *The Adventures of Pinocchio: Story of a Puppet* (Berkeley: University of California Press, 1986), p. 427. I have used this edition where the other standard editions have left out phrases or sentences—often pious expressions or religious references—that are, nevertheless, essential to our understanding of the story.

11. Augustine, *The Confessions*, translated by R. S. Pine-Coffin (New York: Penguin Books, 1961), p. 92 (Bk. 5:2).

12. Perella, trans., *The Adventures of Pinocchio*, p. 443.

13. Pieper, *A Brief Reader on the Virtues of the Human Heart*, p. 25.

14. Pieper, *A Brief Reader on the Virtues of the Human Heart*, pp. 25–26.

15. C. S. Lewis, *Prince Caspian* (New York: HarperCollins, 1994), p. 128..

16. In June 1994, the Colloquium on Everyday Ethics held at the Institute on Religion and Public Life discussed *Pinocchio*. The papers written for that occasion and the discussions that ensued have contributed to this essay. I here want to acknowledge my indebtedness to that forum and the insights of my colleagues.

Chapter 3

1. Robert Coles, *The Spiritual Life of Children* (Boston: Houghton Mifflin, 1990), p. 37.

2. Margery Williams, *The Velveteen Rabbit* (New York: Simon and Schuster, 1983). The text is not paginated.

3. While Williams's story has found its way into nurseries and playrooms for several generations, it is also being used in nursing homes and care centers for the elderly. Students in adult night school courses who work in health and psychiatric care settings have reported that *The Velveteen Rabbit* is a comfort to the old and the infirm. How the Skin Horse and the Velveteen Rabbit become real is like what it is to grow old and still have dignity and worth.

4. Martin Buber, *I and Thou*, 2nd ed. (New York: Charles Scribner's Sons, 1958), p. 11.

5. Roger Sale, *Fairy Tales and After: From Snow White to E. B. White* (Cambridge, MA: Harvard University Press, 1978), chap. 3.

6. Sale, *Fairy Tales*, p. 67.
7. Jack Zipes, *Fairy Tales and the Art of Subversion* (New York: Routledge, 1991), p. 85.
8. I have used L. W. Kingsland's translation of "The Little Mermaid" in *Hans Andersen's Fairy Tales: A Selection*, World's Classics (New York: Oxford University Press, 1984), p. 79. Subsequent page references to the story will be made parenthetically in the text.
9. C. S. Lewis, *Letters to Malcolm* (New York: Harcourt Brace Jovanovich, 1964), p. 121.
10. G. K. Chesterton, *Orthodoxy* (Garden City, NY: Image Books, 1959), p. 102.
11. I am going to pass up the opportunity to pursue the conjecture that there is an allusion here to a young woman's menstrual cycle. That, frankly, does not interest me so much as the fact that allusions to blood and the color red abound in this story, which unmistakably suggest the sacral and redemptive meaning of the same.
12. Sale, *Fairy Tales*, p. 67.
13. Peter Kreeft, *Heaven: The Heart's Deepest Longing* (San Francisco: Harper and Row, 1980), p. 65.
14. Kreeft, *Heaven*, p. 63.
15. See, especially, the story told in 1 Sam. 26.

Chapter 4

1. Aristotle, *Nicomachean Ethics*, in *The Basic Works of Aristotle*, edited by Richard McKeon (New York: Random House, 1941), p. 1058 (Bk. 8).
2. Aristotle, *Nicomachean Ethics*, p. 1088.
3. Kenneth Grahame, *The Wind in the Willows* (New York: Signet Classic, 1969), p. 27. Subsequent references to the book will be made parenthetically in the text.
4. Aristotle, *Nicomachean Ethics*, p. 1058.
5. E. B. White, *Charlotte's Web* (New York: Harper and Row, 1952), p. 165. Subsequent references to the book will be made parenthetically in the text.
6. Aristotle, *Nicomachean Ethics*, pp. 1065–66.
7. Lest there be a misunderstanding, even in the purer sort of mentoral relationship, the formation of that relationship is not merely unilateral. The student or mentee will desire to study under the mentor and may

take the initiative of proposal. However, the mentor decides whether the mentoral relationship will be formed.

8. Felix Salten, *Bambi: A Life in the Woods*, translated by Whittaker Chambers (New York: Minstrel, 1988), p. 57. Subsequent references to the book will be made parenthetically in the text.

Chapter 5

1. Fyodor Dostoevsky, *The Brothers Karamazov*, trans. Richard Pevear and Larissa Volokhonsky (New York: Farrar, Straus, and Giroux, 2002), p. 108.

2. I have used the translation of "The Snow Queen" in L. W. Kingsland, *Hans Andersen's Fairy Tales: A Selection*, World's Classics (New York: Oxford University Press, 1984), p. 229. Subsequent page references to the story will be made parenthetically within the text.

3. Paul Evdokimov, *The Struggle with God* (Glen Rock, NJ: Paulist Press, 1966), p. 78.

4. See, for example, Wolfgang Lederer's book-length study titled *The Kiss of the Snow Queen* (Berkeley: University of California Press, 1986); on Kay's changed behavior, see esp. pp. 23–28.

5. "Unlike his father, who was an atheist, Andersen was a deeply religious person, whose religious beliefs may be summed up by saying that he believed in the existence of a god, in the importance of behaving decently, and the immortality of the soul. This famous triad of God, Virtue and Immortality, which is the basis of theological rationalism, was also the basis of Andersen's religious belief.... Andersen's religion was a primitive and undogmatic one, in which he saw Christ as the great teacher and model to mankind, and Nature as God's universal church." Elias Bredsdorff, *Hans Christian Andersen* (New York: Charles Scribner's Sons, 1975), pp. 297–98. Nevertheless, it needs to be said also that Andersen's religious sensibilities outpaced any sort of simple theological rationalism. There was the mystic in him as well.

6. Nicholas Berdyaev, *The Destiny of Man* (New York: Harper and Row, 1960), p. 23.

7. Dostoevsky, *The Brothers Karamazov*, p. 774.

8. Lederer, *Kiss of the Snow Queen*, p. 183.

9. Kathryn Lindskoog, *The Lion of Judah in Never-Never Land* (Grand Rapids, MI: Wm. B. Eerdmans, 1973), pp. 96–97.

10. Evan K. Gibson, *C. S. Lewis: Spinner of Tales* (Washington, DC: Christian University Press, 1980), p. 136.
11. C. S. Lewis, *The Lion, the Witch and the Wardrobe* (New York: HarperCollins, 1994), p. 34. See also Chapter 2, note 15 in this book.
12. Lindskoog, *Lion of Judah*, p. 96.
13. Gilbert Meilaender, *The Taste for the Other: The Social and Ethical Thought of C. S. Lewis* (Grand Rapids, MI: Wm. B. Eerdmans, 1978), p. 9.
14. Gibson, *C. S. Lewis: Spinner of Tales*, p. 141.

Chapter 6

1. From *A Dish of Orts*, quoted by Roderick McGillis in his Introduction to George MacDonald, *The Princess and the Goblin, The Princess and Curdie*, edited by Roderick McGillis (New York: Oxford University Press, 1990), p. xxii. Subsequent page references to this volume will be made parenthetically in the text.
2. This scene is suspiciously reminiscent of Lewis Carroll's *Alice's Adventures in Wonderland* (1865), published seven years earlier. MacDonald and Carroll were close friends. Carroll's sequel *Through the Looking Glass* was published in the same year as *The Princess and the Goblin*, 1872.
3. See, for example, Nancy-Lou Patterson, "*Kore* Motifs in *The Princess and the Goblin*," in *For the Childlike*, edited by Roderick McGillis (Metuchen, NJ: Children's Literature Association and Scarecrow Press, 1992), pp. 169–82. Patterson also mentions that the spinning wheel and thread being spun are motifs associated with the virgin goddess Athena and the Three Fates of classical Greco-Roman mythology. But these motifs are also associated with Mary in iconography of the Annunciation. A contemporary of MacDonald in England, Dante Gabriel Rossetti, experimented with these and other motifs that we find in MacDonald's story. In his painting *Ecce Ancilla Domini* ("Behold the Handmaid of the Lord"), completed in 1849–50, Rossetti tried to invent a new iconography. In this Annunciation setting, he placed a hand loom at the foot of Mary's bed and a soft blue curtain behind Mary's head, the latter suggesting the ideals of truth and spiritual love. The loom is a loom of life on which is spun the loftiest dreams, or perhaps this is the traditional symbolism of the new life that she will gestate in her womb.

4. The descriptive passages cited in the paragraph are especially reminiscent of Rev. 12:1–2: "After that there appeared a great sign in heaven: a woman robed with the sun, beneath her feet the moon and on her head a crown of twelve stars. She was about to bear a child, and in the anguish of her labour she cried out to be delivered." In the Christian church this passage with its clear allusions to Israel and the twelve tribes has also been interpreted as a vision or sign of Mary. There are other reasons to suspect that MacDonald was employing symbolism through which he intended to suggest the Virgin Mary. In Christian art and literature the moon has often stood for Mary, the Mother of God, who reflects the light of the Son. A comparison with Dante Gabriel Rossetti's poem "The Blessed Damsel" is also interesting in this regard.

5. See the Patterson essay (note 3 in this chapter) and others in McGillis, ed., *For the Childlike.*

6. MacDonald, *The Princess and the Goblin, The Princess and Curdie,* pp. 343–44 n. 5.

7. *Macmillan School Dictionary,* 3rd ed., s.v. "courage."

8. George MacDonald, "The Fear of God," in *Unspoken Sermons* (Whitehorn, CA: Johannesen, 1999), Series Two, pp. 315–16.

9. MacDonald, "Life," in *Unspoken Sermons,* Series Two, p. 311.

10. MacDonald, "Life," in *Unspoken Sermons,* Series Two, p. 311.

11. MacDonald tells two intertwining stories of faith and courage in *The Princess and the Goblin.* One is Princess Irene's story and the other is Curdie's. MacDonald once wrote that "doubts are the messengers of the Living One to the honest. They are the first knock at our door of things, that are not yet but have to be understood. . . . Doubt must precede every deeper assurance, for uncertainties are what we first see when we look into a region hitherto unknown." C. S. Lewis, ed., *George MacDonald: An Anthology* (New York: Simon and Schuster, 1996), pp. 66–67. This is how Curdie's own journey to faith goes. Finally, he does join those others in the story (including his own mother) for whom the grandmother and the transcendent and beneficent reality she represents are profoundly real and a source of hope and courage.

12. Josef Pieper, *The Four Cardinal Virtues* (New York: Harcourt, Brace and World, 1965), p. 140.

13. MacDonald, "Self Denial," in *Unspoken Sermons,* Series Two, pp. 366–67.

14. Pieper, *Four Cardinal Virtues,* p. 140.

15. MacDonald, "The Consuming Fire," in *Unspoken Sermons*, Series One, p. 24.
16. Lewis, ed., *George MacDonald*, p. xxxiii.
17. Lewis, ed., *George MacDonald*, p. xxxiv.
18. Lewis, ed., *George MacDonald*, p. 18.
19. Both MacDonald and Lewis are clear in their conviction that while God, in his infinite being, transcends the words and images through which human beings express and try to make sense of their experience of his self-revelation to them, nevertheless God uses the imaginative and metaphor-making capacities of human beings to bridge the ontological gap that separates creature and Creator. Both MacDonald and Lewis propose powerful sacramental visions of creation. In this sacramental understanding, all creaturely things, including our metaphors of speech, may become windows through which we "see" the Uncreated. Even our physical capacity of sight is a sign and symbol of another capacity of spiritual vision. And while this spiritual capacity has been severely debilitated by sin, faith may remedy the affliction. Thus, through faith's "eyes" we may behold once more the Creative Will behind all things.
20. E. Cobham Brewer, *Dictionary of Phrase and Fable*, 17th ed. (Philadelphia: J. B. Lippincott, n.d.), p. 530.
21. C. S. Lewis, *Prince Caspian* (New York: HarperCollins, 1994), p. 3. Subsequent page references will appear parenthetically in the text.
22. Long ago by Narnian chronology; only several months ago by our (earth's) time.
23. Paul Tillich, *The Courage to Be* (New Haven, CT: Yale University Press, 1952), p. 172.
24. C. S. Lewis, *Surprised by Joy* (New York: Harcourt Brace Jovanovich, 1955), pp. 17–18.
25. Lewis, *Surprised by Joy*, p. 220.
26. Lewis, *Surprised by Joy*, p. 221.
27. MacDonald, "The Truth in Jesus," in *Unspoken Sermons*, Series Two, p. 393.
28. Samuel Terrien, *The Elusive Presence* (San Francisco: Harper and Row, 1978), p. 426.
29. Lewis, ed., *George MacDonald*, p. 28.
30. MacDonald, "The Way," in *Unspoken Sermons*, Series Two, pp. 181–82.
31. Terrien, *Elusive Presence*, pp. 476–77.
32. John Henry Newman, *Miscellanies: From the Oxford Sermons and Other Writings* (London: Strahan, 1870), p. 323 (from the sermon "Watching").
33. C. S. Lewis, *The Last Battle* (New York: HarperCollins, 1994), p. 228.

Chapter 7

1. Jackie Wullschlager, *Hans Christian Andersen: The Life of a Storyteller* (New York: Alfred A. Knopf, 2000), p. 233.
2. Joan Chittister, in *Theological Aesthetics: A Reader*, edited by Gesa Elsbeth Thiessen (Grand Rapids, MI: Wm. B. Eerdmans, 2004), p. 366.
3. *Hans Christian Andersen: The Complete Fairy Tales and Stories*, translated by Erik Christian Haugaard (New York: Doubleday, 1974), p. 203. All subsequent page references to this edition will be made parenthetically in the text.
4. This is likely an allusion to John Keats's "Ode to a Nightingale."
5. Elaine Scarry, *On Beauty and Being Just* (Princeton, NJ: Princeton University Press, 1999), p. 90.
6. Dante, *Purgatory*, translated by Anthony Ensolen (New York: Random House, 2004), Canto 2.
7. Dante, *Purgatory*, Canto 2.
8. Augustine, *Confessions*, trans. Henry Chadwick (Oxford: Oxford University Press, 1991), 29, 30.
9. Simone Weil, "Forms of the Implicit Love of God," in *The Simone Weil Reader*, edited by George A. Panichas (New York: David McKay, 1977), p. 474.
10. Cited in Wullschlager, *Hans Christian Andersen*, p. 229.
11. Cited in Wullschlager, *Hans Christian Andersen*, p. 230. The entry is dated October 7, 1843.
12. Andersen writes in his almanac that he began *The Nightingale* on October 11, 1833, and completed it the following day. Wullschlager, *Hans Christian Andersen*, p. 230.
13. Cited in Wullschlager, *Hans Christian Andersen*, p. 233.
14. Jackie Wullschlager conjectures that Andersen might well have had in mind the Brentved manor house of Count Moltke, where he stayed during this time. *Hans Christian Andersen*, p. 231.
15. In both "The Nightingale" and "The Ugly Duckling," Andersen makes important word choices in order to distinguish the various kinds of beauty from one another. For example, in "The Nightingale" he selects the Danish adjective *praegtigste* to describe the imperial palace. *Praegtisgte* suggests a beauty that gives aesthetic pleasure or has a pleasing appearance. Its literal meaning is "finest" or "most magnificent." So: "The emperor's palace was the most beautiful [*praegtigste*, finest] in the whole world" (p. 203). When, however, Andersen refers to the beauty of the Nightingale's song, he chooses the Danish

adjective *delig*, which literally means delightful or lovely. It denotes a beauty that elicits an emotional response—beauty, that is, that deeply affects the emotions. So when Andersen portrays the loveliness of the natural scene into which the Ugly Duckling is born, the word of his choice is *delig*. But perhaps the most significant use of *delig* occurs late in the story of "The Ugly Duckling," where the duckling is overcome by "a strange longing" when "one evening . . . a flock of beautiful [*delige*] white birds" circles over him. I will return to this scene because it is crucial to an understanding of the quality of the Ugly Duckling that distinguishes him from all the rest of the principal characters in the story. His love of beauty is the kind of love that "is as strong as death" (Song of Songs 8:6). Here again *delig* connotes a beauty that stirs or captures the emotions, a beauty that reaches the soul and even equips it with courage.

16. Weil, "Forms of the Implicit Love of God," p. 474.

17. A little later on the mother repeats this estimate of the Ugly Duckling, though the reader is given the impression that she has become more defensive. Responding to the distinguished duck with noble "Spanish blood," she states: "'He may not be handsome, but he has a good character and swims as well as the others, if not a little better. Perhaps he will grow handsomer as he grows older and becomes a bit smaller" (p. 218).

18. C. S. Lewis, *Surprised by Joy* (New York: Harcourt Brace Jovanovich, 1955), p. 6.

19. Lewis, *Surprised by Joy*, p. 7.

20. Lewis, *Surprised by Joy*, p. 7.

21. Lewis, *Surprised by Joy*, p. 221.

22. Lewis, *Surprised by Joy*, p. 168.

23. Jack Zipes, *Hans Christian Andersen* (New York: Routledge, 2005), p. 69; Jack Zipes, *Fairy Tales and the Art of Subversion* (New York: Routledge, 1991), p. 87.

24. Charles Peguy, "Abandonment: God Speaks," in *Basic Verities: Prose and Poetry*, trans. Ann and Julian Green (New York: Pantheon Books, 1943), pp. 221, 223.

Chapter 8

1. Quoted in John S. Mackenzie, *A Manual of Ethics* (New York: Hinds, Noble & Eldridge, 1901), p. 253 n. 1.

2. Wilhelm and Jacob Grimm, *The Complete Fairy Tales of the Brothers Grimm*, translated by Jack Zipes (New York: Bantam Books, 2003), p. 79. All subsequent page references to this edition will be made parenthetically in the text.

3. Bruno Bettelheim, *The Uses of Enchantment* (New York: Alfred A. Knopf, 1975), p. 9.

4. Ronald Murphy, S.J., *The Owl, the Raven, and the Dove* (New York: Oxford University Press, 2000). I owe more than I can say here for my reading of "Cinderella" to Fr. Murphy's book. particularly his argument about a communion of love that bonds Cinderella and her mother.

5. See Matt. 27:27–31: "Then the soldiers of the governor took Jesus into the praetorium ... And they stripped him and put a scarlet robe upon him, and plaiting a crown of thorns they put it on his head, and put a reed in in his right hand. And kneeling before him they the mocked him, saying 'Hail, King of the Jews!'"

6. Murphy, *The Owl, the Raven, and the Dove*, p. 109.

7. Bettelheim, *The Uses of Enchantment*, p. 251.

8. For example, Matt. 3:16: "And when Jesus was baptized, he went up immediately from the water, and behold, the heavens were opened and he [John the Baptist] saw the Spirit descending like a dove, and alighting on him."

9. At the start of this quote, the German has a biblical cadence in its more literal translation: "It came to pass."

10. "And Samuel said to Jesse, 'Are all your sons here?' And he said, 'There remains yet the youngest, but behold, he is keeping the sheep" (1 Sam. 16:11).

11. Maria Tatar, *The Annotated Brothers Grimm* (New York: W. W. Norton, 2004), pp. 114, 127.

12. Iona Opie and Peter Opie, *The Classic Fairy Tales* (Oxford: Oxford University Press, 1993), p. 127.

13. Tatar, *The Annotated Brothers Grimm*, p. 114.

14. Tatar, *The Annotated Brothers Grimm*, p. 127.

15. Flannery O'Connor, *Mystery and Manners* (New York: Farrar, Straus and Giroux, 1961), p. 41

16. I might add that Christian orthodoxy of whatever stripe, not just Calvinist orthodoxy, is incompatible with modern sentimentalism, which so often leaps over the hard stuff to reach a happy ending. For example, in American romantic comedy, sex rarely if ever leads to pregnancy and ensuing complications.

17. Max Lüthi, *Once Upon a Time* (Bloomington: Indiana University Press, 1976), p. 42..

18. Tim Hilton, *John Ruskin* (New Haven, CT: Yale University Press, 2002), p. 13

19. Hilton, *John Ruskin*, p. 13.

20. Oliver Lodge, in his introduction to John Ruskin, *Sesame and Lilies, The Two Paths, The King of the Golden River* (London: J. M. Dent and Sons, 1907), p. x.

21. This description of the brothers' behavior and the economy they impose is, in fact, the complete inversion of the biblical command: "When you reap your harvest in your field, and have forgotten a sheaf in the field, you shall not go back to get it; it shall be for the sojourner, the fatherless, and the widow; that the Lord your God may bless you in all the work of your hands" (Deut. 24:19).

22. John Ruskin, *Modern Painters* (London: J. M. Dent, 1908), vol. 4, p. 84. The influence of the romantic poets is evident here. I think of Wordsworth in particular.

23. See "A Cautionary Note on the Ghostly Tale," at the back of Russell Kirk, *Ancestral Shadows: An Anthology of Ghostly Tales*, edited by Vigen Guroian (Grand Rapids, MI: Wm. B. Eerdmans, 2004).

24. Cited in *Ancient Commentary on Scripture*, Old Testament, Vol. 2, edited by Mark Sheridan (Downers Grove, IL: InterVarsity Press, 2002), p. 64.

25. Clive Wilmer in his Introduction to John Ruskin, *Unto the Last and Other Writings* (London: Penguin Books, 1995), p. 28.

26. John Ruskin, *Unto the Last and Other Writings* (New York: Penguin Books, 1985), pp. 188, 222.

27. In Christian literature and art the lily is a symbol of purity and resurrection.

28. As the king slips the dewdrops into Gluck's flask, something strange and unexpected happens. The king's features fade, while "the playing colours of his robe form[] themselves into a prismatic mist of dewy light. He . . . [stands] for an instant veiled in this prismatic light," as if covered in "the belt of a broad rainbow" (p. 23), and then, also like a rainbow, he evaporates into the white light. Jesus's Ascension on the Mount of Olives forty days after the Resurrection comes to mind (Acts 1:1–12).

29. Cited by Suzanne Rahn in "The Sources of Ruskin's *King of the Golden River*," *The Victorian Newsletter* 68 (Fall 1985): p. 6.

30. Rahn, "The Sources of Ruskin's *King of the Golden River*," p. 6.

31. Rahn, "The Sources of Ruskin's *King of the Golden River*," p. 6.

32. This needn't amount to a utopian belief that human beings can be entirely righteous in this life. Ruskin explains: "Absolute justice is no more attainable than absolute truth; but the righteous man is distinguished from the false by his desire and hope of justice, as the true man from the false by his desire and hope for truth. And though absolute justice be unattainable, as much justice as we need for all practical use is attainable by all those who make it their aim." Ruskin, *Unto This Last*, p. 194.

33. *Flannery O'Conner Collected Works* (New York: Library of America, 1988), 604.

34. My grandson Harris, at age seven, while riding home from school in the car in the fall of 2020, had this to say to his mother about the matter: "We all know God is going to win at the end of the war, we just don't know how. That's the question."

Chapter 9

1. Maurice Sendak, *Caldecott & Co.: Notes on Books and Culture* (New York: Noonday Press, 1990), p. 46.

2. Sendak, *Caldecott & Co.*, p. 48.

3. C. S. Lewis, ed., *George MacDonald: An Anthology of 365 Readings* (New York: Touchstone, 1996), p. xxix.

4. *The Wise Woman* was originally serialized, and in some editions it is titled *The Lost Princess*. I thank Melba N. Batten for pointing out the original book title in her essay "Duality Beyond Time: George MacDonald's 'The Wise Woman or the Lost Princess: A Double Story,'" in Roderick McGillis, ed., *For the Childlike: George MacDonald's Fantasies for Children* (Metuchen, NJ: Scarecrow Press, 1992), pp. 207–18.

5. *Oxford English Dictionary* (New York: Oxford University Press, 1971).

6. George MacDonald, "Duty-Nothing," in *Proving the Unseen* (New York: Ballantine Books, 1989), p. 49.

7. George MacDonald, "The Last Farthing," in *Unspoken Sermons* (Whitehorn, CA: Johannesen, 1999), Series One, p. 259. MacDonald here paraphrases St. Paul in Rom. 7:19: "For the good that I would I do not; but the evil which I would not, that I do."

8. Gisela H. Kreglinger, *Storied Revelations* (Eugene, OR: Pickwick, 2013), p. 161.

9. George MacDonald, *The Wise Woman and Other Stories* (Grand Rapids, MI: Wm. B. Eerdmans, 1980), p. 1.

10. This is the St. Athanasius Academy Septuagint translation included in the *Orthodox Study Bible* (Nashville, TN: Thomas Nelson, 2008).

11. Again, MacDonald alludes to Rom. 7:19, where St. Paul states: "For the good that I would I do not: but the evil which I would not, that I do." The Wise Woman echoes the same when she says to Rosamond: "Perhaps you will understand me better if I say it just comes down to this, that you must *not do* what is wrong, however much you are inclined to do it, and you must *do* what is right, however much you are disinclined to do it."

12. MacDonald, "Abba, Father!," in *Unspoken Sermons*, Series One, p. 291.

13. MacDonald, "The Truth," in *Unspoken Sermons*, Series Three, p. 478.

14. Stated in more philosophical language: the enlivening, ontological antecedent to all of our righteous willings is the willing that God does.

15. MacDonald, "The Truth," in *Unspoken Sermons*, Series Three, p. 479.

16. Flannery O'Connor, *Mystery and Manners* (New York: Farrar, Straus and Giroux, 1990), p. 79.

17. George MacDonald, "The Hope of the Gospel," in *The Miracles of Our Lord and The Hope of the Gospel* (Clearwater, FL: R. A Sites Books, 2014), p. 134.

18. MacDonald, "Righteousness," in *Unspoken Sermons*, Series Three, p. 585. "What does the apostle mean by righteousness that is of God by faith [in Philippians 3, 8, 9]? He means the same righteousness Christ had by his faith in God, the same righteousness as God himself has" (p. 577).

19. Peter Baelz, "Obedience," in A. R. Vidler, ed., *Traditional Virtues Reassessed* (London: SPCK, 1964), pp. 44–45.

20. George MacDonald, *Donal Grant* (Boston: Lothrop, 1883), p. 9.

21. MacDonald, "Life," in *Unspoken Sermons*, Series Two, pp. 310–11.

22. MacDonald, "The Way," in *Unspoken Sermons*, Series One, p. 185.

23. MacDonald, "The Truth in Jesus," in *Unspoken Sermons*, Series Two, p. 397.

24. MacDonald, "The Truth in Jesus," in *Unspoken Sermons*, Series Two, p. 399.

25. C. S. Lewis undoubtedly borrowed this motif for *The Voyage of the Dawn Trader* in the Narnia series. At the start of the story, Lucy and Edmund Pevensie and their cousin Eustace step into a picture that puts them on board Prince Caspian's ship, thus commencing a transformative journey.

26. Might this name allude to Christ, the Prince of Peace (Is. 9:6)?

27. Dante's *Divine Comedy* is likely an inspiration for this episode, especially the poet's use of *contrapasso*. The literal meaning of *contrapasso* is to "suffer the opposite." In Dante's hands, the more accurate translation might be "a return punishment." When she is sealed inside the hollow sphere, Agnes painfully experiences the loathsomeness and vileness of her own conceit and vanity as if another were inflicting it upon her. Characters in the *Inferno* undergo punishments that agonizingly torment them with ordeals that imitate or mimic in a scornful or ridiculing way the principal sin that they committed in their earthly lives. Thus, for example, those who were uncommitted in life are forced in the Vestibule of Hell to forever chase, but never catch, a pennant while being tormented by stinging insects.

28. MacDonald comments: "The fearlessness of Agnes was only ignorance: she had not read a single story of a giant, or ogress, or wolf; and her mother had never carried out her threats of punishment. If the Wise Woman had pinched her, she would have shown herself an abject coward" (p. 47). This statement may strike our ears at first as a pejorative expression about fairy tales. It is not. Rather, MacDonald is affirming a value of fairy tales in enabling children to experience frightening things at one remove, coming to "know" fear in this way, and practicing how to deal with fear when fear is the correct response to endangerment.

29. George MacDonald, *What's Mine's Mine* (London: Kegan, Paul, Trench, Trubner, 1900), p. 26.

30. We meet the white rabbit early in the story (p. 9). There also she abuses the creature. The white rabbit is an allusion to *Alice in Wonderland*.

31. This reads in full: "In the midst of the street of it, and on either side of the river, was there the tree of life, which bare twelve manner of fruits, and yielded her fruit every month; and the leaves of the tree were for the healing of the nations."

32. Lilies are symbols of resurrection.

33. Note the moon and light motifs. Rosamond is attracted to the beauty of this water lily with the same love of beauty that has previously drawn her in the story to the moon and its light. Nonetheless, greed continues to corrupt her attraction to beauty.

34. See Is. 11:1–9.

35. The mention of "many rooms" is an allusion to John 14:2: "In my Father's house there are many mansions, if it were not so I would have

told you. I go to prepare a place to you." And the notion of her progression through them is suggestive of a process of purification or perfection that continues after death.

36. Her speech and the action that unfolds bring to mind the ninth chapter of John's gospel, in which certain Pharisees judge wrongly and disbelieve the testimony of a blind man to whom Jesus has given sight. They deny the presence of God in Christ, while the blind man declares Jesus to be the Son of God. Whereupon Jesus pronounces, "For judgment I have come into this world, that those who do not see may see, and that those who see may be made blind" (John 9:39). Jesus, of course, means that these Pharisees are spiritually blind. But they, in turn, deliberately misconstrue his meaning as if he is claiming they are physically blind, to which Jesus replies, "'If you were blind, you would have no sin; but now you say, 'We see.' Therefore your sin remains" (John 9:41).

37. "Justice is not, never can be, satisfied in or from suffering. Human resentment, human revenge, human hate may." MacDonald, "Justice," in *Unspoken Sermons*, Series Three, p. 512.

38. MacDonald, "Justice," in *Unspoken Sermons*, Series Three, p. 514.

39. MacDonald, *Hope of the Gospel*, p. 138.

40. MacDonald, "The Consuming Fire," in *Unspoken Sermons*, Series One, p. 24.

41. This is the sense behind the Wise Woman's answer to the king and queen when she first enters the court at the start of the story. "Haven't we given her [Rosamond] every mortal thing she wanted?" they plead. The Wise Woman responds, "'Surely . . . what else could have killed her? You should have given her a few things [spiritual things] of the other sort'" (p. 8).

42. I owe this final phrasing to Stanley Hauerwas in one of his very best books, *Character and the Christian Life* (Notre Dame, IN: University of Notre Dame Press, 1994), p. 15.

43. MacDonald, "The Last Farthing," in *Unspoken Sermons*, Series One, p. 259.

Conclusion

1. Gilbert C. Meilaender, *The Theory and Practice of Virtue* (Notre Dame, IN: University of Notre Dame Press, 1984), 54.

INDEX

For the benefit of digital users, indexed terms that span two pages (e.g., 52–53) may, on occasion, appear on only one of those pages.